WALK A LONELY MILE

BRIAN PAIGE

© 2025 Brian Paige. All rights reserved.

No part of this book may be reproduced, stored in a retrieval system, or transmitted by any means without written permission of the author.

While this book is based primarily on personal experiences, the majority of names listed have been changed to protect the privacy of those mentioned. Certain events have been dramatized for effect as well.

Paperback ISBN: 979-8-9894006-3-8
Hardcover ISBN: 979-8-9894006-4-5
E-Book ISBN: 979-8-9894006-5-2

All photos and artwork by Brian Paige

Printed in the United States of America

ACKNOWLEDGMENTS

I would like to take this occasion to thank a variety of people who mean so much to me: My wife, Amanda, my son, Andrew, my mother, Phyllis, and my brother, Eric. I would also like to thank various friends for helping contribute to the various stories in this book, even if I felt the need to change names at times.

I would like to thank several teachers from Butler Traditional High School from my days there: Ron Orwick, Sherry Ederheimer, Dottie Ballard, and Martha Gutermuth. I have had many other teachers over the years, but these are the ones who believed in me and encouraged my writing.

I would also like to thank Jimmy Humphrey for his film editing help back in 2006, and also for reading and commenting on any piece I send his way. The same goes for Rachel Ingram, who I consider the sister I never had. Rachel is usually willing to read anything I have written and gives quality feedback.

Special thanks to: Michael Scott Williams for editing and proofreading, as well as Danielle Peck and Tatiana Rizo for their terrific beta reads.

CONTENTS

PART FOUR
REUNIONS AND FAREWELLS

INTRODUCTION

I often think back to the fateful summer of 1991 when I was about to turn twelve, and puberty caused my hormones to run rampant. My voice started to deepen, I suddenly found hair in previously unthought of places, and for the only time in my life I acted like an out-of-control fool around girls.

Yes, that summer saw Chad Black, Isaac Long, Jeremy Stigler and me as inseparable friends, thicker than thieves while attending the University of Louisville's *Summer of Adventure* daycare program at the Stoddard Johnston building. Without much goading from my friends, I rampantly hit on the "leader" of the girls, a blonde named Leanne. Neither the boys nor girls had "leaders," but nominally I was one of the main group of boys, while Leanne was one of the more noteworthy girls.

I know my trashy antics had to have embarrassed Leanne. I made no secret of wanting to "bone" her every day, how much she turned me on, and all sorts of sexual remarks. Amazingly, none of the teachers or admins at the daycare called me out on this behavior. Why would they? Act up in school and these transgressions might go on my *permanent record*. I never acted up in school. But summer daycare? They were happy to collect my mom's check each week, so why not?

AUGUST 5, 1991.

I awakened Monday morning to hear the phone ringing with shocking news—my maternal grandfather died while on a weekend trip at Nolin Lake. I was stunned and saddened by the news, Papaw's death being the first of a close family member in my lifetime. I still remember the funeral home down in Clarkson, Kentucky. I remember little about the actual funeral, but mostly this old-style Coke machine with bottles instead of cans. I probably downed ten Cokes that day, sitting alone in the lobby.

My grandfather's death had a profound impact on me, sending me into a dark mental frame of mind for the rest of my middle school years. At the time I wondered if I was being punished for how I acted that summer and vowed not to ever behave that way again. I returned for the last week of *Summer of Adventure*, a subdued experience where we played some kickball, swam at Crawford Gym, and said my goodbyes to the gang. I wanted to find Leanne and apologize to her for my antics, but she had left during my absence and never returned the next year.

Nearly a decade later I made a point to seek out Leanne once I had home internet access. She, too, was a U of L student so I found her email address on the university website. I profusely apologized for how I acted towards her nine years earlier, not in some attempt to ask her out, but to apologize. Her response?

"I'm sorry. I don't remember you at all."

I gave her further details, and she finally remembered me, accepted my apology, and we exchanged a few emails. Leanne is hardly a close friend these days, perhaps that is impossible, but I make sure to follow her dog shelter posts on Facebook to this day.

This is a book about seeking and failing, about loss in various forms. Losing what I already had, or who I had in my life. Some people die. Others drift away over time. Some spontaneously combust, emotionally. Schemes may not work, and sometimes music one enjoyed as a teen fades into the sands of time, but what else is there to do but carry on?

Since my previous book, *Salvaged From the Flood,* ended in mid-2022, *Walk a Lonely Mile* picks up around that time. With a quasi-follow up to my crypto misadventures in the previous book, I share my absurd attempts to use crypto to arbitrage trade Nigerian naira in the

"Nigerian Prince" chapter here. This is a lighter story before the book turns serious the rest of the way, with a couple of exceptions.

The two-part story of creating my own self-produced album, *Sonic Screamer*, was also a chapter I couldn't figure out how to write for *Salvaged From the Flood*. I figured there was room for one major chapter about creative pursuits, and since I had already discussed my script *Welcome to Paradise* in other chapters, I needed to chronicle my botched filmmaking attempt in "The Sub Par Filmmaker," instead of my dubious attempt at music. The first chapter is a nostalgic look back at the alternative rock scene circa 1994, and why I first started trying to record anything at home, with the second chapter nearly twenty years later, when I came back to these bizarre demo tapes and decided to do something with them. The isolation of recording in my room as well as piecing the album together in 2014 fit the theme of this book better.

In the introduction to *Salvaged*, I mentioned there were stories I skipped over because I couldn't find the words to tell them. A fair portion of this book consists of those stories. An entire series of chapters chronicles the complicated and sometimes confusing interactions with a girl in Florida, with details of my trips to St. Petersburg in 2003 and 2004, as well as Orlando in 2008. These chapters are steeped in pro wrestling online geekery of the era, since that's how we first met online and bonded. I had a wistful nostalgia writing about this, especially about the first trip in 2003, especially those first few days. The Florida chapters aren't meant to be a literal "we did this, then we did that" travelogue, but instead fragments of memorable moments.

If the Florida story illustrates a long-term stable relationship which never became fulfilling, the second major story of the book is a deep dive into a much shorter term and chaotic online relationship with a fellow writer and Wheeler and Woolsey fan. I won't discuss too much about these chapters here, but this arc is a payoff to many themes throughout both books: the desire for deep personal relationships, the long running attempts to get my PhD, my attempts to leave Louisville, and projects backfiring when I involve others. While the main storylines of the book are wildly different, both are examples of poor timing in life, dubious communication, and not understanding where I stood with people. I have included the Wheeler & Woolsey piece I submitted to *Classic*

Images as an Appendix, given how central the piece is to the later chapters.

Some characters from *Salvaged* aren't in much of this book (Chad and Isaac in particular), possibly because the theme is one of isolated loneliness. The book concludes with a sympathetic look at Isaac's stressful past year, which ranks along my own 1996, in terms of life altering events.

The goal of the book is not to be bleak or downbeat, even though it is emotionally charged at times. I included cartoon style versions of the front and back cover at the beginning and ending of the book, indicating we are stepping into a world that may not seem quite real. Hopefully readers will find these stories fascinating, heartwarming, hilarious, informative, and yes, heartbreaking. I don't know if everyone feels the need to walk a lonely mile, but after reading these pages, hopefully you will understand why I do.

PART ONE

SCHEMES AND SCREAMS

CHAPTER 1

THE NIGERIAN PRINCE

In the year of our Lord, 2022, I decided to become a Nigerian scammer. Okay, I'm not Nigerian and I wasn't actually attempting to scam anyone, but I tend to think the Nigerian government would frown upon what I attempted to do in order to arbitrage Nigerian naira with the U.S. dollar.

My wife, Amanda, left early every morning for her STEM teaching job at Rutherford Elementary. I had to drop my son Andrew off at Stonestreet Elementary, since his morning Child Enrichment Program at the school had been canceled during the pandemic. I became unable to sub high school classes, which had already begun by the time I took him to school and returned. As such, I found myself with an inordinate amount of time on my hands, which isn't necessarily a good thing.

I have long since been frustrated by my previous crypto debacles and couldn't help but seek out new opportunities to right my previous miscues. During my daily boredom, I did what anyone would do. I searched YouTube for crypto arbitrage videos. What platforms were out there where I could buy low and sell high elsewhere? What angle can someone work to generate profits?

Enter the Nigerian YouTubers. I couldn't ignore these guys. Especially Mr. Arbitrage or Big Classroom. They were everywhere when I searched for crypto arbitrage ideas, constantly discussing methods for using bank cards on Binance or converting cell phone airtime for profits. At first, I didn't understand anything they were talking about, and not just because of their accents. I understood little about the naira, the official currency of Nigeria. But the more I watched, the more fascinated I became in what was going on there.

To make a long story short, during this period of time the naira traded at two different rates. One was the official Central Bank of Nigeria rate, which was the rate you would find if you typed in "USD to NGN" on Google. When I first watched these videos, the official bank rate was in the 450 range (as in 1 USD = 450 NGN).

However, what blew my mind the more I heard about this was there existed a different rate. The so-called black market rate, which hovered in the 740 range at the time I started watching these videos. 740 vs. 450 is an insane difference in rate and could make for an arbitrage opportunity if I could figure out how to capitalize on it. Most of these questionable fellows were using sites such as Binance or the Nigerian based Remitano crypto exchange, which proved problematic, since neither allowed Americans (BinanceUS is a lesser form of the site for U.S. customers).

I analyzed the situation, looking for any way I could leverage naira. If I had to involve crypto websites, fine, but I would have preferred to buy and sell naira without the hassle of involving sketchy overseas crypto merchants. The best potential site I could find for this idea was Mercuryo, more of a third-party payment processor than actual crypto exchange. Mercuryo also had an exchange, and for my purposes they were using the bank rate. Even better, they accepted actual NGN bank transfers from some of the leading Nigerian banks such as Zenith or Sterling.

Sensing huge potential for profit, I attempted to sign up for a Zenith bank account. Alas, as a foreigner I had no chance, and not because I didn't have a Nigerian address to give them. In order to conduct any banking business, I needed to have a Bank Verification Number (BVN). A BVN identifies a particular individual throughout the Nigerian banking system. It isn't like a social security number, which is a basic overall ID number for the United States. As I would later learn, the Nigerian version of an SSN is the National Identification Number (NIN).

But where could I obtain a BVN? Was this even possible in America? Believe it or not, yes. There were locations throughout the U.S. operated by Online Integrated Solutions for the purpose of BVN distribution. I would assume Nigerians in diaspora were the target audience, but nothing on the website insisted on someone being a native Nigerian in order to obtain a BVN. None of the OIS locations were near Louisville, however, with the closest branches being in the D.C. area or Atlanta.

I had zero desire to ever travel through West Virginia again, after various near-death experiences during my time with the U of L debate team, so the D.C. location was out. I rather enjoyed Atlanta during other debate trips, so a trip south seemed a more feasible idea. I sent the Atlanta location an email inquiring about what I needed to bring for a BVN. I needed to make an appointment online, bring the appointment slip, a valid passport with a recent additional photograph, and the $45.00 enrollment fee. This sounded doable.

I got my passport the previous year, ironically because I needed one to attempt to sign up on the South Korean crypto exchange Bithumb. I wanted to leverage the Kimchi premium there, but the whole idea never panned out because the premium fizzled over time, and there wasn't much difference in price between American and South Korean exchanges by the time I obtained my passport. Buying BTC low and selling in South Korea at a profit was the main way the now disgraced Sam Bankman-Fried made his fortune, originally. We had the same idea, but he figured out how to make it work. I didn't have a Korean cell phone or partner in Seoul.

Thinking about a trip to Atlanta for my appointment with OIS, I finally cashed out of the Kentucky Teachers Retirement System in September 2022, retrieving the money these people had been stealing from me for years (10% early withdrawal fee naturally). To celebrate, Amanda and I planned to take Andrew on a fall break trip to Atlanta over the last weekend of the MLB season. The Braves and Mets were set to play a huge series to determine the NL East champions, so I bought tickets for the Sunday night game at Truist Park. Initially we were going to stay the weekend and head over to the OIS office in Roswell (suburb of Atlanta) Monday morning before we left town. As such, Amanda used Hotwire to snag a fairly cheap room in the Perimeter area, somewhere between downtown, Truist Park, and Roswell.

I made my BVN appointment for Monday morning, October 3. In the week before we left, the woman from the OIS office sent me a curious email informing me my appointment was off. In celebration of Nigerian Independence Day, the OIS office would be closed on Monday since the holiday fell on Saturday the 1st. This was a frustrating problem. Now the only way I could get the BVN, the main reason for the trip, was to make an appointment on Friday instead. Now we had to stay Thursday and Friday night in addition to the weekend, so we were spending the entire fall break either traveling to or staying in Atlanta. This trip was starting to cost money.

Thankfully, the trip progressed decently enough, though the mountains as you travel from Tennessee into Georgia can be dicey on I-24. We made decent time until reaching the Atlanta area, where traffic backed up for miles on I-75 due to a car being on fire on the side of the interstate. The I-285 area around the hotel was a chaotic construction zone, but we navigated to the Hilton Garden Inn.

I had a 10:00 a.m. appointment at the OIS center in Roswell, roughly fifteen minutes from our hotel. Amanda was driving by this point, mainly because I refused to drive in and around Atlanta. I couldn't help but notice the sheer amount of cops pulling speeders over on US-19 as we crossed the Chattahoochee River. We could forget about laying rubber on the Georgia asphalt, because we definitely would have gotten caught.

The OIS office sits in a nondescript upstairs office villa. I checked and rechecked to make sure I had everything: passport, application form, photo, debit card. A stern Nigerian woman waited on me upon my arrival, possibly the same one I had been emailing for the previous few weeks. While she didn't put up a fuss about taking my $45.00, I could tell she wasn't thrilled with the idea of this American white boy partaking in the Nigerian banking system. I wasn't the lone white person there, since others were applying for visas. I was certainly the only one there for a BVN, however. She reviewed my passport, took the photo for their records, then did a live biometrics capture.

"So ... what do I need to do now?" I asked. "When do I receive the BVN?"

"You will be emailed your BVN to the address you provided. Should take a few hours."

Odd. No official paperwork sent via registered mail? Nothing printed in the office? Someone's bank ID in Nigeria is sent to an email address in such informal fashion? Within half an hour I checked Gmail on my phone and the BVN email arrived.

The rest of the trip was enjoyable enough. On Saturday we trekked downtown to the Coca Cola Museum, where we sampled some truly horrific soft drinks from around the world, some of which need to be banned by the Geneva Convention. After the museum, we walked across the street to Olympic Park and did some sightseeing.

On Sunday we headed to Truist Park for the Braves/Mets game. I secured a handicapped parking space at the garage after talking to a myriad of Braves employees on the phone. Truist Park is a sexed-up carnival of a baseball park with mountains for kids to climb, batting cages, blaring music, and lunacy at every turn. By the time we reached our seats I had a tinge of anxiety from the bombardment of stimuli. As I predicted, the Braves had taken the first two games in the series from the Mets to force a tie atop the NL East. We had our usual cheap seat view, and Andrew couldn't see much of the action. The Braves won the game 5-3, and thus the NL East. Neither team went anywhere in the playoffs, as the Phillies won the pennant, despite fourteen fewer victories.

Problems with my plan arose once I returned. I emailed Mercuryo customer service, inquiring about their NGN rates, to which they responded the rate was no longer available and they were re-evaluating what to do with the Nigerian market. Regardless, I went ahead with the plan to apply for a Zenith account, as well as Sterling Bank, two of the top Nigerian banks. The problems I ran into were confusing. Zenith had a five-page application to fill out, but as I would learn time and time again, you need a Nigerian cell phone to do anything relevant in the NGN banking world. I gave OIS my U.S. cell number, so I always entered the incorrect country code on these applications. Further, banks like Zenith insist on tokens (6-digit pins) and I could not figure out how to get one. Sterling went much the same, though I finally managed an entry level One Bank account on the app.

Several other banks refused anyone without a local address or Nigerian passport. I finally found one, First City Monument Bank, who processed my application and granted me a Tier 1 account. This proved to be a serious problem, since Tier 1 is trash. 50,000 NGN limit per transaction and a cumulative balance of 300,000 NGN, which is like telling someone in America you can only deposit $70.00 at a time and hold $400.00 or so in your account at a time. Was this a joke? FCMB also demanded the token nonsense as well, since I needed one to verify my account to increase my limits, but I couldn't get the token without being in the country or having the proper cell. Without a token I couldn't increase my limits. I thought I would go mad.

Other banking apps such as Mintyn or Alat by Wema were also pointless, giving me the same Tier 1 status. Wema offered me a domiciliary account, which meant I could only transact in USD but not NGN. Kuda proved a better app. I at least got verified at a somewhat higher level after giving them a bogus Lagos address I found on a random address generator website. For all I know there's a random mailbox in Lagos with a plethora of Kuda Bank letters addressed to me.

Regardless, I needed to see how any of these accounts worked, even by transferring a small amount. I bought some BTC and signed up for Paxful, a truly sketchy website/app where people from all over the world deal in crypto. On Paxful, one can be scammed in a variety of ways: shady crypto traders, people selling bogus gift cards at a 70% discount, bogus Visa and Mastercard numbers, or those phishing for PayPal accounts to defraud. Name the scam and you'll find a scammer of your choice.

There are legit traders there as well. Make sure to check their feedback and reliability. I deposited this trivial amount of BTC on Paxful, linked my FCMB account, and opened a trade. No response. The problem I immediately ran into was few of these Nigerian traders wanted to trade with me. Even though I gained verified status on the site using my BVN, most traders knew I was an American and may well have thought *I* wanted to con *them*. Eventually, I found a legit trader who took my offer.

I was shocked at how amazingly fast the Nigerian banking system operates. I had the NGN in my FCMB account within five minutes. Incredible speed and efficiency compared to the tedium of American banks, where wiring money via bank transfer takes days to clear. We are living in the banking stone age. At least I knew I could complete a trade. I completed a few more trades on Paxful so I could gain some feedback and open myself up to more trading opportunities, since some major sellers block those without much feedback. I was never scammed on Paxful, but the biggest annoyance came from sellers who had discounted rates too good to be true. I tried opening a trade and invariably these swine would then attempt to negotiate a higher rate. When I refused, they dragged out the time limit for the trade. Paxful blocked U.S. customers in April 2023 due to regulatory concerns. A similar site, Noones, emerged, and I signed up for it. Noones didn't accept Americans either, but my BVN and a rented Argentinian phone number from an SMS website gained me access.

But what did this matter? I was no closer to achieving the real endgame goal of flipping the NGN back into USD at the coveted bank rate, nor did I have any access to the prime debit cards from any of these banks to potentially use a U.S. dollar card with naira deposits at bank rate. I analyzed other options such as Flywire, but the website seemed more about students overseas being sent money from home. I could hardly send myself money that way since I was no longer a student, and besides, there were limits on how much NGN can be sent. The CBN wasn't making this easy.

I finally solved my transaction limit problem after watching another YouTube video about the Grey.co website and app. Grey is a multi-currency platform where one can deal in U.S. dollars, British pounds, Nigerian naira, and a limited amount of other African currencies like Kenyan shillings (no deposit, only withdrawal on KES). Grey offered $5,000.00 daily limits in USD, or the equivalent in these other currencies, which more than suited my needs. The irony? I didn't even need the BVN. Since the site dealt in USD, I gave them my standard driver's license and signed up for the platform. I also did the same on another app platform, LemFi, which offered better exchange rates than Grey.

For much of 2023, I felt stuck. I couldn't figure out how to gain access to the bank rate. Using LemFi I could easily deposit USD with my debit card and flip it into NGN without a problem, but I needed another way of flipping back into USD and making a profit. I found a currency management platform, Kantox, and attempted several times to call various numbers, asking what I needed to do to gain access to Nigerian bank rate. Kantox was one of the few online platforms dealing in the coveted rate. I finally reached someone, but he told me they didn't deal with NGN much and he couldn't help me.

I also tried Convera, another fintech currency exchange platform. I couldn't get a hold of anyone at the various U.S. phone numbers, so I finally called a Canadian number. I finally talked to someone after a long wait.

"Hello, do you offer naira to USD at bank rate?" I asked.

"Yes, we do. What type of business do you run in Nigeria?"

"I don't have a business in Nigeria, or any registered business, yet. I'm trying to figure out the feasibility of arbitrage trading naira by converting USD at the black-market rate, which everyone uses, and then converting back at the official rate."

"In that case we can't help you. We deal in multi-million-dollar businesses here who sell actual products, goods, or services. However, you have a decent idea here."

Amanda had long since been perplexed at all of this. "I have no idea what you are trying to do with all this Nigerian nonsense. But then none of this stuff you try ever works."

Nigeria's banking system became a complete dumpster fire in 2023. Bizarrely, the government tried to eliminate traditional currency in favor of e-naira, a digital form of currency which few people adopted. The experiment was a fiasco. I never understood the purpose, nor did e-naira apply to me, anyway. More frustrating, the news hit in mid-2023 that CBN was desperate to unify the bank rate with the black-market rate to wipe out the black market once and for all. For all intents and purposes, the black-market rate *was* the rate. Most Nigerian businesses used black market rate. Even banking apps like Grey used it. The solution was to give up and use black market rate as the official rate, so CBN set the official rate around 750. This achieved nothing short term, since the black market merely shifted past 1,000. All the Nigerian government achieved was a devaluing of their own currency.

Since the chasm still existed between bank and black-market rate, I kept studying the situation. I found another video discussing Swap by Flutterwave, which used bank rate for conversions. Shock of shocks, I managed to complete a transaction this way, a trivial $20.00 deal where I deposited onto LemFi, flipped into NGN, then sent the NGN to the Wema account Flutterwave gave me. A few days later my U.S. bank was credited. I made a few dollars. The problems were thus: I couldn't repeat these transactions easily, since each took days to clear, because as I mentioned, U.S. banking still operates in the stone age. Further, after YouTube videos were out discussing how to do this transaction, the Flutterwave Swap site was flooded and inoperable for long stretches at a time. After a few weeks of this, the site gave up and posted a notice saying, "We are out of funds for today, try again tomorrow at noon."

Flutterwave's main website was a decent idea, if I could figure out how to register as an individual seller on the site. I tried registering as an American, since USD was available on the site, but I couldn't get anywhere. I contacted customer service repeatedly, but nothing they said or did ever made sense. I became fed up and told them to disregard my current application, but I would try again with the BVN under Nigerian registration. I managed to verify the BVN but hit the wall once they asked for a National Identification Number.

I had long since realized I needed the NIN as well, if I wanted to do anything worthwhile, increase banking limits, gain a decent debit card with any of these banks, or apply to Flutterwave. I searched online to see if this was feasible, and even after reading up on the issue, I wasn't crystal clear whether a non-native could obtain one. Sure, random people from neighboring countries might be able to show up at a location in Nigeria and be rubber stamped, but how could I do this in America?

OCTOBER 3, 2023

I made a last-ditch effort at this entire ordeal on fall break. I found the address of a Nigerian immigration service in Lexington and called to set up an appointment to inquire about the NIN. I convinced Amanda and Andrew to stop at this place, since we were driving through Lexington on our way to Asheville for the break. I brought my passport, debit card, and BVN. The location wasn't an office of any sort, but instead a residential house a couple of miles off I-75. We pulled into the driveway, and I knocked on the door. A thin, middle aged, Nigerian man answered.

"Hello, who are you?" he asked.

"We've talked on the phone. I'm here about getting an NIN. I have my passport and BVN with me." He looked at me as if I had three heads.

"But sir, you are not Nigerian."

"Do I have to be? Nothing on your website directly stated I needed to be. I obtained the BVN, after all."

"How were you allowed to get the BVN?"

"I gave OIS my passport and money. They were fine with it."

"But ... you are not Nigerian. The software inside has a box to check stating 'Nigerian origin,' and I can't seriously say that in your case."

"Bottom line this for me. Are you willing to help me or not?" He paused for a moment.

"Well, no. Not usually. But maybe for one thousand dollars."

Unbelievable. Even someone acting in a quasi-official status for the Nigerian government ran a scam of his own.

"Sorry, I'm not interested." We left immediately. Once we returned from fall break I toyed with the idea of signing up for a local Louisville based NIN distribution, which were infrequent but happened at a local immigration center on occasion. However, they demanded a fee up front, and since I wasn't sure if they would give me the NIN slip even after paying them, I dropped the idea. Over time, I forgot about the NIN, the BVN, or anything else to do with Nigerian banking.

As far as the naira goes, eventually the CBN managed to unify the bank rate with the black-market rate. Both now hover around the 1,500-

1,600 range, a complete and utter destruction of the currency, which brings to mind the hyperinflation of post WW1 era Germany. But no major war caused this. On the contrary, these fools seemingly crashed their currency on their own.

My attempts at making huge profits and becoming a Nigerian prince were ill fated, another poorly thought-out plan in a series of them. Knowing an opportunity, even a fleeting one, is out there but being unable to navigate the red tape and nonsensical bureaucracy was incredibly frustrating. Now if you'll excuse me, I must go. I have more YouTube crypto arbitrage videos to watch. One of them has to work someday ... right?

Chapter 2

Sonic Screamer: The Demos

What in God's name is that racket?!

— My mom, anytime in 1994

Let me take you back to a time when alternative rock ruled the charts, and my creativity, from a musical perspective, was in full flourish. Mind you, I have never taken a guitar, drums, or piano lesson in my life. I can't play any instrument. I'm not a vocalist whatsoever. But hey, why let a complete and total lack of musical talent stop me from delving into the world of music?

I never cared much for popular music in middle school. I drifted so far out of the mainstream during those years as to not know any relevant songs or albums. I was slightly young for the initial popularity of bands like Nirvana or Pearl Jam, but by the time I reached high school I was more inclined to be interested.

For Christmas in 1993, I had two CDs on my list which excited me: Nirvana's *In Utero* and Pearl Jam's *Vs*. Technically, I opened those a day or two earlier when we visited my paternal grandmother's house in Henderson. She looked negatively at the bizarre baby imagery on the back of *In Utero*, nor was she happy to see a song called "Rape Me" on the album. As far as my parents, eh, they didn't care.

I vividly remember listening to these CDs once we were home. I put on *Vs.* first, since I figured it was less abrasive than the Nirvana album. After the album played, no one in the room was especially thrilled. My dad's verdict: "I mean, you can listen to it, but that's all. Nothing bothered me about it, but I wasn't compelled, either. Anyway, why don't you listen to the other CD on headphones? We're going to bed."

So, I did. I put on a pair of headphones and cranked up *In Utero* on the stereo system. Our stereo was one of those early '90s massive systems with a CD player, dual tape decks, a record player, and AM/FM radio. My life has never been the same since. From the opening of "Serve the Servants" I was blown away. Forty-one minutes later, and I sat there, not believing what I had heard. I quickly made a tape off the CD and wanted my dad to listen to it in the car. This time his verdict? "Those boys are too hard for me. It held my interest, though." Ah. I found something to terrify my parents. After all, who wants to listen to music with their parents when they are fourteen? Hell, if I wanted that, I could have kept listening to the Spin Doctors.

That Christmas, my brother Eric received a rather curious present of his own, namely a cheesy Fisher Price kid's keytar, complete with a microphone headset. The keytar was shaped like a kiddie guitar, featuring various buttons for keyboard sounds, as well as a demo button which played "It's a Small World" incessantly. Eric also received a kiddie tape recorder. He never thought of anything to do with these presents, but I certainly did.

As 1994 dawned, I became immersed in this exciting world of alternative rock music, in due part because 1994 was an amazing year for the genre. Every week some all-time classic album was released, featuring songs still in heavy rotation to this day. Alice In Chains' *Jar of Flies*, Beck's *Mellow Gold*, Soundgarden's *Superunknown*, Nine Inch Nails' *The Downward Spiral*, Stone Temple Pilots' *Purple*, Green Day's *Dookie*, The Offspring's *Smash*, Weezer's self-titled debut, and so many others.

The two albums which struck my fancy in terms of an approach I wanted to do were *Mellow Gold* and *The Downward Spiral*, alongside

In Utero. The Beck album fascinated me because at times it felt like this guy's absurd home demo recordings were done with minimal production, except a major label decided to release this to the masses. *Mellow Gold* is hilariously brilliant. One criticism of grunge or alternative rock was that the music sounded too depressing. In the case of some bands that might be true, whereas Beck was laugh-out-loud funny. "Truck-drivin Neighbors Downstairs" is still one of the funniest songs I've ever heard.

The *Downward Spiral* isn't necessarily one of my favorite albums these days, mainly because I can't stomach the lyrical content anymore. It's the perfect album for a rage filled teen and also holds the record for the album my parents ordered me to turn off in the quickest amount of time. Once the intro to "Mr. Self-Destruct" finished and the song truly kicked in, they were mortified and immediately yelled, "Turn that crap off now!" Trent Reznor was doing something right.

The most fascinating aspect of Reznor was the idea of him as a one-man band. Sure, NIN were also an actual touring band, but in the studio Reznor did everything. Since I had zero musical training, I could hardly audition for someone's band. The only person I knew at school in a band was Chris Owens, singer/guitarist of Snoit. I wasn't taking any of this seriously and had no designs on a musical career, so the Reznor method of being a one-man band and trying things at home seemed the way to go.

I first attempted a recording in the Spring of 1994. I played around with the keytar for a while, trying to figure out what this thing could do. One critical aspect revealed itself when I accidentally placed the microphone next to the speaker and ear-splitting feedback resulted. From a kid's instrument, no less. Oh, I was going to have fun now. The first "song" I recorded was little more than me blathering lyrics from "March of the Pigs," and the aforementioned "Truckdrivin Neighbors." Midway through I busted out my feedback solo and tried playing a few notes on the keyboard.

The bizarre nature of this recording was evident once I played it back. The awful kiddie recorder messed up the basic sound and the music played back ultra slowly and freaky, akin to the songs parents would be *sure* had some Satanic elements. I played this for my mom, as well as a second instrumental (with some feedback of course). Her mouth dropped. "Is that you? How did you even *do* something like that?"

For the next few days, I kept recording bizarre songs featuring titles such as "Hair," "Teeth," "Skills," "Jurassic Prick," and the like. I had no idea what I was doing, hammering away on this keytar, creating feedback, and I even dragged out an older Casio keyboard and played some of the demo patterns. I titled this demo tape *The Beatnik Vampire*, a wacky comic character I created while bored in Mr. Orwick's Algebra 1 class.

I couldn't wait to have some of my classmates listen to my twelve song epic demo, lasting little over twenty minutes. Jim Hitchens, the closest thing I had to a decent friend in high school, was the first victim. I let him borrow the tape, and his review the next day proved revealing.

"I laid down on my bed with headphones on, put your tape in my Walkman, and a few seconds later I was so shocked I fell off the bed. What the hell *is* this!?"

Ah, perfect. I wanted to freak people out with these recordings. I also subjected Jessica Herbert, with whom I had several discussions of popular music, to various demo tapes as I recorded them, to which she replied in rather puzzled fashion, "Um, these have been ... interesting."

Owens, for his part, was not a fan. He took this stuff seriously, and he resented a total hack amateur, who had zero idea what he was doing, trying to record demos. He listened to these early tapes I recorded, which also included demos titled *Masked Man* and *Bathroom Noises*, but wasn't shocked, and didn't find them funny.

Early on in the recording of *Bathroom Noises* the mic for the keytar died, and I sadly could no longer conjure up feedback, which limited what I could do. Hence, the title of the demo. I used the washer and dryer as drums, flushed the toilet on one song, made fart noises on another, and other inanities. My attempt at a concept album, but not one of my better efforts. Since the mic died, and I hated the crappy kiddie recorder, I ceased recording ... for the time being.

I wanted two things for my birthday in August: a new keytar with a working mic, as well as a decent tape recorder. Shockingly, my wishes were granted, and by the time school started up again I was back in business. One of the early attempts included Chad Black sitting in on acoustic guitar for a few songs recorded in my grandma's basement, though he knew as much about playing guitar as I did keytar. I also tested the new keytar and tape recorder by recording the most insanely loud fever dream of a "song" you can imagine. Classic end of album extra track noise. I played the tape back in front of the hall bathroom door while Chad took a dump. When he came back downstairs, I told him I had been busy while he was indisposed, to which he replied in deadpan fashion, "Yeah, I heard that."

My first solo attempt with the new equipment was the *Guber Boy* demo. The demo was largely forgettable, mainly serving as a test of the new keytar and recording. The sound was bone crunching now, so this alone created solid improvement.

As Keith Richards said about punk rockers in 1977, "They're going to get better. You can't *not* get better." That was true here, as well. I started to figure out how to play this thing. In the following months, I developed my own deranged style of playing on the kid's keytar. Instead of using the mic for merely feedback, I discovered playing notes while using the feedback created wild distortion. Further, I leaned into the demo button, but instead of letting it play the same irritating song, I kept hitting the button repeatedly while also playing the keytar. This gave a wild, crunching effect which sounded like an entire band playing multiple instruments. The mix of this approach with the softer acoustic numbers became the original demo tape, *Sonic Screamer*. I even started writing full-fledged lyrics for some songs while bored in homeroom, such as "Smoking Rope." I can still recall these Parental Advisory level lyrics:

And once I was a little boy ...
Hey, you
I know you
You're the kid from the neighborhood
You're the one that's always smoking rope
Hey, you
I know you
You're the one I caught that's been fucking my daughter

18

Hey, you
I know you
You're the one that fucked my wife
Hey, what's up?
I know you
You're the kid that's smoking rope
I know you from way back when
You're the one that fucked my dog
Hey, you
I know you
You're the kid that's been smoking rope

I kept plugging away and recorded another demo, *Beats R Us*, which even Owens found to be one of my better efforts. "Well, at least you are learning how to put together a memorable riff or two," he said, with faint praise. Another classmate, Justin, was in a Christian rock band, and he volunteered to see what he could do with *Beats R Us* in a professional studio. After a while he gave up, noting, "There isn't anything I can do here. There's no actual coherent song structures on the tape." As I would later prove, there were songs, but they needed a backbone added to them.

I recorded one last demo tape circa 1994, *Treble Rebel (AKA The Black and Tan Tape)*, a title taken after Jim Hitchens jokingly referred to me as such a rebel after listening to my first demo. I ran out of blank audio cassettes, and my parents weren't in a rush to buy more, given what I had been doing with them. I typically recorded these demos in my bedroom with the door shut, but there's no way they couldn't hear the insane racket being created. I would surmise the neighbors down the hall probably heard as well, though no one complained, oddly enough.

Treble Rebel was the most adventurous and wild demo I recorded. I figured out how to do the style I attempted but also created crazier songs where I played the demo button, keytar, *and* used the mic to create feedback all at once. Was this stuff unlistenable? Of course. That was the point. I started creating a different type of feedback by placing the mic on the back of the keytar, creating an uncanny underwater feedback noise in the two instrumentals, "Submarine 1 and 2" songs.

I could tell the mic was going out again during the recording of this demo tape. By the time I finished it had kicked the bucket. I had abused the hell out of this kiddie equipment, doing experimental noise music never intended. By late 1994, my enthusiasm waned for recording music, anyway. I was out of ideas. I had exhausted what I could do on the keytar, so I quit recording.

Over the years these demos stayed in my bureau drawer, and on occasion Eric and I would pull them out and listen to them for a laugh. Make no mistake, these unedited demos were hilarious if you were in the right mood. When Amanda and I first met, I had her listen to *The Beatnik Vampire,* as she laid on my bed at my apartment with headphones on and prosthetic leg off. Seconds later she was in tears from laughing. But for the most part, these tapes sat in a drawer collecting dust for years, and I never had much interest in doing anything with them.

Alas, similar to my own interest in recording demos, the early to mid '90s alternative rock boom was destined to fade, even if I hoped at the time it would last for years. I feel a deeper and deeper sadness about the death of Kurt Cobain as the years pass. I still remember being on spring break when the news broke on April 8, 1994. Given how huge of a Nirvana fan I had become in such a short amount of time, Cobain's death hit hard. I recall even Owens being deeply affected the next week at school, and he never showed much genuine emotion over anything.

The alt rock movement of the 1990s was a special time—until its inevitable post Nirvana slide into mediocrity by decade's end. I only wish I'd realized it at the time. Maybe I would have had more fun and appreciated those years more. But the '90s wasn't a decade about having fun. That was the '80s. The '90s carried a type of cultural inferiority complex, always trying to mean something, even while everything felt vaguely unsatisfying. The rage was palpable. I felt it. But why, and against whom? I didn't know. Cobain exemplified that feeling of inscrutable angst, the "Voice of a Generation," who mostly spoke in cryptic lyrics only he understood. In the end, Cobain defined the ultimate cultural failure of the '90s: a decade with so much potential, yet so little of it actually realized.

The first movie I recall steeped in '90s era nostalgia was *Juno.* I laughed out loud at Jason Bateman's character saying his favorite song was the Sonic Youth cover of "Superstar" from the Carpenters tribute album circa 1994. I used to tape *120 Minutes* back then on a weekly basis and my dad occasionally watched some of the videos with me. One week they hyped the epic debut of that Sonic Youth cover, and my dad took special interest, since he always swore Karen Carpenter was the greatest singer he'd ever seen in person. Even drunken WKU frat boys stopped dead in their tracks when she started belting. Imagine the sheer horror he felt as the bizarre feedback started on the Sonic Youth version, then Thurston Moore's eerie whisper of the lyrics. Dad sat stunned, mouth agape, before finally ranting, "Jesus Christ, what is this shit? Someone take the mic from that asshole! Hell, they have a girl in the band! Let her try and sing it!"

People romanticize the era now, but here's the truth: the '90s is a far better decade to look back on than it was to live through. Sure, there are TV shows and movies set in 1995, celebrating the dawn of the internet age, but I wonder—how would a young person today react if they hopped in Doc Brown's DeLorean and traveled back in time to 1995? They would probably find it boring. And they would be right. 1995 *was* boring. There was no YouTube back then, so if you wanted to watch a music video MTV never played you had to call The Box, spend 99 cents, and hope it played an hour later. Yet that boredom was filled with small moments that only became special years later in hindsight. I recorded these demos mainly out of sheer boredom. What I wouldn't give to be bored like that again.

CHAPTER 3

SONIC SCREAMER: THE ALBUM

For the audio clips and music videos described in this chapter check out
https://www.youtube.com/@demosonicscreamer7340

AUGUST 2012

Amanda, Andrew, and I finally moved away from Tanglewood
Apartments and into our new patio home, which lies in a sleepy area in
back of Waverly Hills Sanitarium. Once our belongings were in place
and in working order, school started back up. I started my first full year
of subbing, but in August there weren't many jobs on the sub website as
of yet. Andrew started Life Church daycare, so I found myself with time
on my hands. Now that we were settled into the new house I had what
to look forward to, exactly?

Eric sometimes came over to visit and hang out in the afternoon for
a few hours. One afternoon I decided to rummage through the old
drawer and found all my demo tapes. We spent a few days listening to
these hilariously primitive cassettes until a fascinating thought occurred
to me.

I wonder if I could do something with this stuff?

I started thinking. What exactly could I do with nearly two-decade-old demo tapes? The vocals were incoherent on several songs, since the mic on the kid's keytar had the same speaker as the keytar, so the music and the vocals were fighting for breathing room. I also recall practically drooling on the mic at times, my performance being so intense.

The first idea I had was to digitize the tapes using a direct hook up from the stereo system to a laptop computer using the microphone slot on the computer. I used the Audacity program to create audio files. I tried my first tape, *The Beatnik Vampire*, using such a setup, to see whether the idea proved viable or not. I digitized the tape without incident, but when I played back the audio the new files were unusable. I heard incessant tape hiss, breaks in the sound, and imperfections too large to ignore. The idea of direct transfer wasn't going to work, but what about indirect transfers? By this I mean live captures via Audacity using a small microphone to pick up the performance, as though I could transport myself back in time to 1994 and record digitally. Thus, I bought a cheap $3.00 mic for this process.

I spent the next few weeks playing the tapes out loud on the stereo for the microphone to hear and record in Audacity files. The results were a mixed bag. My earliest recordings were so primitive and painful to listen to that they weren't salvageable. While I transferred them over to aup3 files, I planned nothing much beyond using these songs to amuse friends and guests. I knew that stuff sucked. More disappointing, the songs using acoustic guitar didn't work with this rinky-dink setup. The cheap mic couldn't pick up acoustic guitar (or electric either - I had Eric bring his guitar, and I tried to record him, with no success). Therefore, I decided any of the songs using acoustic guitar were not viable. Whenever Chad didn't play the acoustic, I tried to play keytar *and* acoustic guitar all at once, while scream-singing at the same time. In 1994 I didn't have a program such as Audacity to record these tracks individually, nor did I even have a four-track recorder.

There existed no particular urgency with this project. Whenever I had some down time, I opened a file on Audacity and sifted through the dreck to find usable songs in order to piece together a full album. The problems were numerous. On most songs I missed notes or had to turn off the keytar to stop the demo button from playing, since bits of "It's a Small World" infected songs and had to be trimmed out. Audacity is fairly easy to use once you get the hang of it, allowing the user to zoom in and quickly eliminate a shaky section, then replace it with a similar section to create a more flawless end result.

While the acoustic guitar songs were unusable, I was stunned at how crisp and powerful sounding these keytar-oriented noise songs were, once transferred to Audacity. The forgettable *Guber Boy* tape especially sounded clear and potent, which made sense, given its status as the first recording I made after receiving the new keytar and tape recorder. None of the songs by themselves were anything thrilling, but I noted a particularly strong thirty seconds of instrumental, as well as a shockingly jarring scream. Bits and pieces to augment other songs, easily edited out of one file and into another. In the case of a couple of those thirty second clips, I could easily loop those four times to create a two-minute instrumental song.

There was no escaping one key fact: These songs had nothing to them, instrumentally speaking. What I mean is they weren't the product of a full band. They needed something else for structural backbone. As my mom said when I played the files for her, "They don't make no sense!" Amanda loathed having to hear these demos, long since not finding any of these songs amusing. "They're screechy and terrible!" she ranted.

Enter a Yamaha electric drum kit. Amanda surprised me with this for a Christmas present in 2013, given she knew what I had in mind. I planned to do quite a bit, as this absurd lark started becoming a serious project. I spent the holidays figuring out which songs were viable enough to add drums, which meant a decent amount of the non-acoustic material from *Sonic Screamer*, eight of the better cuts from *Beats R Us*, and various songs from *The Black and Tan Tape*. *Guber Boy* provided a few minutes of instrumentals, and one song "I Coulda Been Somebody." I planned to use the crazed noise I used to torment Chad but wasn't sure where it would work.

I had a rather bizarre setup to record the drums. Typically, I played the drums in the back bedroom on days I wasn't subbing, thinking up catchy drumbeats for a particular song. I used a variety of settings on the Yamaha kit, but don't ask me what the names are of them individually, since I've long forgotten what they are beyond a numbered setting.

Most settings give you a basic drum sound, a deeper bass drum sound, and two other pads used for cymbals and what not.

Eric helped on occasion. He came up with the military style drum beat for "Beware the Deep Voiced Commando," so I gave him a co-writing credit. Sometimes he might press play or record as I would add the new drum track to the existing files. I usually listened to the song on headphones, while hammering away on drums to keep up. I could always hear a faint amount of the song on the drum track bleeding in from the headphones, but once I matched the sound this wasn't notice-able on a final cut.

I may not be a professional drummer, but drumming is the only thing I could do in a band at a high level if I wanted to learn. If I screwed up, I could always edit out a mistimed strike and replace it with a better version on Audacity. The one song I never played correctly on drums was "Cold Turd." The keyboard riff on the song was too quick for me to keep pace. I couldn't fully keep up the pace no matter how many times I tried. Frustrating, since the song was one of the original high-lights of my old demos.

I became a perfectionist, spending weeks analyzing each song for off kilter notes, clipping the audio, replacing poor areas of songs with better parts from other songs which worked better. "Knife" was a problematic song since the ideas I had originally weren't possible, due to the limits of the crappy kid's keytar. I usually had to shut off the keytar due to the demo button and the song playing. I edited out instances where I turned off the instrument to resume playing after a bellowing scream, then also edited the chaotic attempt at a feedback bridge near the end of the song. I played the song so many times I had to have driven anyone else in the house crazy.

One dilemma was the ambient noise on all of the tracks. Not just the original cassette-based demos, but the newer drum tracks, as well. One of the benefits of Audacity is the ability to utilize noise reduction. I would highlight a baseline of ambient noise, then use it to remove the noise from the entire song. Ironically, I titled one of my tracks "Noise Reduction," a song which I drastically edited from a ponderous four minutes down to a leaner, crisper 2:22. I also conjured up a techno remix of that song as well, done by doubling the speed of the drum tracks to create an aggressively wild version of the song. Again, "Cold Turd" provided the problem here. Try as I might, I never could entirely remove the hissing from the intro to the song, not without compromising the keyboard notes as well. Such is life.

Eric wasn't overly thrilled with the mixes after all the noise removal. "You've made this sound so much less fascinating," he said. Had to be done, though. My mom had a far different opinion after listening to a nearly finished mix of the album. "This 'music' of yours has made my heart race so fast I'm close to having a breakdown," she said. I was on the right track, after all!

Since the beginnings and endings of the demo tracks all sucked, I used the drumkit and Audacity trickery to mask this fact. Clacking the drumsticks together, adding odd, staggered sounds to the end of songs, anything to hide the fact that I had to turn off the keytar originally and stop the song dead in its tracks. I recall playing the instrumental "Hellish Beat" for Isaac at one point and asked for his analysis.

"Needs more cowbell," he said.

"Totally," I replied. So, I added a cowbell effect to the beginning of the song. I planned to use another instrumental, "Pioneer Stock," as the album opener, but decided to use "Hellish Beat," instead. The idea of beginning an album with cowbell being too irresistibly amusing to ignore.

There was also the matter of having so many instrumentals. I had five other instrumentals I wanted to use, but didn't know how to sequence them. I felt they were decent enough to add drums, but I couldn't stop the album dead in its tracks five different times for instrumental interludes. What if I combined all five of these into one ten-minute epic? I put together a prog rock style suite titled "Metamorphosis" with five subchapters:

1. Submarine
2. Anarchy (a condensed version of the crazy noise previously mentioned)
3. Scrambled Brain
4. Chaos
5. Submarine 2

Oddly enough, this lunacy does tell a story, if you know what to listen for, starting ominous but slow, descending into a state of anarchy, then complete madness and chaos, before relaxing again with the eerie, repetitive, echo feedback.

Most of the songs were slightly over two minutes in length, primarily because I originally played until the timer on the recorder reached 100 and then I would stop. Usually, I ran out of ideas by then anyway. I settled on nineteen total tracks, eighteen of which were blistering and crazy, and then the album-closing five-part epic. Rancid's ... *And Out Come the Wolves* is one of my all-time favorite albums, and while musically there isn't much in common other than the number of tracks, the sequencing (minus the epic) was what I strove for. The one song originally on *Beatnik Vampire* making its way
onto the album, "Don't Take Away My Happiness," was a song pieced together from a couple of incarnations I recorded. "Jungle Bellow" became the looniest standard song on the album, a stitched together hybrid of different drumbeats, the mind boggling scream lifted from *Guber Boy*, and a crazed feedback outro.

I planned on doing a physical and digital release of the album, titled *Sonic Screamer*, since I found that title the coolest of my original demo tapes. Rather absurdly, I decided on the artist name Demo, though in hindsight I wish I hadn't, since there is also another artist named Demo, and this became a bone of confusion on Spotify when the site tried to categorize my album on his page. I wonder if I can switch those around and have the artist name Sonic Screamer and the album called *Demos*? (Note: In April 2025 I resubmitted the album on CD Baby for this purpose, as well as changing my YouTube clips to reflect this update).

CD Baby was my choice of release, primarily because they could provide CDs physically, but also distributed the album to iTunes and other online streaming platforms for $35.00. I had to trim "Metamorphosis" a few seconds to sneak under the ten-minute length for iTunes, lest it be considered an EP. The iTunes aspect wasn't especially expensive, roughly ten bucks to list the album there. I spent slightly more to also release the "Noise Reduction" remix as a single on iTunes.

Something I learned while figuring out iTunes vs. CDs is the difference in file quality between those two methods. I exported the files as

MP3s for iTunes, which is a condensed version of the original Audacity file. I can't recall now if MP3s were all I could use on iTunes or CD Baby. Compact discs use WAV format, which is not condensed, and provides a considerably better quality of sound. I wondered if many users of iTunes even understand they are buying a lesser form of music with MP3s? When given the option, always opt for a lossless audio file such as WAV or Apple Lossless.

I decided to order a run of 100 CDs from CD Baby, some of which I would distribute myself to local record stores on consignment, while selling the rest myself. This provided a definite challenge, since a physical release requires album art, so I had to work on this as well. Amanda had a beat-up old clown doll she dragged out of mothballs. This clown seemed appropriately freaky looking, so I thought of propping him up in a child's chair for a pose in front of my mom's bedroom door. I tinkered endlessly on Pixlr, PicMonkey, and a few other websites for filters, vignette settings, and text. The vignette setting gave the cover a look as though someone with a flashlight aimed it at this freaky clown. The iTunes cover is not the same as the eventual CD cover, looking cheerier and more normal. And who wants that?

I used the same basic font and style for the back cover, listing each track. What could I do about a booklet? I had no coherent lyrics to include. Half the time I had no idea what I screamed out anyway. No credits, aside from myself and Eric for his contribution to one song. But I needed something as a gatefold, even a trivial design such as the first Weezer album, which had a booklet consisting of no other pages than the gatefold. I decided to film a few seconds of Waverly Hills with my HD camcorder on a snowy February day for future use, a shot impossible now, since a house blocks the vantage point. But in 2014 there were less houses in the area, and I could get a wintery shot of the eerie sanitarium. I applied a nighttime filter and more vignette to the picture, then decided to use it for the gatefold.

I wanted a clear background on the inner CD casing, so I needed another picture design as a background. I had a pic of a few framed photos of my grandparents, which I used a similar blue filter as the rest of the artwork, and then applied a wild kaleidoscope setting to make it look hallucinatory. Quite the imagery.

If I wanted to own the rights to the album, I also needed to do some registrations. I applied for *Sonic Screamer* to be registered at the Library of Congress, as well as buying a twenty-five pack of UPC barcodes for $25.00 from Speedybarcodes.com. Don't waste money buying expensive bar codes. I provided one for iTunes, and also one for CD Baby's physical release, but those clowns screwed up and assigned me one of their own UPCs, so my CDs all have the wrong bar code on the back. Later, they remedied this problem by sending me a series of stickers to place on the cellophane wrapping for each CD. No wonder CD Baby discontinued physical media.

Upon my receipt of the discs, Eric was floored. "I can't wrap my head around this. It's so cool to see the end result of something I helped create." Personally, I was frustrated at seeing an incorrect barcode, so I couldn't enjoy holding the CD in my hands. A few days later the two of us made the rounds to various indie record stores around Bardstown Road and Frankfort Avenue, dropping off five copies a piece at stores such as Better Days, Underground Sounds, Guestroom Records, and Matt Anthony's. I never checked back with any of these stores to see if they sold any copies. I tend to think they didn't, since I've seen a few copies pop up on eBay in recent years, which is the only way new copies could be online.

I pondered the idea of a vinyl record release as well, but after looking online at a few record pressing websites quickly gave up on the idea. 100 CDs cost me about $190.00. The same 100 copies on vinyl cost roughly $1,000.00. Rant time: I have never, and will never, understand the appeal of vinyl records. Frankly, the bizarre surge in vinyl in recent years baffles me. Vinyl is an outdated form of listening to music, as well as an expensive one. Purists will have you believe records sound better than CDs, which I assume is an urban legend dating back to the initial awful CD mastering jobs done on classic older albums. For example, *Sabbath Bloody Sabbath* had a terrible original CD mastering, with sound so low the listener could barely hear the album. Subsequent remasters of those albums on CD were much higher quality.

For newer music recorded in the past thirty-five years, few major releases were ever done with the idea of mixing down to analog for a vinyl release. Sure, these albums have been released on vinyl, but if they are using the same WAV files I used, would they not be losing quality by pressing them on vinyl instead of a CD? Personally, I could never get past the record scratching sounds on vinyl, finding those more frustrating than cassette tape hiss. Frankly, I tend to think the music industry wants to sell vinyl records at a prestige price far beyond the cost of a CD, so labels push vinyl now. For any independent artist or band, however, vinyl is a costly way of doing business merely to impress the hipster crowd.

Some of my friends also bought CDs, including Isaac and Kate buying five copies for friends of theirs who professed an interest. Isaac said of the final album, "This isn't too bad. A perfect counter to the bass filled car stereos you hear on the road." His curious praise pointed at the biggest fundamental problem the album had, however: It didn't suck enough. Make no mistake, I wanted a terrorizing experience for the listener, an antagonistic experience that would clear a room if one put the album on. I cranked up each Audacity setting so far I would single handedly win the Loudness War without anyone putting up a fight, even if I did normalize the overall sound before submitting the album to iTunes or CD Baby. This isn't an album to be listened to with noise canceling headphones. Find a cheap boombox and crank this CD up and let the volume kick your ass. What I lacked in budget I made up for in sheer volume.

I also joined Radio Airplay in April 2014 and posted the album there. Oddly enough, I managed to reach the Top 10 in the Louisville area on the site and gained some fans from other countries in the process. Did these people not understand the entire album was *supposed* to suck? That I had zero musical talent?

To bolster *Sonic Screamer*, I also filmed a couple of music videos for YouTube, which I edited on the old Windows Movie Maker. I long considered "Smoking Rope" my best song, so it made for an ideal first "single" of sorts. I used the evil clown to great effect in this video, as the first-person character encounters the clown at every turn while trying to escape my mom's house, until the camera collapses to the ground. Cue the video shot of Waverly Hills to fade out. I released both a color and B & W version of "Smoking Rope." I tend to think the B & W version is creepier and better, but it has fewer views on YouTube than the color version.

I created another music video for the song "Bon Jovi Sucks," which has zero to do with Bon Jovi. It was my attempt at doing a harsh, riff filled song full of screaming similar to Nirvana's "Scentless Apprentice," so listen to the song with that in mind, if you dare. The title originated from hearing the dreary Bon Jovi ballad "Always" in late 1994. "How dare Bon Jovi have a new song out!" I thought. "Don't they realize this is 1994 and they should go away now?"

The video has nothing to do with Bon Jovi either, instead featuring a ragged doll pondering the decline of the city he lives in while hanging himself in the garage. We see shots of empty buildings, XXX motels and the like to illustrate a decaying city. At the end, the doll's owner places his body in a plastic bag and tosses him in the trash. Some of the YouTube comments on the video crack me up, with one saying, "This song is a rip off of KMFDM." That would be difficult, considering I've never heard a single KMFDM album. At least accuse me of ripping off "Scentless Apprentice."

After filming this video, I ran out of steam. The album became a drain on time and finances, especially considering few people bought any copies from me. Whenever Amanda and I discuss housecleaning, she always starts with, "There's a box of crap in the closet that should be the first thing to go," referring to the box of unsold CDs.

Amusingly, students at Manual High School stumbled upon my YouTube clips and I gained somewhat of a cult following for a while. I recall the guitar teacher at YPAS (Youth Performing Arts School, part of Manual) telling me, "Some of the students were talking about your songs. I think you're becoming famous. Oh, and you are right. Bon Jovi does in fact suck."

In 2016, while I was student teaching at Holy Cross High School, some of the kids found out about *Sonic Screamer* and occasionally made murmuring comments while I was teaching. This led to the awkward conversation among the admins as to whether "Cold Turd" had a deleterious effect on the youth of the Archdiocese of Louisville. I can hope.

I have never recouped my investment from the physical release. My royalties from the various platforms? About $17.00. *Sonic Screamer* wasn't about making money, but more about its two-decade long journeyof creation. I've never had any official reviews of the album, so I have no idea whether it's any good or not. I sent a copy to the music critic of Leo - a local newspaper I thought would give the album a chance. I never heard back from him. Judging by the YouTube reactions, the opinion seems split 50/50, which is a shame, since I was gunning for 100% dislike. The full album on YouTube has an amusing comment by a former Manual student: "Bro, you need to release another album of these bangers!" Sorry, no can do. Well, not unless someone happens to have a 1994 era Fisher Price keytar.

The cover of my first demo tape, The Beatnik Vampire.

Another absurd demo cover, Guber Boy.

The cover of my demo compilation tape, Tree Head.

Final album cover of Sonic Screamer (2014, updated April 2025).

PART TWO

ROCHELLE

CHAPTER 4

THE GIRL FROM PINELLAS PARK

NOVEMBER 16, 2023

"Coming to Louisville in May."

I received that text message today. How long has it been? Fifteen years? Sixteen in May? So much has changed since I last saw Rochelle. Went back to grad school for my master's. Got married and had a kid. We've texted each other sporadically over the years, though always slightly at arm's length. As I stared at my phone looking at this text, many memories came flooding back, some of them as vivid as the day they happened. Others were like something from a half-remembered dream, fragments of time from a previous era when we were close.

Sometimes in life you randomly stumble into people who wind up meaning a great deal purely by chance. After my unsatisfying trip to Los Angeles in August 2001, I felt unsure of what to do next. Should I apply to film schools for graduate work, or get a boring job somewhere like Enterprise? I made an odd decision on that front and plowed full blown into selling movies on eBay, fifty listings a week, by early 2002.

I still tried finding local girls to date online during this time period, and AOL profiles were a help. Back then the situation wasn't hard to scour your city for profiles on AOL and match entries with similar interests. If locals didn't pass muster, why stop there? Expand the search to the entire country, which I did in late 2001. On a lark I did a nationwide search for the following: Female, wrestling fan, Rob Van Dam, WWF. One of the sillier screen names repeatedly popping up was Spinarooni-Sucka, and since I was bored that evening I sent an instant message.

"Hey, I saw your profile and that you are into wrestling. Wanna talk? My name is Brian."

"Yes, I am a big fan. I'm Rochelle."

From there we chatted about the current storylines going on in the WWF, namely the business killing fiasco known as The WCW/ECW Invasion. Rochelle was hilariously gung-ho about these various McMahon family soap opera antics, even as I bristled at those angles and wanted better in ring action. Her attitude towards wrestling seemed about like mine nearly a decade earlier, when I accepted angles like Papa Shango putting a curse on the Ultimate Warrior, which made Warrior vomit green puke on Saturday morning TV.

"Wait up, Rochelle. How old are you exactly?"

"Twelve!"

"Nice talking to you, bye. I'm twenty-two and shouldn't talk to you." I closed the IM, figuring I'd never hear from her again. A few minutes later, she messaged me back wanting to know if she had done something wrong. I told her no, but a twenty-two-year-old guy chatting with a twelve year old girl online could be considered questionable. I acquiesced to continuing to chat, but noted, "Well, if we talk, let's keep our talks to wrestling."

We kept our conversations to wrestling for a couple of months, but as 2002 dawned, we started talking about a variety of things. I confided in Rochelle about my lame recent attempts at dating, my various eBay dealings, or my family situation regarding my dad's recent hospital stay. In turn, Rochelle told me various things about herself, as well. Rochelle lived in Pinellas Park, Florida, which is a suburb of St. Petersburg. Pinellas Park is similar to the Okolona area here in Louisville, in terms of socioeconomic status. Rochelle lived with her mom, Jessie, in an apartment fairly similar to Tanglewood, as well as a roommate Rochelle didn't like.

The more I heard, the more fascinated I became. Jessie was a stripper in Tampa for about fifteen years. Rochelle was the product of a fling Jessie had with a rocker who played in the house band at the strip joint. As Rochelle bluntly said, "Yep, I'm a bastard." Once Rochelle was born, Jessie faced losing custody if she didn't clean up her act, so she sobered up and went back to college. Jessie obtained a master's degree and now worked as a social worker for the State of Florida. There's the cliched joke of meeting a stripper working her way through college, but in this case it was the truth.

Over the course of 2002 I began to look at Rochelle as my kid sister. She was three weeks younger than my brother Eric, but smart as a whip, and savvy for her age. If she needed help with some homework, I was glad to help. If something troubled her, I was glad to listen, and vice versa. I even started sending her a bunch of movies in an attempt to turn her into a fellow classic movie geek. I started with easier stuff to get into like the Marx Bros. or Busby Berkeley musicals, then made my way to Wheeler and Woolsey movies. I think she enjoyed most of these movies, especially the "Big Bad Wolf" music number from *Cockeyed Cavaliers* ("I hummed the song to myself all weekend at my grandma's").

When my family vacationed in Myrtle Beach, I made sure to mail Rochelle a postcard. When Rochelle left on a big vacation in New York City with her grandma, she made sure to send me a postcard informing me of her trip. "We saw Lady Liberty, oh and I also met Tommy Dreamer at WWE New York!" The WWF became WWE, due to losing the court case with the World Wildlife Fund. Rochelle and I both loathed the new WWE name. Hell, I *still* loathe it. When Rochelle got back from NYC and saw me online, she sent an IM of nothing but grinning emojis.

At various points we came up with silly names for each other. I was Yogi and she was Boo Boo, though I can't recall why. Sometimes I called her Raquel as a Latin variation on her name, or silly stuff like Kroger, after the grocery store. She countered with Karry for Kash n' Karry down there. I also called her hoss, since the term was bandied about on WWE TV frequently during that time period.

We talked less over the weekends as 2002 progressed, since she and Jessie were spending time at her grandfather's horse ranch, the Morgan Ranch. The ranch was located in Sumter County, about eighty-five miles away from St. Pete, and about forty-five minutes from Orlando. Rochelle spent weekends learning to train horses, riding, and any other chores needed to be done.

By late 2002, we hit upon an idea. What if I came down to St. Pete for Spring Break in 2003 and watched *WrestleMania* with them? We discussed this possibility on AIM. Around this time Rochelle changed her screen name to TripleH4Ever since Triple H was by far her favorite wrestler in the world. We had several debates about Triple H and his backstage politicking, especially in late 2002 and early 2003, where one could definitely argue he buried potential main event talent like Rob Van Dam and Booker T. Let's not even get into the Katie Vick fiasco.

"Where would I stay though? A hotel?"

"You could stay with us at the apartment," she replied.

"I'm not sure. I mentioned my previous trip to L.A. It didn't go well. Besides, isn't inviting someone to stay for a week usually something reserved for family?"

"You *are* family. Sometimes I think about you and whether you are happy, whether you are having a good life. But yes, stay with us. I will practically tie you up to make sure you don't leave!"

"And your mom is okay with this?" I asked, feeling moved.

"Sure, she trusts you. I did ask her if she planned to sleep with you, though."

"Uh, what now?"

"She said, 'Rochelle, give me more credit than that.' I said, 'But you slept with Brent!'" Brent was a cowboy at the ranch, about my age, and also from Kentucky. I never met him.

"I don't know what to say, Rochelle," I replied.

"Eh, I think Brent may have given her hepatitis, anyway."

"I recently started my website but haven't had much business yet. I can always post an away message and not list anything on eBay, so that part is no problem. I'll make the arrangements. Take care of yourself, hoss."

"Please don't say hoss. I hear that name constantly from Jim Ross as it is!"

"You should come up with a new screen name. RochelleTheHoss."

"I'm not doing that as an AOL screen name!"

"Pretty please?"

"Okay, I might do it later!"

Before I thought of making plans, I felt as though I should get Lasik done on my eyes. I was sick of wearing glasses, and if I traveled to Florida and likely headed to the beach, I wanted to look my best. I booked an appointment with Bennett and Bloom for a consultation at the Suburban Hospital area office. An old Butler classmate of mine, Kendra Gillum, worked for Bennett and Bloom and checked me in. "So, do you still talk to anyone from Butler?" she asked.

"We don't have enough time for those stories," I replied.

Kendra looked puzzled but took me back to meet Dr. Bennett. It was a routine visit to go over the costs and procedure. I was doing pretty well on eBay so $1600.00 an eye didn't bother me. I had another visit near St. Mary's and Elizabeth Hospital to dilate my eyes and get the necessary prescription. I worried about being too young for the procedure at age twenty-three, but they were willing to perform Lasik on anyone over twenty-one.

The actual procedure should have been mundane, with a few days of recovery. The right eye proceeded without a hitch, but during the procedure on my left eye something went wrong. Apparently the laser went off its track and zigzagged across my retina. Bennett had to stop the procedure. This apparently happens once in a blue moon. I had to wear contact lenses for protection in my left eye for about six months while it healed. Then we would try again, but with the safer PRK process instead of Lasik. What a mess. I stumbled around for the next six months with blurry vision on one side, and 20/20 vision on the other. I had frequent headaches. I thought of suing them, but after talking to a few lawyers they said as long as Bennett fixed my eye when he said he would I didn't have much of a case. Upon telling Rochelle about this misfortune, she replied, "Oh, those idiots! Sue them anyway!"

During December 2002, I decided to start my own website, since I had been temporarily suspended by eBay for selling bootlegs. I knew enough HTML to code a rudimentary site, where I posted pictures of actors, and listed commercially unavailable movies I had in my collection. This was the dawn of Cabbageboy Movies, with the idea being to sell some movies on eBay and drive those customers to more movies on my site.

I copied a few of my demo tapes and sent them to Rochelle and she didn't seem to hate them, but instead said, "They weren't *that* bad, but you sound like you are dying." For her part, Jessie mostly listened mouth agape.

In early 2003, I made my plans, one blurry eye and all. I booked the trip for March 23, a Sunday, through Tuesday, April 1. I can't remember why I didn't leave the day after *WrestleMania*. Unless I felt I needed one extra day to wind things down? I had no idea what to expect from this trip. I had no particular agenda this time. No life changing goals. I wanted to hang out and have fun.

Around this same time, my mom had to put my grandmother in the Franciscan Nursing Home. I had noticed Mamaw slipping mentally for a couple of years, but throughout 2002 she had gotten worse and worse. Alzheimer's had set in. There would be days when she would forget to eat anything other than a few chocolates. While I never had a problem visiting my dad whenever he was in the hospital or nursing home, this became too much. I never saw her at Franciscan during the time she was there. Mom went out of some sense of daughterly obligation, but I couldn't bear to see Mamaw so far gone she didn't recognize family members.

I vividly remember the moment I realized Mamaw was becoming senile. For years she talked of how much she enjoyed the movie *Laura* when she first saw it in 1944. She was a big Dana Andrews fan, finding him a handsome man and a solid actor. I brought her a VHS copy of the film and stayed the night at her house. Half an hour into the film Mamaw turned to me and asked, "Which one is Dana Andrews?"

My dad didn't especially care either way if I flew down to see Rochelle, and Mom was too preoccupied with what was going on with my grandmother. Instead, I used a fellow college basketball fan from Union County, Fran, as a sounding board for this trip. Fran was a few years younger than my mom. "If her mom was about ten years younger I would advise you not to go," she said. (Jessie was forty-five).

For his part, my old friend Chad Black said, "You should take them out somewhere nice for dinner."

"Yeah, we can go to McDonald's," I jested, as we both laughed.

I left for Tampa on March 23rd. U of L lost in the NCAA tournament to Butler that day and I felt deflated, as my mom dropped me off at the airport. The airport in Tampa is set up rather oddly compared to other airports I've seen. Upon arrival, I entered a shuttle area, the Sky Connect, which quickly moves arriving and departing passengers back to the main airport, where the bagging area, airline desks, and shops are located.

Tampa was dark when I arrived. I hadn't talked to Rochelle or Jessie about where I should meet them. As I later found out, they tried to call me the night before, but I was online at the time. This being the last gasp of the dial up era, the attempted call kicked me offline, so I never heard from them. I made my way to the baggage claim and waited for my grip.

"We've been looking everywhere in the airport for you," I heard a female voice say from behind. I turned around. It was Rochelle. She was slightly thinner than I expected, with long brown hair that had a slight reddish tinge in certain light. She greeted me with a hug. The moment was oddly subdued, but then again it had been a long trip. I felt like I had met someone I had known for years, rather than someone I had just met in person for the first time.

The baggage claim isn't a far walk to the car waiting area. Jessie parked right outside the door in her Chrysler Sebring with the engine running. Rochelle sat in the front passenger seat. I put my bag in the trunk and got in the back seat. Jessie wore glasses for nighttime driving. I must admit, when I saw her, the first thing crossing my mind was if I could picture her as a stripper. Somehow, I couldn't envision it. She gave me the once over as I buckled in.

"Well, you're about what I figured you would be," she said. Was this meant as a compliment or an insult? We took off from there and headed back to the apartment in Pinellas Park. Unfortunately, we traveled in the dark, since the trip across Tampa Bay to the St. Pete side is gorgeous in the daytime. Once we arrived at Breezeway Villas, I unpacked and checked the score of the Kentucky/Utah NCAA tournament game. UK won by twenty.

Jessie cracked me up when I mentioned wanting to watch UK's

tournament games, asking, "Is that soccer or golf?" as though UK meant the United Kingdom instead of the University of Kentucky. Hilarity ensued trying to explain the complex rivalry of U of L and UK to them. Back then, I didn't hate UK, but cheered for them as more or less a second team unless they were playing U of L. My mom was a huge Rupp's Runts fan as a teen, with Pat Riley being her hero. By the time Calipari started all the one and done trash, UK became tough to like. While I previously educated Rochelle on the fine art of filling out a bracket, this concept was foreign to Jessie.

Jessie was baffled by my *lack* of an accent, noting Brent the ranch hand had a thick southern accent. Jessie had a slightly California stoner style of speech, rather than anything native to Florida.

"Jessie, you do realize Louisville is a pretty big city, and not everyone is a redneck?" I offered.

I took the futon couch in the living room near the TV, unfolding it for a bed. Rochelle and Jessie had to take one bedroom, since they had a new roommate named Barb living in the back bedroom. Barb was a middle-aged woman who worked at the Kash n' Karry grocery store. Apparently, Jessie had kicked out the previous obnoxious roommate. Barb was much better.

The next morning Jessie had to leave for work, as did Barb, which left Rochelle and me at the apartment. We passed the time going to the pool at the complex, as well as her introducing me to *Grand Theft Auto: Vice City*, and the *8 Mile* soundtrack. Rochelle had a basketball, so we played at the nearby court onsite. She could play rough at times, which I have to admit surprised me.

"You play like some goon from Cincy!" I laughed. "Is Huggins going to recruit you?"

The first day also presented a dilemma which hadn't factored into my thinking, possibly due to my lack of success with females. Rochelle seemed enamored with me, to the point where if I tried to get a drink from the fridge, she jumped up and wrapped her legs around me. If we were on the futon watching TV, she would snuggle up to me. This was a tricky situation. I didn't want to reject her or hurt her feelings, but given Rochelle's age, there was a limit on what was appropriate or, frankly, legal. I thought back to my revulsion at Arianne telling me about an older guy taking advantage of her at age thirteen, and I refused to go down that path. Besides, Jessie invited me to her home and put her trust in me not to do anything stupid.

Jessie took off early from work to take us out to see the sights. We drove down the coast by the Gulf of Mexico, venturing through Treasure Island, St. Pete Beach, and Madeira Beach. Pinellas Park is an area no different from Louisville. But then you travel to the coast, and it is *amazing*. Yachts galore, beautiful white sand beaches, hotels, inlets, the list is endless. If there was ever an area of this country I instantly fell in love with, it would be the Gulf area beaches around St. Pete. I remember feeling amazement at seeing The Don Cesar, a famous pink hotel resort standing out on the coast in breathtaking fashion. I've never been there, but it's still a goal. Rochelle and I played miniature golf at a place called Polynesian Putter, but Jessie didn't. She stayed in the car.

We parked at a public lot and walked on the beach. The Gulf waves are fairly timid compared to the Atlantic Ocean, and the sand is so fine as to almost look white. The weather on that spring day was practically perfect, reasonably sunny and about eighty degrees. I had cut my foot before I left home, so the Gulf water helped heal it.

"I felt down after U of L lost yesterday," I said to Rochelle. "But today has been so great." Later, we headed to Lake Seminole Park nearby, where Rochelle and I played an impromptu game of volleyball. During one volley I flopped backwards and fell to the ground in foolish fashion, and Rochelle howled with laughter. To be honest, so did I. Before heading back to the apartment, we stopped by Checkers for some food (Checkers is Rally's where I'm from).

Rochelle's grandma stopped by the apartment for a brief visit, since she lived in Hernando County about an hour away. She was a charming, gray-haired woman in her 60s, who greeted me and made me feel welcome.

"Nice to meet you, Brian. I've heard a lot about you," she said.

"Hopefully good things," I joked. She nodded, then sauntered across the room to talk to Jessie, and left Rochelle and me alone on the couch. We scoured a recent issue of Pro Wrestling Illustrated, then Rochelle put on her *Best of Triple H* DVD so I could see his WWF debut match vs. "Rock N Roll" Buck Zumhoffe from 1995.

47

"After this, can we watch the Flair/Steamboat match?" I asked, examining the box. "It's an extra feature on the DVD. At least then we could see a *good* match." Rochelle shot me a wry look. We also watched *Monday Night Raw* when we got back, the "go home" show for *WrestleMania* on Sunday.

Looking back, I probably should have rented a car, since I depended on Jessie to drive us around, though with one enhanced eye driving in a strange city wasn't a great idea. Rochelle and I spent most of Tuesday at the now defunct Pinellas Square Mall, looking around various shops and going to see *Chicago*, which recently won Best Picture at the Oscars. I enjoyed watching Rochelle's reactions to certain moments in the film, such as the reveal of Richard Gere as the shoeshine boy instead of the dapper gent.

We did not bother with the ice rink at the mall, however. I might be willing to fall down in a heap playing volleyball, but there were limits to my willingness to be embarrassed. The mall had the distinct feeling it had seen its best days, and indeed by mid-2004 the mall closed. At the time I noticed several vacant storefronts.

As we stood outside the mall waiting for Jessie to pick us up, we discussed the movie. Having seen the 1942 version *Roxie Hart*, I was familiar with the story.

"*Chicago* was okay, but I'm a little baffled as to why it won Best Picture over *The Two Towers*," I pontificated. "I guess they are saving Best Picture for the third *Lord of the Rings* movie."

"The movie was fine. I might be interested in seeing *Roxie Hart*, since you mentioned it," Rochelle said. "I might want to see this Rob Zombie movie coming out soon, *House of 1,000 Corpses*. I've heard that the movie's so bad it probably shouldn't be released, so I must see it."

"I mean it's a movie directed by Rob Zombie. What else could be expected?" I pondered.

That night I met Callie, Rochelle's best friend, and fellow wrestling fan. Callie was a semi punk rock girl, with occasionally pink hair, though blonde on this occasion. I say semi because she was more of a mall type punk, rather than a serious one. But then how many thirteen-year-old girls can be serious punk rockers? The three of us headed to Sunrise Lanes, a bowling alley in the area. This was the one time on the trip I played babysitter, as we bowled and played pool. Amusingly, neither seemed to be big fans of Avril Lavigne when she popped up on the radio at the bowling alley.

"What the crap is this, 'It's a damn cold night' stuff, anyway, dude?" Rochelle asked.

"'Complicated' is okay," Callie replied. "But this new song is such a ballad, dude." For whatever reason they enjoyed calling each other dude.

The next couple of days were fairly peaceful, as Rochelle and I hit the pool yet again, ate at a Chinese buffet, and rented *Barbershop* from the nearest Blockbuster. I had to use my mom's membership card, since I never had a Blockbuster card of my own. Back when I first wanted one they wanted bank statements, utility bills, and a DNA sample just to be a Blockbuster member. They wanted a "more exclusive clientele," and they got it, all right. Now no one goes there.

Around the time *Barbershop* ended, Jessie and Barb left to go out bar hopping, which seemed like a curious thing to do on a Wednesday night. However, Jessie planned on heading to Daytona Beach on Friday, clear across the state on the Atlantic Ocean side. After that, a journey to the ranch to see Rochelle's grandfather and tend to the stables.

"Okay, you two. We are heading out. No hanky-panky while we are gone," Jessie said. I was taken aback by the remark but didn't reply. Neither did Rochelle. Given some of Jessie's curious hints, I had previously wondered if she thought I was gay. Earlier in the car while dropping us off at the Chinese buffet, we heard a gay themed news story on the radio and Jessie made sure to turn the volume up. As we exited, she then quipped, "See you later, girls!"

Upon the middle-aged duo's exit, Rochelle immediately put on a DVD of *The Princess Bride*, which we both counted among our favorite movies. The futon pulled down like a bed, and Rochelle once again nuzzled up to me while the movie played. This was a test, one which became harder not to fail. I was leery of letting this go too far, which didn't go beyond Rochelle draping a leg around mine on the futon.

At one point during the movie, Rochelle lifted up my U of L T-shirt to look at my back. I had made mention in our online conversations about my terrible back acne some years prior, so she was curious about the scarring.

"Honestly, it isn't anything off-putting. Why are you so self-conscious about your back?" she asked.

"I just am," I said, slowly pulling the shirt back down. After the movie ended, Rochelle bid me good night, left the room and went to bed. I turned out the lights in the living room and crashed on the futon. Around midnight, Jessie and Barb returned.

"Rochelle!" Jessie exclaimed, as if she expected her to be sleeping with me on the futon. Startled, I popped up. Upon seeing me alone she nodded in approval. Jessie and Barb retreated to the back bedrooms. Jessie had been testing me, all right.

Those first few days in St. Pete were a special time. Everyone needs a happy place they can think about when feeling stressed, and those days are mine. Whenever I had feelings of anxiety during the pandemic, especially late at night, I would transport myself back to those days and feel serene. This trip seemed like the opposite of my trip to L.A., where I was met with ambivalence by the person I journeyed there to see. Some days in life have a magical vibe to them, the type of days where one feels nothing but warmth, love, and respect. The rest of the trip would have its ups and downs, but those first few days were full of magic. I wish I could find a way to bottle the feeling. The sort of days when you feel like fireworks are going off inside your head.

CHAPTER 5

A TRIP TO DAYTONA

We spent Thursday hanging out and watching either NCAA tournament games or *WWE Smackdown*. The games of particular interest to me were UK vs. Wisconsin and Marquette vs. Pitt, with the winners facing off on Saturday in the Elite 8 for a spot in the Final Four. I've never had the same anxious terror watching UK the way I do with U of L, mainly because they aren't exactly my school. U of L games have been known to drive me up a wall. Earlier that month, I became so livid over U of L being screwed by the refs in an overtime loss at DePaul I punched a hole in my bedroom wall. I related this story to Rochelle and Jessie during the UK game.

"My God, Brian. It was just a game!" Rochelle said.

"Don't give him a hard time, Rochelle. I can tell he feels like a fool for having done that in the first place," Jessie replied.

"This season began so amazingly for U of L," I said. "We started the season 18-1 and rose as high as #2 in the AP Poll, only to then have the wheels come off. Maybe we weren't that good, but we also lost Ellis Myles to an injury. The DePaul fiasco was the last straw, and it sucked to be ripped off against a scrub team. Chad and I attended the previous U of L/DePaul game back in January, and we crushed them by almost thirty points."

"Rochelle, are you still wanting to go to veterinary school in Kentucky?" Jessie asked, changing the subject. Rochelle didn't respond either way, but all of this talk seemed presumptuous. When I was in seventh grade I wanted to become the starting first baseman for the Chicago Cubs.

As we were having this conversation, UK star Keith Bogans sustained an ankle injury against Wisconsin. UK won the game, staggering to a 63-57 win over the Badgers. The Wildcats would have bigger problems in the form of Dwyane Wade and Marquette, who pulled off a mild 77-74 upset of #2 seed Pitt.

Callie came over to stay all night, since she asked to go with the three of us on the upcoming trip to Daytona Beach, and then subsequently, to the Morgan Ranch. With Callie over, she and Rochelle crashed on the futon, and I wound up having to sleep on the smaller couch. That night was the first time I ever slept in the same room with two females, albeit on a different couch. Jessie had the bedroom to herself for a change, while Barb's boyfriend Eddie came over to visit her in the back bedroom. Sleep didn't come easy to me on this occasion, possibly due to residual excitement from the Sweet 16, or general unease about the sleeping situation.

Nothing daunted, the four of us headed out for Daytona the next afternoon. Jessie had to work in the morning but took off early around lunchtime. Before we left, Rochelle and Callie amused themselves by listening to some random CDs, including *Weird Al Yankovic's Greatest Hits* and *Billy Idol's Greatest Hits*. Apparently, Jessie was a big Idol fan, which made sense, given his best work is classic '80s stripper music.

Daytona is about two and a half hours from Pinellas Park, so there was plenty of time to converse. Jessie drove while I rode shotgun in the passenger seat. Rochelle and Callie sat in the back and either chatted with each other or listened to music on headphones.

"So how do you like Florida so far?" Jessie asked.

"It's been great. Never been to Daytona Beach. All I know about Daytona is the racetrack, but I've never been a big NASCAR fan. Louisville isn't far from Indy, so I would say the Indy 500 means more where I'm from."

"Rural Florida is more country than people realize," she replied.

"The ranch is away from the crowd, a slice of heaven on earth. We'll be in Orlando soon, which is known for Disney and tourists. The southern part of Florida around Miami is heavily Hispanic. Cuban. But I would say Daytona fits in with the redneck part of the state. I am worried about the crowd there during spring break though, especially being Back to College Week."

"Are you looking forward to the pay-per-view on Sunday?" I asked.

"You bet. I can't wait to see Brock Lesnar beat up Kurt Angle," she replied. "But don't tell me any spoilers."

"Jessie, I can't give you spoilers for *WrestleMania*," I chuckled. "The event hasn't happened yet. All I can tell you is there is a high probability Brock Lesnar will defeat Kurt Angle for the WWE title. I can't stand Lesnar, not since he beat my boy Van Dam at King of the Ring. RVD isn't even on the main card Sunday."

"Well, he'll get his chance at some point," Jessie said.

"As far as the Lesnar/Angle match goes, I would be willing to bet Brock busts out the Shooting Star Press. I saw him do it in an OVW match before a *Smackdown* taping two years ago. That move was insane for a 290 lb. man."

"Sounds amazing!" Rochelle said. Callie nodded in agreement.

Jessie turned on the radio. Heart's "Magic Man" played. She seemed to approve.

"I may be in the minority, but I prefer Heart's 1980s stuff to their '70s era heyday," I said.

"Yeah, but the '70s stuff is when I first listened to them. Better to get stoned listening to," she jested.

"Maybe so," I said. "I think the '70s Heart output meanders too much, and they aren't technically proficient enough to do jam sessions. They aren't Zeppelin or Sabbath here."

"Zeppelin is great. Black Sabbath though? Too much for me, aside from *Paranoid*."

"Yeah, not sure how many chicks would be into Sabbath thirty years ago." We both chuckled.

Soon after, we entered Orlando on I-4. The traffic was hectic on a Friday afternoon during spring break, but we managed to barrel through without incident. As I would later learn, one can also use toll roads to bypass most of the Orlando traffic, but our particular route didn't involve tolls. I noticed a wildly fancy two-story McDonald's by the interstate, as well as the single ritziest Waffle House I had ever seen. Here I was used to the run-down dive of a Waffle House down the street from where I lived.

As we entered Daytona Beach, I couldn't help but be astounded at the sheer size of the racetrack. As you enter town, you see the track and then drive past the entirety of it before finding a road to the beach. I had been past Churchill Downs several times, though I've never been there for a race, but the Daytona track seemed to dwarf the Downs in size.

We found ourselves on the main drag by the hotels on what is now known as Jimmy Buffett Memorial Highway. Upon people watching, I couldn't help but note a curiously high number of black college aged people walking the streets. I wasn't especially alarmed, but Jessie soon realized what was going on.

"Aw, man. I must have misheard. It isn't Back to College Week in Daytona, but instead Black College Week! That's what the guy on the phone told me!"

This development wasn't a big deal to me, nor to Rochelle and Callie. I caught a vibe from Jessie that she wasn't entirely comfortable, however. Regardless, we found a public parking lot and hit the beach. Jessie mostly sat on her beach towel and read a book, while I let the waves crash into me like I usually do at Myrtle Beach. Callie and I buried Rochelle in the sand and had a laugh at her trying to dig herself out and rinse off all the sand.

After venturing into some of the local beach stores and seeing a plethora of Confederate flag memorabilia, along with the usual marijuana themed shirts in such venues, Jessie decided we weren't going to spend the night in Daytona after all. She never mentioned the Black College Week aspect, but instead, what were we to do about sleeping arrangements at the hotel? I have to admit I was curious, myself. Instead, we were going to eat dinner in Daytona, then head to the ranch, over ninety miles away.

Upon seeing a local Red Lobster, I recalled Chad's advice about treating them to a nice dinner.

"Let's stop here. I'm starving. I'll even pay for it, myself."

I didn't have to ask twice. The wait was a half an hour at minimum, but we didn't mind.. Once we were finally seated, I ordered the steak and lobster combo I used to always order at Red Lobster before it became priced out of all feasibility. Jessie, Rochelle, and Callie split a large fish and shrimp plate.

At one point I spilled Sweet'N Low on the table and noticed Jessie bristle ever so slightly.

"Sorry, I'll clean it up," I said.

"No big deal," she replied. "Just reminded me of a stupid joke my ex-boyfriend Tim used to do in restaurants. He used to open several sugar packets and place them in lines, then pretend to snort it like cocaine. I swear every man I've dated was either an alcoholic or a drug user."

"You'd probably get along with my uncle Monty," I replied. "He spent most of the 1980s and first half of the '90s being one of the foremost marijuana dealers in Florida. He moved back to Kentucky for a while when the FBI caught onto him, but I think he lives in New Port Richey now."

"Poor bastard. I recall hearing about having some family up in Kentucky," Jessie said. "Wouldn't it be wild if we were related?"

"Oh God, I would kill myself!" Rochelle exclaimed.

I said nothing, merely blushed and continued eating. The total bill amounted to $90.00 or so, which I casually paid, having learned my lesson from grumbling about restaurant checks with Arianne in L.A. After paying up, we left and headed out back on the road.

As we left Daytona, Rochelle handed me a CD to insert in the car stereo, of all things a compilation of current WWE wrestler themes. The idea of these two thirteen-year-old girls in the back seat jamming and singing along to Reverend D'Von's theme song still cracks me up to this day. The time was here. We were at the precipice. I had been worried about this part of the trip. We were about to head to the Morgan Ranch.

CHAPTER 6

THE MORGAN RANCH

The four of us arrived at the Morgan Ranch late that evening. I have hazy memories of the trip, other than navigating our way through some of the toll roads around Orlando. During this time period one still needed to either insert money or wave a card at the toll booth to proceed, unlike today where a camera scans the car as you pass.

The Morgan Ranch was a full-scale horse farm with ninety acres of land, trailers for workers who lived on site, barns for the horses, a horse arena, and the main house. Rochelle's grandfather John was nowhere to be found, but on a Friday night he may have been out socializing with friends. Even in darkness the full scale of the compound stunned me.

After unpacking, Rochelle, Callie, and I made our way to the barn and stable area. Rochelle wanted to tend to her horse, Sonny, before turning in for the night. I wanted to check out the entire grounds, but in the dark there was an ominous feeling to it. There were huge lights around the arena to be sure, but not so much around the stable stalls. The night darkness and quiet were infrequently broken up by the outside lights and the occasional horse's neigh.

For the second straight night I got little sleep, this time due to the various cats in the living room. I had to take the couch near the TV, yet all night Rochelle's cat Gulliver and another cat fought each other.

Screeching, clawing, and the like. After a while I dozed off from exhaustion if nothing else. Everyone else turned in, since Saturday was usually a big day at the ranch, with various guests paying for horse rides, and workers mulling about.

I awakened in the morning to hear Jessie conversing with Grandpa John, who spoke with a deep, commanding voice, similar to former U of L football coach Howard Schnellenberger. He even looked somewhat like Schnellenberger, with a similar mustache, though not as tall and intimidating. John gave me the once over, a sly smile on his face.

"Looks like we have a live one here. Get yourself some breakfast," he said.

To say I felt ill at ease around John would be an understatement. When I previously mentioned visiting the ranch concerned me, having to meet Rochelle's grandpa worried me the most. I didn't know what Rochelle and Jessie had told him about me, who I was, or why I was there. If he had asked, I doubt I had the answers he wanted, anyway.

Rochelle awoke early and tended to some of the horses, though I believe Callie was still asleep in one of the guest rooms. I saw little of Callie during the day. She either kept to the office computer or otherwise out of sight. I had the feeling she was as ill at ease at the ranch as me.

I ate some cereal while John tried to strike up a conversation.

"How come you didn't want to shop for a Tampa Bay Buccaneers Super Bowl shirt?" he asked.

"I'm not a fan of the Bucs," I replied. "I'm more of a fan of the Colts and Peyton Manning. We get Colts games on local TV in Louisville. Bengals too, but they usually suck."

"I've been a fan of the Buccaneers since they were an expansion team in the '70s," he replied. "I always dreamed of them getting to the Super Bowl. Well, they finally did. And they won the motherfucker. That team has driven me to drink over the years, but thankfully I have my AA meetings now."

After eating, I noticed all of the guests arriving, as well as the workers. I roamed outside and watched the proceedings, but suffice it to say, this wasn't my scene. I wasn't comfortable around these people in the least, almost as if you dropped me into the Yellowstone Ranch and told me to mingle with the cowboys.

I overheard Rochelle previously discuss one of the teenage ranch hands, some kid named Dory. Apparently, a hard worker for John on the weekends. While standing on the porch I glanced at the barn and noticed Rochelle and Dory chatting and smiling at one another, Rochelle playing around with his cowboy hat. Wait, was I jealous? I had no business being jealous. Now I felt confused, not knowing how to feel about Rochelle, the ranch, or anything else.

I retreated to the office and surfed the internet most of the afternoon, at least when Callie wasn't in there. The computer did not have AOL installed, but instead Microsoft Explorer. I wanted to chat with Fran about the upcoming UK/Marquette game, so I foolishly downloaded AIM and signed in. This was a mistake.

"So, do you think UK wins this one today?" Fran asked.

"Not really," I replied. "Not with Bogans hurting. U of L tangled with Wade and Marquette twice this year and both games were thrillers. UK has won so many games in a row they seem due for a loss. Who wants to see Marquette get killed by either Arizona or Kansas in the Final Four?"

After avoiding the crowd all day, I walked back to the living room in time for the start of the game. By this point things had died down outside, so John sat back in his easy chair and turned on the TV. He switched the channel to Fox News to watch coverage of the recent invasion of Iraq.

"Did we win yet?" he asked, facetiously.

"Can I watch the Kentucky basketball game?" I asked. "This is the Elite 8, winner heads to the Final Four."

"What, you want to watch a bunch of million-dollar niggers shoot a basketball?"

I was stunned by that comment. Mind you, such language wasn't exactly foreign to me. My dad, being from small town Kentucky, used occasional racial slurs, but hearing one from someone I barely knew in such a dismissive tone caught me off guard. I sat down on the couch quietly, not knowing what to say next. Finally, I mustered up a lame reply.

"Well, in theory these are college guys not being paid." This being the days before NIL, when players were being paid under the table, instead of out in the open.

"All right, soon to be millionaires, then. Go ahead. Turn it on."

I was on pins and needles but sat down to watch the game as best I could. And what a fiasco to witness. Marquette raced out to a dominant early lead, blowing past UK defenders, with Dwyane Wade going out of his mind going for a triple double (twenty-nine points, eleven rebounds, eleven assists). U of L tormentor Steve Novak also hit five 3s that day. With the game out of hand at the half, I had seen enough.

"You can watch whatever you want," I said. "I've seen enough." John turned off the TV instead.

"Jessie mentioned you had never been on a horse before. Do you want to take a ride?" he asked.

"Sure. Make sure the horse is tame, since I have no idea what I'm doing, and don't want to be thrown."

Jessie and Rochelle saddled up a horse for me as I observed all the steps. They adjusted the girth, then the saddle, cinched it up, and soon enough, I was set to go. I managed to mount the horse well enough, and they pointed me in the right direction to ride around the ranch.

"Tug on the reins when you want to stop, and he'll stop for you," Rochelle said. "He's tamed."

No kidding. As I took off around the grassy field I couldn't help but think they gave me the creakiest, oldest nag in the stable. The ride went decent enough for a beginner, as I tried to take in the scenery while also keeping control of the horse. The area around the ranch is beautiful. I later learned Florida is one of the horse capitals of the United States. Not on par with the area around Lexington, but in the same ballpark.

Upon my return to the house, Jessie and John were interested in how my ride had gone. By this point they were at the dinner table eating, so I sat down with them.

"How did it go?" Jessie asked.

"Well, I was a little nervous, but overall, not too bad," I replied. "The horse thankfully wasn't too fast or excitable. Mostly limped along."

"What do you mean by *that*?" John inquired. "Are you saying we put you on a broken-down horse that needed to be put down due to being lame? Broken leg?"

"Um ... no" I responded. "Slow going I suppose. I don't know."

Jessie could see me drowning here, so she attempted to throw me a life preserver.

"Dad, he didn't mean anything by that."

"Jesus, Jessie. What if someone from the county heard him say one of the horses walked with a limp. We have buses of school kids who come here for horse rides. That could cost us money. They could shut us down."

I was mentally done with this experience. I shut down and stopped talking. John left a short time later. Now I would be able to exhale. I think his passive aggressive attitude towards me masked some inner thoughts he didn't want to discuss. His honest thoughts were probably more like, "Okay, you little prick. Which of these girls are you trying to fuck? My daughter or my granddaughter? Because I'm thinking about cutting your nuts off and feeding them to you."

By nightfall, we packed up our stuff and headed out, but not after watching Kansas pull the upset over Arizona in the other Elite 8 game to set up the Final Four matchup no one possibly wanted between Marquette and Kansas. Hey, I am going to watch the NCAA tournament at all costs.

As we approached Tampa, Jessie's cell phone rang. John called, sounding pissed about something or other. I couldn't make out everything being said, but the call sounded something like this:

"Who the hell installed this bullshit on my computer? It keeps popping up!"

"I don't know, I wasn't in there," Jessie replied. "Did Callie mess with something?"

"I think it might be the AIM I installed earlier," I said. "Tell him to uninstall the app, since it may keep popping up automatically. Sorry I didn't do that myself, but I forgot."

He continued ranting at Jessie for several more minutes until she finally hung up the phone. Jessie now issued a rant of her own.

"Why does he do this bullshit? Here we are, happy as hell, heading home. But he has to come up with something minor and turn it into a crisis. I'm sick of it. He can go piss up a rope for all I care."

She kept this rant going the rest of the way back to Pinellas Park. I never complained. It was music to my ears. Rochelle and Callie sat quietly in the back the rest of the way.

Once I returned home, I remember talking to my dad about this experience with Rochelle's grandfather. As my dad noted, "Let's see. He's a die-hard Republican. Kind of a racist. Rich. Overbearing. Grandpa Joe would have loved this guy. They would've been great friends."

Some weeks later, I discussed my experience at the ranch with Chad. He joked to me, "If that man had treated me the way he did you, I would have taken a piss on the side of his barn. Maybe ask him if he wanted a drink."

"He said he was going to AA meetings though ..."

"That's why I would ask."

Chapter 7

WrestleMania XIX Sunday

The big day of *WrestleMania* finally arrived. After the trip to Daytona and the ranch our enthusiasm was waning. I noticed a subtle change in Rochelle after we returned from the Morgan Ranch. She wasn't mean spirited towards me or hostile, but she seemed a little distant. When I looked at her face to face, I noticed a slight sadness in her eyes, and the pep in her voice had dimmed. Deep down she realized the ranch experience left me uncomfortable. She hadn't even been privy to the tense interactions I had with Grandpa John.

In prior months Rochelle talked of having a practice wrestling match with Callie and wanted me to critique what they were doing. Callie apparently had a homemade ring in her backyard where she and Rochelle performed moves on each other. That afternoon, Rochelle hopped on AIM to chat with Callie and relayed some bizarre developments.

"Callie says her family doesn't want Brian around," she said to Jessie. "They aren't comfortable with him being at their house. I've wanted to do this practice wrestling match for months, but now it's off."

This was the first outright disapproval I had faced from anyone in Florida, and while I said nothing, I can't say I understood this sudden rejection from Callie's mom. I didn't know her, and she didn't know me, yet she previously signed off on her daughter being at the bowling alley with me, sleeping ten feet away overnight on a futon, or taking a trip to Daytona Beach. All of these events occurred without incident, so I was slightly offended at not being welcome at her home. I was weary of Callie being around, so if she didn't come over for *WrestleMania*, that was fine by me. But all of this drama seemed to dampen Rochelle's spirits.

After a dinner consisting mainly of Ramen noodles, we were set to watch the highly anticipated PPV. Even Barb ventured into the room here and there to check out some of the matches. She was excited for the Hulk Hogan vs. Vince McMahon "Legend vs. Boss" match, more so than the rest of us in the room. The Hogan/Vince feud was the primary storyline going into WM, but in reality WM XIX had no true main event. Rochelle, being a massive Triple H fan, was most excited about Helmsley's World title match vs. Booker T.

Personally, I *hated* Triple H during this time period. Not in a positive way of him being a dastardly heel getting heat, either. Most smart fans of that era viewed Triple H's title reign circa 2002-03 as The Reign of Terror, where he buried credible opponents. Tonight's victim, poor Booker T., was buried leading up to the show in a quasi-racist storyline, where Triple H made thinly veiled remarks about how, "People like you aren't main eventers. Dance for me, Booker!"

I had no particular rooting interest in the PPV. As noted, my favorite wrestler, Rob Van Dam, wasn't on the main card, instead reduced to teaming with another Triple H victim, Kane, in a pre-show tag title match, which they lost.

For her part, Rochelle spent the entire show sitting at the computer chatting online with Callie. They were still arguing about not being able to execute their practice match earlier in the day.

"Rochelle, the show is on," I said. "Don't worry about Callie. This Pay Per View is why I'm here. Why not come over and watch it on the couch?"

She didn't respond, but instead kept typing away at Callie and half watched the show. Occasionally, I walked over to the computer and saw glimpses of their conversation. "My parents don't want him around."

"Not coming over for *WrestleMania* later." "Yeah, well I'll see you at school then. Or not."

I spent more time discussing the PPV with Jessie or even Barb at times. During the Shawn Michaels vs. Chris Jericho match, I noted to Rochelle and Jessie, "Just watch, Shawn will win this one. I can see him in the booking meeting now arguing he has to go over since Triple H will win as a heel, so the card needs him to win to balance the show with a babyface win."

"I wish the Trish match had gotten more time," Rochelle said.

"Oh, come on, Rochelle" Jessie retorted. "This Jericho/Shawn match is actually serious business." Twenty minutes later, Michaels defeated Jericho, as predicted.

"You were right about the Shawn match," Jessie said. "But how do you know about the Triple H deal?"

"I read online that WWE is signing Bill Goldberg to be Triple H's next major feud," I replied. "Hunter can't lose tonight, even though he should."

"Oh, shit. Not Goldberg!" Jessie groaned. "Can't stand him."

As I figured, Triple H defeated Booker T. after hitting him with the Pedigree and waiting thirty seconds to cover him. Rochelle cheered since her main man won, while the rest of us shook our heads.

Barb was amusing. She must have been a major Hogan fan dating back in the '80s, because she ranted heavily during the match, wanting him to pulverize Vince. "Yes, Hulk! Beat him up, make him bleed!" And so, he did.

After The Rock finally bested Steve Austin on his third try at *WrestleMania*, the time arrived for the main event: Brock Lesnar challenging Kurt Angle for the WWE title.

"Angle shouldn't be wrestling," I said. "The guy has a broken neck and needs surgery. I'm worried about him being in this match, to be honest."

The match was decent enough, given Angle's limited condition. Once it reached the climax, the time arrived for Lesnar to attempt his epic Shooting Star Press (an inverted flip splash from the top rope usually done by cruiserweights).

"Okay, check this out!" I yelled. "I saw him do this in person."

Rochelle and Jessie gathered closer to the TV. Lesnar lurched up for the move, flipped in mid-air ... and crash landed on his neck, not fully rotating and nearly breaking his own neck in the process. He eventually recovered and hit another move to win.

"Well, that sucked," Jessie said. "After all the buildup he didn't even hit the move."

The fascinating aspect of *WrestleMania XIX* is that it is considered one of the better WMs, yet I've never especially considered it as such. Even watching the DVD a month later yielded no new insights, and didn't add to my love of the show. Had I become too jaded? Too much of an internet smart mark?

As a product of late 1980s wrestling, I felt sorry for Rochelle. Being ten years younger than me, Rochelle comes from a generation who grew up watching wrestling for the Vince Russo style "sports entertainment" craziness and storylines more than the actual wrestling. My brother Eric would also fall into this category, but I at least have shown him older shows, like Mid-South, World Class, and Memphis, so he has more of a schooling in classic wrestling booking, and not just the modern stuff. The single biggest dilemma wrestling has had since the late 1990s is the theory that every segment or match has to have a storyline behind it, that the wrestling matches themselves are secondary. People who became fans during the late '90s and early '00s were chiefly interested in story-lines, and as such weren't as likely to remain lifelong fans.

CHAPTER 8

THE PARTING LETTER

I figured on being tired after the PPV, which is one reason I didn't fly out immediately the next day. In retrospect, I probably should have. Spring Break ended by now, and in theory Rochelle should be back in school. Jessie let her stay home on Monday, so Rochelle and I both slept in. I never entirely understood Jessie's social work job with the State of Florida, since she seemed to take off early when need be.

Rochelle was still distant. Not moody to the point where I felt the need to ask if something was wrong, but a notable change in her demeanor had occurred. I wondered if I had done something she disliked, but she wasn't angry. Vaguely moody, there seemed to be something under the surface I couldn't understand.

Since Monday was my last full day, Jessie planned a trip to the St. Petersburg waterfront area. Rochelle wanted to see the recent Stephen King film adaptation *Dreamcatcher*, though I can't recall why. In the afternoon we made our way down to the waterfront to the AMC theater for the film.

The film was inconsequential, and I can barely recall much other than Morgan Freeman being an unhinged general dealing with King style monsters or aliens. The events after the film are what stayed with me even to this day.

After the movie, we walked by the nearby shops. We stopped outside a bridal store, which Jessie made sure to notice.

"That's a wonderful dress. Maybe someday I'll still wear one, huh Rochelle?" Rochelle gave a slight smile.

Rochelle wanted to eat at a bizarre restaurant called Dish in downtown St. Pete. I've still never been to another place exactly like Dish, and probably won't again, since the place closed in 2007. After eating there, I can understand why. Dish was an Avant Garde style restaurant, where you didn't order from a menu. At first, you headed to the salad bar, but then subsequently you would gather up your own meats, vegetables, and sauces and take the plate of raw materials to a chef in the center of the restaurant. He would then cook your food in front of you. This wasn't a Japanese style Hibachi grill. I can't describe the food, since it had no discernible genre. The food didn't taste awful, but it wasn't great. After you used one plate, you were done. No seconds.

The last order of leisure brought us to the St. Pete Pier. By this point the sun was going down, darkness setting in. Jessie, possibly needing her own Lasik enhanced, squinted as she tried to navigate the tricky streets to the pier.

"Where am I going? I think we might be lost," she said. Rochelle responded with a comment which sucked the air out of the car.

"You're not very smart, are you?"

Jessie was irate and let her know it. I sat in the passenger seat, dead quiet.

"How dare you speak to me like that, you little bitch! You think because you get mostly As and Bs you are smart, or know what it's like to be an adult? I happen to have a master's degree and am plenty smart, so you will never talk to me like that again or it's your ass!"

Rochelle was wrong in what she said, but Jessie continued on like this the rest of the way to the pier, to the point of overkill. I wish Rochelle had apologized for the comment and we could move on, but she never did. Once we arrived at the pier, Rochelle walked away from Jessie and into a souvenir shop. I tracked her down.

"Rochelle, are you okay?" I asked. "You probably shouldn't have said that, but I think your mom overreacted."

"Yeah, it happens sometimes."

We didn't linger long at the pier. Darkness had set in and we couldn't see the Bay, so the two of us walked to the end of the pier and back and decided to call it a night so we could head back to the apartment for the post *WrestleMania* edition of *Raw*. One fact ran through my head as we headed back to the apartment: I had stayed one day too many.

Jessie's an interesting woman. On one hand she could be exceedingly generous and personable to be around, yet when crossed she had a temper that scared me. This rant directed at Rochelle wasn't like the one directed at her own father when we were traveling back from the ranch. I enjoyed that rant. There was humor to it, nothing mean spirited and dark. But this tirade? It was dark. Ugly. It showed a side of her I hadn't seen before and hoped I would never see again.

Tuesday went along fairly uneventfully. Rochelle went back to school, with Jessie also back at work. Since my plane didn't leave until 5:00 p.m., I had plenty of time to pack and reflect on the trip. I mostly talked with Barb, watched TV, and listened to her Steve Miller music downloads. Her boyfriend, Eddie, also stopped by again, and seemed baffled as to my continued presence.

"Are you *still* here?" he asked.

"Yeah, but I leave later today," I replied. "Ready to go home."

Since I had plenty of time, I decided to write a farewell letter. Most of the letter reflected on my time down there, thanks for having me, so on and so forth. But one paragraph caused a rift with Rochelle going forward, one where I discussed my problems with her grandfather. To wit:

"You all go up there every weekend and you do all these chores around the ranch, but you are little more than unpaid labor."

We rushed to get to the airport on time, as my departure time caused a rush for Jessie to drive back from work, pick me up, and head to the airport. Rochelle and even Callie joined on the trip, since apparently the two of them smoothed things over at school and were planning to hang out that evening after I left.

The group walked along with me to the Sky Connect shuttle area, which is as far as they could go. Before I left, I pulled Rochelle into one of the convenience stores and took the letter out of my pocket.

"I wrote this for you," I said, handing her the letter. "Don't read it until I'm gone, though."

"I won't."

I gave Rochelle a hug, waved the group goodbye, and boarded the shuttle. I arrived back in Louisville without incident around 11:00 p.m. that night.

Once I returned home, I tried to decompress but had little time to fully reflect on the trip, or what it meant. Within weeks I finally had my left eye fixed by Dr. Bennett, this time with PRK instead of Lasik. Since the eye was permanently scarred by the botched procedure, Dr. Bennett decided PRK was the safer procedure, since it didn't involve lifting the corneal flap. My eyes have never been right since that initial procedure, though. A year later I had to have an enhancement on my right eye, probably because I shouldn't have even done Lasik in the first place. My eyes were still changing for the worse. In 2005 I gave up on Bennett and Bloom and took my business to LasikPlus for another enhancement on the left eye, since Bennett didn't guarantee lifetime results without charging extra.

Another, far more serious matter, concerned us, as well. By May 2003, my grandmother was at death's door. Her dementia had been rapid, to the point where she stopped eating and gave up. I recall on Friday, May 23rd taking Eric to eat at Tumbleweed, and somehow, I had a feeling as if something terrible had happened. When we arrived home, my mom received a call from Franciscan with the news that she needed to head over there because the end was near. If there's one thing about my mom, she knows how to deal with tragic events. She never cried when my dad had the stroke. If she cried over Mamaw's death, I never saw her. Maybe she did, but not in front of the rest of us.

The funeral took place at Owen Funeral Home on Dixie Highway. The various Durbin and Logsdon family members from my mom's side of the family were in attendance, having made the drive from various rural parts of Kentucky. The ceremony didn't do her justice, mainly because none of us knew what to tell the funeral director to say beyond routine plaudits. I mostly remember my dad arguing with my mom's distant relatives over George W. Bush and the War in Iraq. While I admired his antiwar stance, I'm not sure heated political debates were appropriate, given the occasion. Aside from political discourse, dad also found time for some profound thoughts shared with the group.

"I thought she would outlive me," he said. Given his stroke in 1996, she nearly did.

"Florence dying at eighty-one isn't a big shock," one female relative said. "I was shocked when Aubrey (my maternal grandfather) died at age seventy-two."

My mom left with the funeral procession for Clarkson, Mamaw's old hometown, an hour away from Louisville in Grayson County. She preferred for me to take my dad and Eric back home to the apartment, so I did. As we left the funeral home, I turned on the radio and The Offspring's "Gone Away" was playing. An appropriate song for the occasion, no doubt. Later that night we watched, of all things, the Arnold Schwarzenegger action movie *Commando*, to lighten the mood.

I kept Rochelle in the loop for all of this news. She expressed sympathy in the wake of my Mamaw's passing, yet we were never as close after I came back to Louisville from the trip. For her part, I don't think she enjoyed my letter, mainly the paragraph about the ranch and her grandpa. We did an autopsy of the trip during the summer while talking on AIM.

"What were your favorite parts of me being down there?" I asked. "Least favorite?"

"I enjoyed most of the time you were here, but I would say the time at the ranch was my least favorite," she replied. "I could tell you weren't comfortable there."

"I certainly wouldn't live there. At most I would visit for a day or so, like you all already do. I'm too much of a city person. I felt your grandfather did not like me at all, so I acted out in the letter."

"I love Pappy with all my heart, and if you want to stay in contact with me, you will not try to come between him and me. He does need to get used to the idea of me bringing guys around. Believe it or not, he liked you."

"Should I come back down there again sometime?" I asked.

"I don't think that would be a good idea."

I knew what she meant and didn't press my luck. For the time being

I was content chatting with Rochelle if I saw her online, but I had no time to worry too much about her. My family planned to move into my grandma's house, and I had some decisions to make about the future. Those decisions would shape the next nine years of my life.

CHAPTER 9

TRAGEDY STRIKES

Upon my grandmother's death in May 2003, my family had some major decisions to make, or at least I did. After years of living at Tanglewood, my parents were all too glad to leave the apartment complex behind and move to Mamaw's house, once my mom took ownership. The main dilemma concerned its total lack of handicap accessibility for my dad, since there was no ramp for his wheelchair, and no walk-in shower. The apartment didn't have a decent shower for him either, so he mostly had to be rinsed off when necessary. The process of moving took several months, since my mom used her inheritance money to renovate the house: a wooden ramp from the driveway to the front door, a newly constructed back room to the house, which became my dad's room, and a second bathroom with a walk-in shower.

For my part, I kept my distance from the entire situation. I didn't know what to do yet, but with friends like Chad and Isaac imploring me to get my own place, I figured the time might be right to do so. My first instinct was to stay at Tanglewood and move to a one-bedroom apartment there, but there weren't any available units. I checked some other places, including a room at a house down near Phoenix Hill Tavern, but the house didn't interest me.

A unit finally became available at Tanglewood, and in October 2003

I moved into my own apartment at the same time my family moved out and headed to my grandma's house. For anyone keeping score, I started out in #304, then moved to #306 after being flooded out in 1997, and then lastly to #607 in 2003. Between my website and eBay paying the $409.50 rent per month plus utilities, rent wasn't excruciating. Thankfully, the apartment was on the second floor, so I never had to worry about flooding again. Chad helped me move most of the furniture from the old apartment to the new one, as long as I helped him move in a few months, as well.

"Hey, I'm helping to move your ass, so help me move, too," he said, while lifting a desk.

"Yeah, I will," I replied. "But this is the first time I've voluntarily moved, whereas this is like the tenth time you've moved."

"After we get the main stuff moved, we're going to have to go to a store to find some other furniture," he said.

A few nights later Chad and I checked out the recently opened Meijer on Preston Highway near the Gene Snyder Freeway. After leaving I had splurged for several major pieces, such as a futon of my own to serve as a secondary couch in the living room, a massive desk for working at home consisting of a main surface and several stacked areas for papers and files, and a combo record /CD/cassette player. These items totaled several hundred dollars, and the futon in particular frustrated us putting it together, but by the weekend I was set to go.

But go where? After the initial hoopla, the cable and internet installed (bye-bye dial up, hello high speed), and belongings unpacked, a sad sense of lonesome permanence crept in. Occasionally a friend, such as Chad or Isaac, might stop by to watch a game or wrestling, but otherwise I was alone for days at a time. I made the trek to my mom's house on the weekends to do laundry, since the apartment didn't have a hook up for a washer.

I had yet to convert my movie collection to DVDs, so for the first year at the apartment I still copied movies for my site and eBay on various VCRs. At some points I had three different TVs hooked up to multiple VCRs, one in the living room, one in the bedroom, and another auxiliary setup by the kitchen table. Frankly, I always found the process easier to dub tapes than to burn DVD-Rs. Wearing out a VCR was no big deal - you replace it with another cheap VCR. But keeping movie ISO files on the computer and consistently burning discs was a good way to destroy your hard drive.

During these tumultuous times, I talked less and less with Rochelle. We never had a major blow up, but I saw her online less than before, and the conversations were brusquer than before. Was she still bothered by my largely inconsequential letter? Mad at me for suggesting track and field might not be her forte, upon hearing of her less than stellar results? I felt the need to do something again, since otherwise I chatted up the usual parade of freaks populating early 2000s AOL. For her part, Rochelle worked officially for her grandpa on the weekends and was being paid to do so.

Around March 2004, I started reflecting back on the previous year's trip, and how much I wanted to recapture the feeling I had those first three or four days in Pinellas Park. Even though I was unsure whether I was welcome or not, I sent Rochelle an email with a new plan of action.

"I have been thinking lately about the trip and last year. I know you said you didn't feel my coming back was a good idea anytime soon, but I think everything would be okay. Obviously, it is too late to come back for spring break like last year, but how about the first or second week of June after school is over?"

The next day I received her reply.

"I talked to my mom, and we think it would be possible for you to come down on the dates mentioned. Let us know the details, and yes, you will probably have to head to the ranch again."

A serious sounding email, but at least in the affirmative. Not wasting a moment, I quickly booked a flight for the second week of June. I was heading back to the Tampa Bay area for a sequel I hoped would surpass the original.

MAY 11, 2004

I had my itinerary for the return trip to Florida set for June 6-12. Planning the trip was going reasonably well, but when I checked my email that night I noticed one from the Morgan Ranch address. The contents of what Rochelle had to say stunned me.

"I had to write to tell you pappy had an accident while cutting down a tree at the ranch. He had to be flown to Orlando and is in the hospital now on life support. If he dies, I don't know what I will do, hon. He means so much to me."

Apparently, John was chopping down a tree at the ranch by himself, and somehow the tree fell on him. I never understood the exact details, but the accident proved fatal, and he died later that night at age sixty-five. I wrote back offering condolences, while asking for the phone number at the ranch, which Rochelle provided in a follow-up email. The next day I called, and Jessie answered.

"How are you holding up?" I asked.

"I mean ... we're still shocked at what happened, but we're surviving," she replied.

"Anything I can do? I'm not sure what though. About the upcoming trip ... do you want me to cancel or postpone and come down some other time?"

"No, you don't have to do that. Things will be in flux, but changing the dates on the plane ticket would cost you money. For the time being we will probably be going back and forth from the apartment to the ranch, but we'll still be able to do some fun stuff."

"Okay, I'll keep the ticket. But I'm sorry about your loss. How is Rochelle handling things?"

"She is coping, but I can tell she's broken up. You're coming down might be a good thing to get her mind off what has happened."

"I'll think up some stuff to do to cheer her up."

"I'm looking forward to seeing you again."

"Take care."

Even after the call, I had misgivings about the trip. I remember when my grandfather died in 1991, and how sullen and withdrawn I became in the weeks following his death. I was never diagnosed as being depressed, but in retrospect I wonder. In his case, he went to bed and didn't wake up the next morning. Certainly nothing as shocking and upsetting as being crushed by a falling tree.

I spent the next few weeks figuring out what to do on the trip. Anything to boost Rochelle's morale and hopefully make her happy. I definitely wanted to take some funny movies, so I packed DVDs of the funniest Zucker/Abrahams/Zucker movies: *Airplane, Top Secret,* and *The Naked Gun.* I especially wanted Rochelle to see *Top Secret,* since the film may well be my pick for the funniest movie I've ever seen.

From what I could gather, Rochelle had changed somewhat in the past year. While she was firmly entrenched in horseback riding and duties at the ranch, she became wildly obsessed with *CSI* and wanted a career in forensics instead of veterinary work. *CSI* had become appointment viewing for Rochelle and Jessie, though the show would be in reruns by the time I vacationed down there.

Rochelle was also hugely into Harry Potter by this point, reading all the books currently published. Nothing new, but she took her fandom to the next level during this time period. She even wrote some fanfic pieces that she shared with me, some of which were fairly amusing if you want to read PG-13 teen steamy romance plots between Hermione Granger and Draco Malfoy. Luckily, the latest film, *Harry Potter and the Prisoner of Azkaban,* was due to be released on June 4, so we would definitely have to see it.

I wanted to check out a Tampa Bay Devil Rays game. I had never been to a major league game before 2004 (though early era Rays barely qualified as major league). Sure, I had seen countless Triple A Louisville Redbirds games at old Cardinal Stadium, but I had never been to a major league game. Cincinnati is fairly close to Louisville, but I've never liked the Reds whatsoever, so the idea never appealed to me. I asked Rochelle a few days later if going to a Devil Rays game was on her to-do list.

"Sure, that would be great," she said. "I always wanted to play softball, but my mom never let me. She worried about me being hit in the head by the ball."

"I know what it's like," I said. "I was beaned in the head at the 1993 district All Star tourney at Prairie Village and was never the same player. Imagine laying on the ground seeing stars while those punks from Blue Lick were cracking jokes. 'Aw, poor baby. Did he get hurt?' I doubt something so intense happens when we go. The San Francisco Giants will be in Tampa that week, so even if the Devil Rays suck, we can at least go to see Barry Bonds."

"Oh, lord. Bonds. Hasn't he been in the news for being on steroids or something?"

"Yep. And I plan on buying tickets for the left field bleachers so we can heckle him all night! Do you have any ideas?"

"We have season passes to Busch Gardens. My mom and I can get in with those, but you would still have to pay your own way for admission."

"Sounds fun, I haven't been to an amusement park in ages, probably since I graduated from middle school. Try and take your mind off what happened though. If you need to talk, I'll be here."

Despite the tragic occurrence, the trip was still on as planned. I hoped to make it the rare sequel surpassing the original. I would will this to happen, if need be.

CHAPTER 10

THE SEQUEL CAN'T MATCH THE ORIGINAL

I left for St. Pete on Sunday, June 6. The trip to the Tampa airport went smoothly, yet upon arrival this time I did not find an eager Rochelle waiting at the baggage claim but instead had to venture outside and find Jessie's car. Gone was the functional but uninspiring Sebring, and in its place a new updated 2004 model. Upon finding the new car in the dark, I heaved my bag into the trunk and hopped in. Instead of driving across the Bay, we headed towards I-75 inland.

"Where's Rochelle?" I asked.

"Yeah, she's at the ranch right now with Dani," Jessie responded. "That's where we are going."

"I have no idea who Dani is. Rochelle hasn't mentioned her. I mostly knew about Callie."

"Dani is a newer friend of Rochelle's, same age. She's from Leesburg. She's been helping out at the ranch lately."

I knew of Leesburg, due to the town being where Ozzy Osbourne's guitarist Randy Rhoads died in a plane crash in 1982.

"How about Callie? I noticed Rochelle hadn't mentioned her lately."

"Something happened between her and Callie. They aren't as close as they used to be. Rochelle hangs out with some other girls, now."

I wasn't necessarily sad to hear this news. I didn't mind Callie or anything, but after a point she became an intrusion on the last trip.

"If I had known we were headed to the ranch right now I would have flown into Orlando instead of Tampa. Isn't Orlando closer?"

"No way you could have known. Keep in mind I have to take off again tomorrow morning and head back to St. Pete for work. But I will be back tomorrow evening to pick you and Rochelle up."

"Okay, whatever fits your schedule."

"You stirred up a hornet's nest with your letter last year. But hey, dad started paying Rochelle after we told him about what you said." Of all the things to take from the letter, this minor point? I thought it a mere incidental detail.

The trip lasted roughly an hour and a half from St. Pete to the ranch, but almost half as far from Orlando to the ranch. The logistics of this trip were already bonkers. Spending a whole day at the ranch the first day wasn't what I had in mind either, but such is life.

I crashed once again on the couch in the living room, though I can't recall why, since there should have been a spare bedroom. Yet again I barely slept, having to stay on guard from Gulliver and another feuding cat threatening each other on the nearby kitchen counter.

I didn't see Rochelle until the next morning. Jessie had already taken off for St. Pete and we wouldn't see her until she journeyed back after work. After eating breakfast and getting dressed, I walked outside to find Rochelle and Dani already in the arena, riding their horses. I leaned against the wooden fence and smiled at the duo riding and training. If there is one thing I know for certain, Rochelle loved her horse Sonny.

"God, I love this horse so much!" Rochelle exclaimed. "I'd marry him if it wasn't against the law!"

"I remember a Jerry Springer episode about that subject some years ago," I bellowed. This was the first time I walked around the Morgan Ranch in broad daylight without a crowd of people around. Finally, I took in the beauty of the scenery, and how relaxed the environment could be minus so much chaos going on.

As the day progressed, I met an older blonde woman named Sue, who had been helping out at the ranch as part of her community service for a drug arrest. Sue was in her late 50s or early 60s. I swear every grown adult I met in Florida had to be either a recovering alcoholic or drug addict.

I helped Sue and Rochelle lift some hay to the barn area, while Gretchen Wilson's main hits "Redneck Woman" and "Here For the Party" blared on the radio. Out with Eminem and 50 Cent, in with the country hits of the day. To me, this seemed to be trading one version of crap for another. I noticed a "Save a Horse, Ride a Cowboy" bumper sticker on the wall, as well. I've never been a big country music fan, but at least in the 1990s I found most of the artists respectable and didn't loathe the genre. Acts like Wilson or Big & Rich though? Country lost me.

"I'm glad to meet you, Brian," Sue said. "John did so much for me, helping me out of my legal trouble, and letting me work here at the ranch." Who was this woman? Was she Grandpa John's girlfriend? I knew he had been married and divorced a few times, but no details otherwise.

The only food we had the rest of the day was some quasi-homemade hamburgers Rochelle cooked on the grill on the outside deck, an area surrounded by netting to keep bugs away. For a sunny June day, the weather wasn't terribly hot. No more so than Louisville, albeit less humid. Rochelle and Dani also rummaged through John's death certificate paperwork on the outside table.

"Where did you get these patties?" I asked.

"We know someone who works at McDonald's in town" Dani said. "We get all sorts of free food, but in this case, we have to cook it ourselves."

"These burger patties don't look like McDonald's to me. More like White Castle. But you all don't have White Castle down here, do you?"

"No, we have Krystal down here," Rochelle replied. "I know someone at school who flat out loves Krystal burgers, but I've never had any."

"I live right by a White Castle," I said. "Technically, White Castle and Krystal are not related companies. They serve different areas of the country. I think London, Kentucky, is the one place I've seen where an exit has both a Krystal and a White Castle. Pagan luxury, I say."

Rochelle and Dani laughed at my discussion of fart burger joints. I took a look at the paperwork, as well.

"I didn't realize he was originally from Connecticut," I noted, reading the papers. "I noticed the rusty old car with an outdated Connecticut tag on the lawn. Mother's name is Gonchar. What sort of name is Gonchar?"

"Czech, I think," Rochelle added.

Later in the evening, Jessie picked up Rochelle and me, and we headed back to Pinellas Park. Dani's mom retrieved her in the meantime, while I gathered my belongings to finally unpack back at the apartment. As Jessie exited the car, Sue couldn't help but admire the new auto.

"Loving the new car, darlin," Sue said.

"Hey, what can I say? I've had a financial windfall of sorts, and the old car had to go. Besides, I bought this one with a good interest rate." If there's one thing I can say about Jessie, she definitely had a touch of Barbara Stanwyck moxie in her. Even looked slightly similar, with more of a Florida tan.

Rochelle and I grabbed our stuff, and we were off to St. Pete.

"Who is Sue?" I asked Jessie.

"You may know by now she had a drug charge and worked at the ranch for my dad as community service. But she was his girlfriend, as well. I swear he would talk about humping her half a dozen times a day. I do wonder where she was the night of his accident, though. The man was lying there dying. So, that's who Sue is."

Jessie stopped there and we changed the subject to anything else. "Okay, everyone," I said. "Who is the worst band of the past fifteen years? I nominate Korn."

"Callie likes Korn," Jessie chuckled.

"I'm not surprised," I replied. "Wonder if we should check out Clearwater this week?" I pondered. Jessie and Rochelle didn't reply to the question.

We arrived back at the apartment late that night in time to see the finish of Game 7 of the Stanley Cup Finals, as the local Tampa Bay Lightning won their first championship with a 2-1 victory over the Calgary Flames. My trips must be a good luck charm for the Tampa Bay area. The last trip happened right after the Buccaneers had won their first Super Bowl. We were away from the ranch and back in St. Pete, so I felt more at ease.

Barb moved out a few months before, so Rochelle regained her old room. Since Rochelle earned money from the ranch, she helped pay a portion of the rent. The dilemma became, well, Rochelle now had her room back, and as such spent more time there as the week progressed, and less time in the living room with me.

My sense of ease lasted until the next morning. As the day progressed, I noticed the AC hadn't been cycling in the apartment. This being Florida in June, the villa started heating up. Jessie was at work, but as before she would stop by to check on us at various points throughout the day. Once again without a car, though I can't recall why this time. Stingy, I reckon.

I decided to show Rochelle *Top Secret*, despite the apartment heating up. She didn't respond well to the film. Maybe the heat sapped her sense of frivolity? The humor in the film didn't appeal to her? Cheering her up from the recent tragedy was going to be tougher than I thought.

Thankfully, Jessie rescued us from the hot apartment after lunch and dropped us off at the Pinellas Square Mall so we could see the Harry Potter movie Rochelle was chomping at the bit to devour. At least the theater was air conditioned, and thankfully Rochelle responded to *Prisoner of Azkaban* positively. Therein laid the slight frustration, however. As the film unspooled, Rochelle would occasionally whisper at me, "This is a fun scene," or other tidbits.

"Have you already seen this?" I mumbled.

"Yeah, sorry, but I couldn't wait," she whispered.

Jessie picked us up after the movie, and much like the previous year, we headed back towards the Gulf beach area, mainly Redington Beach, but all of those various beaches along the coast blur together after a point. As we walked in the white sand I couldn't help but notice Rochelle kept her distance from me, preferring to walk alongside Jessie. At one point, she wrote "I 'heart sign' Sonny" in the sand. I started to understand that Rochelle's priorities had changed in the past year.

After this abbreviated beach outing, Jessie once again stopped by Lake Seminole Park and took a brief drive, though with the sun fading, we never left the car. Everything from the mall trip, the beach, and now the brief tour of the park felt like a washed-up band playing their greatest hits in routine fashion. There was little spark to Rochelle. She wasn't mean or disagreeable, but I couldn't reach her. I tried to be there for her the best I could, but I lacked the tools and know-how.

Thankfully, Jessie called the apartment office and reported the AC problem. But for the rest of the night, I roamed around shirtless at the apartment due to the heat. Rochelle glanced at the mail she brought from the ranch. One curious letter from a horse activist group came with a shock headline, "Donate now! Only you can prevent wild horses from being rounded up and slaughtered!"

"This sounds like the opening scene of *Billy Jack*," I jested. Rochelle had zero idea what I was talking about, but Jessie laughed.

I decided not to bother showing the other movies I brought and instead watched the Lakers vs. Pistons in the NBA Finals, while Rochelle mostly watched TV in her room. The next day shaped up to be fun at least, since we were heading to Sunrise Lanes again for bowling, and then Rochelle and I were going to the Devil Rays/Giants game at Tropicana Field. The bowling alley trip was fairly uneventful. Once again, I couldn't help but notice Rochelle's slightly sullen demeanor. We also played a few games, and I won enough tickets for a pair of vampire teeth. I had an amusing idea for later.

Since Jessie wasn't picking us up for a while and ballpark food is absurdly expensive, we decided to walk across the street to the nearby Waffle House. This location lacked the palatial splendor of the one in Orlando, but still better than the one down the street for me back home.

Jessie had a knack for knowing when to pick us up. We met her back at the bowling alley parking lot, whereby I inserted the wacky vampire teeth as I entered the car and yelled "AHHHHHH!" Jessie was startled at first but then cracked up laughing.

"I bet you've been waiting all day to do that!"

CHAPTER 11

A NIGHT AT THE TROPICANA

Tropicana Field was one of those multi-purpose toilets of a stadium. I am shocked that it still exists in MLB, though Hurricane Milton recently ripped away the roof. Believe me, I know my multi-purpose dumps. I used to frequent old Cardinal Stadium at the fairgrounds, mainly for Redbirds games, but also the occasional U of L football game. UK defeated Duke in the 1998 Elite 8 at Tropicana, right around the time the Devil Rays came into existence.

The Devil Rays were still little better than an expansion team, having nothing but awful losing seasons and low attendance. From 1998 to 2007, the team lost between 92 and 106 games each year, so you have to admire their consistency of crap. The dilemma with Tampa Bay having an MLB team is that the area is a Yankees town, historically speaking. The Yankees hold Spring Training there. There are numerous transplanted New Yorkers in the Tampa area, so those people still prefer the Yankees. The Devil Rays drew two and a half million fans their first year, but once fans had a look at that motley expansion crew, they quickly lost interest. By 2003, the team drew a little over one million fans at the gate, slightly more than 13,000 fans a game (and who knows how many of those are bought by ticket brokers, companies, and season ticket holders who don't show up).

I've been to Louisville Redbirds Triple A games as a kid attended by more people.

Bonds and the Giants brought out the fans. There were twice as many people as they usually drew, without any special promotion. I made sure to buy two tickets around the left field bleachers for $30.00 each, so we could heckle Barry Bonds in the outfield. The irony of the Giants being the opponent wasn't lost on me, since I recall the time a decade earlier when the Giants toyed with the idea of leaving San Francisco for Tampa Bay. San Fran ponied up for a new stadium, and the idea went by the wayside. Hence Tampa Bay receiving an expansion team.

Jessie didn't want to go. Maybe she wasn't a baseball fan, or didn't want me to buy three tickets. She knew to pick us up a little after 10:00 p.m., since the game would run roughly three hours.

As the bottom of the first inning resumed, the Giants took the field. However, Bonds was nowhere to be found. Some other random dude played LF.

"Aw, crap," I said. "Tampa is an American League team. Since Bonds is old, he's probably the designated hitter tonight."

"Eh, no big deal," Rochelle replied. "We can heckle whoever this guy is instead, if you want. I remember hearing at school that The Undertaker and his wife had sex in the bathroom at Tropicana Field. Wonder if that was true?"

"Men's room or women's room?"

"I don't know more than that."

The dilemma of paying money to see a particular baseball player is that the famous player in question may not do anything special. Bonds went 1 for 5, with a lone single being a grounder up the middle. Speaking of old guys, Fred McGriff was the DH for the Devil Rays in 2004, playing out his career.

"Hey, the Crime Dog!" I said, as McGriff came up to bat. "Hopefully this man still has something left in the tank." McGriff proceeded to strike out, looking like a shell of himself.

"Maybe not," Rochelle replied.

Rochelle had an amusing cluelessness about baseball. One of the Giants hit a popup in foul territory behind home plate, and the Rays catcher threw off his mask and ran after the ball but came up short. Rochelle was baffled.

"Why would you even go after *that*?" she asked, indignantly.

"What do you mean?" I asked in return.

"Why did the catcher bother going after that?" she asked again. "What the crap?"

"I still don't understand."

"Why waste energy going after something like that?" she reiterated.

"Uh ... to get the man out?" I replied, confused by this question. I never answered to her satisfaction. She was also amazed at anyone in the outfield making routine plays.

"Wow, our catchers are really good!" she said, meaning the outfielders.

"Yeah, these are routine fly balls, though. We'll see if someone makes an amazing play." No one did.

The player who stood out to me was Carl Crawford. He was the best player on the Devil Rays during that era, the lone All Star level talent they had. In 2004 Crawford led the league in triples and stolen bases, the type of exciting player every team needed. The lack of speed at the heart of Moneyball has always been a problem for me with that style of play. To Billy Beane, speed costs money the A's didn't have, but the Devil Rays were a low payroll team as well, and managed to have one guy who could run, steal, and excite the crowd.

Jessie started calling Rochelle's cell around the time the 9th inning rolled around. The Tampa closer sucked and blew a 3-1 lead. As such, the game headed to extra innings.

"Your mom won't like this, but we're headed for the 10th," I said. Thankfully, the Devil Rays put two men on in the 10th and won the game with a base hit, 4-3. I can imagine how grouchy Jessie would have been if the game became a fifteen inning marathon. Amusingly, this epic extra inning win sent the Devil Rays on a (then) franchise best twelve game winning streak. As I said, I am good luck for Tampa sports teams.

When we returned to the apartment, the AC had been mercifully restored.

"Hallelujah!" I exclaimed. "Let's bask in this nice, cold air."

"You won't believe what caused the problem," Jessie said. "A snake slithered into the outside unit and fried the AC!"

"Well, we know what's for dinner tomorrow, then," I replied.

"I have a gift for you," Jessie said. "Since you are a baseball fan and all."

Jessie darted to another room and came back with a framed picture of 2002 era Devil Rays first baseman Steve Cox. She handed it to me.

"Thank you very much!" I said. I couldn't help but wonder to myself, *Who the hell is Steve Cox?* I have the picture in a closet somewhere, even if I still have no idea who Steve Cox is (note: Cox played four uneventful years for the Devil Rays from 1999-2002 and was a career .262 hitter. Thanks baseball-reference.com).

Chapter 12

My Own Confusion

Since we planned to enjoy Busch Gardens on Friday, Thursday was a tranquil day. An important day, however, as a turning point in how I approached Rochelle. Thus far, she hadn't been hostile or angry with me, and I was glad to see she and her mom were getting along better than on my previous trip.

Rochelle slept later than she did the previous year. She had her room back, and due to summer break had no urgent need to wake up. With Jessie at work, I felt the need to roust Rochelle around 10:00 a.m. As I entered the room, she seemed startled and even slightly taken aback that I entered, a problem with not having clear previous boundaries.

After we ate some cereal, Rochelle retreated back to her room and sat on the bed. I rejoined her.

"Can we talk?" I asked.

"Sure," she said.

I knew something needed to be said, but what? The lack of being able to verbally express myself reared its ugly head again, so I decided to try a tactic which worked fairly well when I used it on Tracy Bowen back in high school.

"Hang on," I said. "I'll be right back."

I found a piece of paper and pen in the dining room, then headed back to Rochelle's room. I started writing and we took turns responding to each other.

Is something the matter? You have seemed distant since I came down here.

I handed her the paper and pen for a response. She took her time but started writing.

Nothing is wrong. Been through a lot lately, that's all.

I have noticed the way you stopped giving hugs and affection. Did you not want me to come back down after all?

Well, no. That isn't it. But you and I can only be friends right now.

I understand. Kinda confusing right now.

We will have to see what happens.

I stopped writing and shuffled back into the kitchen. I wadded up the paper and threw it away. I left Rochelle to her own devices while I flipped through channels in the living room.

A few hours later Jessie dropped us off at a local pet store so Rochelle could look for a pet toy for Gulliver to use back at the ranch, instead of brawling with other cats. As Rochelle perused the aisles in the back of the store, I walked up to her somewhat forlorn.

"Rochelle, I'm sorry."

"For what?" she asked, slightly annoyed.

"For everything."

For the first time on the trip, she gave me a hug.

I didn't even know why I apologized, but I felt it needed to be done. Not finding what she came for, Rochelle soon called Jessie, and we left the store.

With no other plans on the docket, we ended up back at the mall. Rochelle had an interest in seeing *Raising Helen*, a Kate Hudson vehicle I've never bothered to watch since then. The other notable excursion was a trip to the Hot Topic, where I bought a vinyl copy of Nirvana's *Bleach* album, probably my most enduring memento from that trip, aside from the Steve Cox framed picture. Records were roughly the same cost as a CD back then, about $15.00.

One meaningful change I noticed was Rochelle's newfound disinterest in wrestling. Aside from the occasional mention, wrestling didn't seem to hold her interest anymore. I watched *Smackdown* that evening alone in the living room. Jessie watched something else in her room and Rochelle the VMAs on MTV back in her room. At various points, I tried to lure her up front with some tantalizing action transpiring onscreen.

"What do you think of the Yeah Yeah Yeahs?" I asked, walking into the room to see the band playing.

"The song 'Maps' sucks," she stated. "The Beastie Boys performance wasn't bad though, for old guys."

I left the room.

"Hey, RVD gave John Cena a spin kick! This is getting exciting!"

No dice. She didn't seem to care much. Then again, this *was* 2004 era *Smackdown*, one of the worst wrestling programs ever broadcast for mass consumption. Her disinterest didn't surprise me. As mentioned, Rochelle was one of these younger fans who became interested in wrestling for the crazy storylines more than the actual wrestling. A major aspect of our shared experience seemed to be going by the wayside, and I had no idea how to replace it.

CHAPTER 13

BUSCH GARDENS AND BEYOND

By the last day of the trip, I had a feeling that the entire trip had been a misfire. It hadn't been a disaster, and in some ways we did a few more activities. The music was good but played out of tune. I had one last day which we were going to spend at Busch Gardens. However, the logistics were insane. The trip is a half hour from Pinellas Park to the amusement park in Tampa, but as the day barreled on there was far more in store, travel wise.

Overall, I much prefer St. Pete to Tampa. Mind you, I haven't spent much time in Tampa, aside from flying into the airport, but passing through on the way to Busch Gardens I seemed to see nothing but strip joints and used car lots. Tampa was like Pottersville in *It's a Wonderful Life*, if George Bailey had never been born.

"I read online that Tampa is one of the ten most dangerous cities in America," I said, while we were driving through.

"Oh God, yes!" Jessie replied. "Tampa has become a terribly dangerous city." For what it's worth, I felt safe enough. No more dangerous than the Preston Highway area here in Louisville.

"Mom, isn't that your old club?" Rochelle asked, as we passed one of the many strip clubs.

"Yes, it is," Jessie groaned, not especially wanting to relive those years.

Busch Gardens was the single strangest amusement park I have ever seen. The entire motif of the place is African, the décor and pageantry wildly cool. As you walk along there are plenty of sights to see, an entire area copying the Serengeti Plains, Moroccan themed areas, Egyptian themed areas, and the like. While walking through the experience, it's not uncommon to have flamingos or geese walk along with you. Given the two hundred species of wildlife, the place doubles as a zoo about as much as an amusement park. Rochelle and Jessie used their season passes at the gate, while I had to fork over $35.00 for admission.

Adding to the bizarre environment, the park at that time was still owned by Anheuser-Busch, and as such, guests were allowed free beers. The policy seemed hazy to me, but Chad informed me previously of his visits there a couple of years earlier, when he moved to Clearwater on a lark, and worked for Budweiser.

"Oh, man," Chad said. "You can get trashed there if you know how. They have various stations set up around the park, and we used to get free beer at each of them. They never checked whether we had already gotten our one freebie. We kept going station to station and rode the coasters while drunk off our asses."

Jessie passed on most of the intense roller coasters and left those to Rochelle and me. We rode the Kumba, a crazy corkscrew coaster leaving riders alternatively exhilarated and queasy. The Gwazi was more my speed in its original wooden form, which reminded me of Thunder Run at Kentucky Kingdom. The Montu, another intense coaster, goes upside down and into corkscrews. As a general rule, I tend to avoid coasters where I have to go upside down.

After a few of these, I started to feel queasy. We sat down at one of the picnic table areas and regrouped.

"You can go inside and get a free beer," Jessie said.

"I doubt that" I replied. "It is almost ninety degrees today, and riding corkscrew roller coasters after drinking beer doesn't sound like the greatest idea." I passed on the free beer.

Rochelle and I walked into an arcade area to cool off. I spotted a photo booth in the corner of the room.

"Want to take some pictures?" I asked.

"Sure, let's go," she said.

We had three pics made in this booth. The first was a fairly serious shot of us looking at the camera, but the other two were absurdly wacky. In one, I goofed around, giving Rochelle bunny ears, and in the third she mugged for the camera. These silly pictures were one of my enduring memories of the trip, but I wound up losing them while moving in 2012.

Jessie joined us for the water themed rides, such as the Congo River Rapids and the Stanley Falls Log Flume. The Congo ride involved strapping yourself into a raft and journeying down a hectic, rapid filled stream. We were drenched by the time it ended. The Log Flume was fun as well, and as we plummeted down the slide to the water below, I braced by placing my left hand on Jessie's leg. She didn't seem to mind.

After being soaked we mostly walked around the park to dry off before leaving. Oddly enough, the park also had a Dale Earnhardt, Jr. race car displayed, a curious outlier in an otherwise exotic themed park. Rochelle was oddly thrilled at the car, which I found curious, since she had never mentioned being a NASCAR fan.

"We need to find you a real job," Jessie said.

"How do you mean? Here?"

"Why not?" she asked.

"Oh, I can't move down here full time," I said. "Not right now, due to my family situation. You know about my dad being in a wheelchair from the stroke, but I also need to be around to help my mom deal with my brother."

"You aren't trying, though," Rochelle said.

"I know I have to do something, eventually," I replied.

"How is Eric these days?" Rochelle asked.

"He didn't have a quality middle school experience," I replied. "Three lousy schools in three years. Thomas Jefferson Middle for 6th, Southern Middle in 7th, and once they moved to my grandma's old house he attended Stuart for 8th. He hates school, and more than once I needed to spend the night to ensure he left for school the next day."

Once we were dry, we left the park. As we were leaving, Jessie's cell phone rang. She answered.

"Wait, what is she doing there already? She's there by herself? Ugh, we will have to pack up and head there later tonight."

"What's up?" I asked.

"Talked to Dani's mom. Apparently, she is already at the ranch for the weekend, but no one else is around. We are going to now have to go back to the apartment, pack up for the weekend, and head over there."

"That doesn't make any sense," I said. "Keep in mind I leave tomorrow morning, so you would then have to drive me from the ranch all the way back to the Tampa airport. If I had known this ahead of time I could have flown into Orlando and saved some mileage."

"Mom, don't we also need to drop by Kevin's house?" Rochelle asked.

"Oh, yeah. We need to do that before leaving for the ranch as well. This Kevin kid is an at-risk teen my dad signed to work at the ranch this summer. I'm going through with the deal."

So, to recap this insanity: We had to drive back to Pinellas Park, thirty-plus minutes away, hurriedly pack, stop by this Kevin kid's house for Jessie to talk about his starting date at the ranch, gas up, then head over eighty miles to the ranch for the evening. In the morning, Jessie would have to drive me back to Tampa for my flight, only to head back to the ranch. Why, exactly, was Dani at the ranch alone in the first place? I had no idea.

After all of these errands back in St. Pete, we arrived in Sumter County as the sun was going down. There isn't much in the way of fine dining in the area, so we stopped at a Subway off the interstate, where I was so starved I bought a footlong chicken breast sub and practically inhaled it. Between spending all day at Busch Gardens and all this bizarre back and forth travel, I was completely exhausted. So exhausted I couldn't even think straight. By the time we arrived at the Morgan Ranch gate I was barely coherent.

"Can you get out and lock the gate?" Jessie asked me. I staggered out of the car, then locked the gate. The problem? I stood on the wrong side, so I had locked myself out. Rochelle and Jessie laughed out loud while I opened the gate once again, stepped inside, and locked it correctly.

I have hazy memories of that night. I recall Rochelle, Jessie, and Dani watching a rerun of *CSI*. Rochelle was enthralled by the Gil Grissom/Sara Sidle blossoming romance storyline. Since I didn't care about *CSI*, I tasked myself with writing another parting letter while sitting at the dining table.

I can't recall the exact specifics of the second letter, but I know it didn't have any particular impact the way the first one did, a fitting conclusion to a trip that didn't have the same impact the first one did. I commented on how we tried to make the best of things during a sad time in Rochelle's life, be wary of this Kevin kid during the summer, and so on. I concluded by saying I needed to stay away for a while.

Jessie and I had to rush the next morning, even waking up at the crack of dawn. Once again, I barely got any sleep on the couch at the ranch, being so tired I couldn't sleep. While we rushed to make it to the Tampa airport on time, the situation soon became obvious. I couldn't make the gate in time for departure. Jessie found the airline phone number and gave them a call while we were en route.

"Yes, I was wondering if you could change a flight at the last minute. I'm trying to rush someone to the airport for a flight, but we can't make it."

After listening for a moment, Jessie pressed on.

"That's right, he needs the next flight out to Louisville, Kentucky."

"I don't relish having to do this, but I could pay $100.00 to change flights," I said.

After discussing the matter for a few more minutes, Jessie hung up the phone, apparently satisfied with the end result.

"They changed your departure to the next flight, since there were plenty of empty seats. No extra charge."

"Okay. I should have booked a slightly later flight, anyway. I'm still thinking about how foolish I looked last night, locking myself outside of the gate."

"Hey, it happens to the best of us. Funny as hell, though."

The trip to the airport was baffling once we reached Tampa. We traveled on back roads, and even right past the University of South Florida. Jessie managed to find the parking garage and grabbed a spot.

"Thanks for having me again," I said. She nodded in approval, bidding me adieu, and I exited the car to the airport.

The trip back proved uneventful, though once I finally returned to my apartment, I needed a nap and crashed. Once again, no rest for the weary, since I now needed to take dirty clothes over to my mom's and wash them, so I could then pack for my family's usual yearly trip to Myrtle Beach. My mom put the trip off for a week so I could visit Florida again.

At the time, I felt the second trip to see Rochelle was a failure. On the surface the trip sounds fairly decent. The plans I had in mind mostly came to fruition in terms of the activities we did. The death of Rochelle's grandfather couldn't help but dampen the occasion, and by the time I returned home I wondered where things stood. I wasn't sure what Rochelle and Jessie were doing about living arrangements going forward. As my dad said of Jessie, "She needs to watch out for fortune hunter types. She is an heiress now." Technically, the ranch ownership split three ways between Jessie and her two brothers. I have never met either of them.

Rochelle and Jessie moved to the Morgan Ranch by the time school started in August. This decision was made easier by the landlord at the villas refusing to renew their lease, due to needing more space, since he was getting a divorce. As such, Jessie had to commute to St. Pete five days a week from the ranch, which is quite a drive.

Once we returned from Myrtle Beach, I had some soul searching to do. What was I even *doing* anyway? The more I analyzed the situation, the more I couldn't help but feel that visiting Rochelle again in the near future presented a Catch 22 situation. I had no desire or inclination to stay at the ranch for an entire week. Also, I wasn't sure what to do about Rochelle because continually visiting in the next few years offered two main scenarios, neither ideal. The first involved Rochelle acting towards me the way she did the previous trip, which could lead to trouble. The second involved Rochelle being distant, the way she acted on this trip, so why spend money on a plane ticket to Florida for more of the same? Going back required a purpose.

While I still cared about Rochelle, I decided not to worry about any further trips to Florida for the time being. I posted a profile on the local website Louisville Mojo and within a week found someone sane and decent, who happened to live around the block from my mom's house. That would be Amanda, who soon became my girlfriend. I was destined to travel back to the Sunshine State, but for the time being Rochelle and I needed to stay as far apart as the poles.

CHAPTER 14

ONCE MORE, WITH FEELING

I distanced myself from Rochelle after returning from Florida in June 2004. We still talked on AOL if I happened to see her online, but once she and Jessie moved to the ranch full time and Rochelle started high school, we drifted apart. This time period coincided with me meeting Amanda, and also my various attempts at applying to film schools, the aborted attempt at making a film of my script *Welcome to Paradise*, and the usual family related drama.

And yet ... I thought about Rochelle every day, even when we weren't actively talking online. Mind you, she hardly dominated my thoughts by any means, but at some point in the day I would wonder how she was doing, whether she was happy in Sumter County, or how things were going at the ranch.

In the Spring of 2007, WWE announced Orlando as being the host of *WrestleMania XXIV* on March 30, 2008. Tickets went on sale in November 2007, so plenty of time to consider whether I wanted to go. That summer I started emailing Rochelle a few times, gauging whether she was interested in going to *WrestleMania*, since the Morgan Ranch isn't far from Orlando. We started talking on the phone as well about some of the current WWE storylines.

"Am I to understand Edge is now the champion on *Smackdown,* and he's married to Eddie Guerrero's widow?" she asked.

"Yeah, pretty much," I replied.

"That sounds incredibly bizarre, but I have to admit I'm interested."

"So, do you want to go to *WrestleMania* if I can grab the tickets?"

"Sure! Sounds like it will be a great show. I'll be glad to see you again. Did I mention my dad is now living here at the ranch?"

"No? This is the first time I've heard about him living with you, but we haven't been able to talk as much lately. I didn't know he lived in Florida. Now that you mention him though, I'm not surprised."

"What makes you say that?"

"Let's face it, Rochelle. Your mom has been largely alone on a ninety-acre horse ranch without much help otherwise. Your uncles aren't around much, are they?"

"Not really. My dad's wife kicked him out."

"Your dad had nowhere to go, and Jessie needed a man around the ranch, so she felt desperate enough to take him in."

"You hit the nail on the head."

"Hey, I've never met your dad, so this will be an interesting experience."

We left things there for the time being. Eventually tickets went on sale, and I needed to know how many to buy. Rochelle mentioned her dad hated wrestling so I figured he had zero interest, so I planned to buy three tickets, and they could reimburse me later. I wanted to buy the cheapest seats I could find, since my website sales were declining circa late 2007/early 2008. In truth, selling classic movies was a dying enterprise. I ran out of feasible movies to sell. New DVD releases cut down the market for bootlegs and I had constant frustrations over being kicked off eBay or PayPal over disputes.

"Can you buy four tickets?" Rochelle asked, sometime later.

"I suppose so. Who is the fourth person going?"

"Dory. Did I not tell you? He's living with us now."

Okay, this was a monkey wrench thrown into my plan. In the back of my mind, I felt the need to see where I stood with Rochelle now that she was eighteen. I barely knew Dory from my previous trip to the ranch in 2003, but Rochelle mentioned a while later that he moved back home to rural Ohio. He returned to Florida, and he and Rochelle were an item. I couldn't fathom the idea of him living there with Rochelle as a couple, given she was still a senior in high school. I knew people from HS who cohabited, but they were in a shotgun situation, due to a teenage pregnancy. But then, Jessie never did play by the same rules as most of society, so once I thought about the scenario more, I wasn't shocked she allowed him to live there.

Once I heard this news, I probably should have called the whole trip off and not bothered with buying the tickets, but I bought them anyway. On one hand I wanted to experience *WrestleMania* in person. On the other, I had to know where I stood with Rochelle, once and for all.

Another problem: I was fat. During the previous few years, I ballooned well over 200 lbs. After the holidays in 2007, I hovered around 230 lbs. I could barely walk up a flight of stairs without losing my breath. I was hopelessly out of shape and figured if I wanted to make a good impression with Rochelle I needed to exercise and start dieting. Frankly, I needed to do those things anyway, regardless of the trip.

Here is a rundown of what I did on my diet, starting in 2008. I cannot vouch for how well any of this may work for other people, but this strategy worked for me.

1. For breakfast, I ate two waffles with syrup and drank a glass of orange juice.
2. Lunch presented a big problem in terms of empty calories, so I cut out eating much for lunch and also stopped drinking any soft drinks for lunch. For lunch, I usually ate two kosher pickle spears, two pretzel rods, and a glass of milk. Later, I realized the milk added calories, so sub in either water or unsweetened tea. Nasty Arizona tea to be specific.
3. I rode five miles on the stationary bike in my mom's basement every day, or at least most days. Not a huge investment of time, twenty to twenty-five minutes a day riding, but it made a world of difference. I spent far too

many years being stationary, at a desk in front of my
computer.

4. Dinner could be a variety of things. I largely cut out fast
food, though you can eat some as long as you cut out the
cokes and such. Eating homemade fish and rice, chicken
dishes. We all need to have a daily intake of calories to
survive, so eating a solid dinner is a must.

5. One small piece of candy for dessert. At night, I drank tea.

6. As a dietary supplement, I took Hydroxycut. I started out
taking as many as four pills a day, two for breakfast and two
for lunch. Eventually I cut down to three a day (breakfast,
lunch, dinner), then by the end down to two pills a day.
Those pills aggravated my stomach after using them too
long.

While I refused to go on a crash diet and lose a massive amount of
weight, I managed to bring myself down to around 200 lbs. by the
second half of March when I headed to Florida. I kept going well into
the summer and finally reached 170 by the time we left for our usual
Myrtle Beach trip. I managed to stay on the diet for another year or so,
until the realities of grad school set in and I ate and drank excessively
once again. But as of March 2008, I felt better, and set out back to the
Sunshine State. Was this trip the start of a new chapter between
Rochelle and me—or the final chapter?

CHAPTER 15

RETURN TO MORGAN RANCH

Looking back now, the 2008 trip to the Morgan Ranch was fascinating in terms of how little circumstances had changed since 2003, even though so much had changed in reality. Here I was journeying back to see Rochelle during *WrestleMania* season, the NCAA tournament's Sweet 16 and Elite 8 rounds serving as a backdrop. Instead of UK's downbeat flop against Marquette, my alma mater U of L was making a run. The Cardinals were set to play Tennessee the evening I arrived in Orlando. I corresponded via email a few times with native Tennessean and ESPN's *Around the Horn* panelist Woody Paige about this game. Woody assured me U of L had zero chance, due to poor free throw shooting. I even had some playful banter back and forth with some UT fans on the plane, joking that U of L needed to smack the Vols around.

The Orlando airport doesn't stand out in my mind the way Tampa's does, aside from the incessant construction going on throughout the terminal as I arrived. For the first time, Rochelle picked me up by herself, now having a license and her own car. By now, we were used to meeting this way, so the reaction was fairly subdued. We hopped in her navy-blue Chevy Malibu and took off for the ranch.

"You'll have to forgive my drunken father if he says something stupid to you when we arrive," Rochelle said. "Can't stand him." An ominous sign to be sure. I had been worried about a potentially jealous boyfriend wanting to kick my ass. A 6'3", 200+ lb. cowboy shitkicker, no less.

"Duly noted. I have no idea what to expect here, but I would at least like to watch the U of L game tonight. We can flip back and forth between the game and *TNA Impact*."

"Yeah, we can do that. Here's the turnoff for the road we need."

Instead of venturing down the sparsely populated Florida Turnpike toll road, I wish we could have kept going towards I-4. Keep going and not look back. But no, within the hour we had arrived back at the ranch.

I wouldn't say the reception I received was chilly, but instead, no reaction at all. Once we arrived, I didn't see Jessie, Dory, or Rochelle's dad, Scott. The only greeting was from a different pet than what I remembered, an ugly pug dog who ran up to me panting and frothing.

Full disclosure: I am not a dog lover. I may well have an undiagnosed phobia against dogs. Merely being around a dog causes my heart to race and my blood pressure to spike. Pug would prove to be a nuisance to me on this trip.

"Come over here, silly!" Rochelle said to her dog.

Yet again, I found myself having to sleep on the couch. I moved my suitcase into a spare room. Jessie emerged from her own bedroom and greeted me.

"Hey, there. Hope you had a good trip. I would let you use the spare room, except my brother uses it when he comes here, and he might not like you staying there. Oh, and I owe you money for three tickets."

"At this point, I'm used to the couch," I replied.

As this disjointed evening wore on, Rochelle and I watched some of *TNA Impact* on Spike until the time came for the U of L game, which started late.

"One thing I like about TNA is they at least have some decent women in their Knockouts division," Rochelle noted.

"Yeah, they do," I said. "They also typically have better tag wrestling than WWE. But that's what you do if you are an alternative product. Figure out what WWE doesn't care about and focus on those divisions."

Rochelle's dad popped in and out of the living room, not saying a whole lot, or even introducing himself initially. Ah, another parallel back to the 2003 trip in the form of a bizarre passive aggressive response at the Morgan Ranch. I never saw Dory at all that night, which was probably a good thing.

I was wiped out from the trip and didn't see the entirety of the anticipated U of L vs. Tennessee game. U of L opened up a decent lead in the second half against an ailing Chris Lofton and Co., so I crashed on the couch and fell asleep. They still had a couple of feuding cats, however, which clawed at each other on the nearby kitchen counter. Once the sun rose, I checked ESPN for the final score of the game. U of L won 79-60 and now faced North Carolina in the regional final on Saturday. The poor free throw shooting hadn't hurt us as much as Woody Paige predicted.

The next morning was a fairly sedate one. Jessie still commuted to her old state job back in St. Pete, which had to be awful daily travel. Rochelle left early for school, since spring break in Sumter County didn't fall on the week of *WrestleMania*, the way it did in 2003. Dory was off at work at a local bait and tackle store. Rochelle's dad and I held down the fort at the ranch most of the day.

"Hi, I'm Scott," he said, as I finished my cereal at the dining room table.

"Hey, I'm Brian," I replied. "Do you know why I am here?"

"Yeah, you all are going to the wrestling show on Sunday. For the life of me I don't get it. What do Jessie and Rochelle see in that crap?"

"I can't vouch for them, but I started watching as a kid and never grew out of watching. Never been to an event the size of a *Wrestle-Mania*, though."

"Walk with me. I have to tend to these horses. I'll bring the dog and take him outside."

From there we strolled over to the barn and stable area, where Scott found several bales of hay in the back of Jessie's new Dodge Ram. The two of us emptied the back of the truck, and Scott heaved a bail over the fence area for the horses in the nearby field.

"Come on!" he yelled, waving his hands at the horses. "Come on!" A few listened, but some didn't. Scott looked slightly discouraged.

"Anything wrong?" I asked.

"I have to get back into corrections. I can't deal with these animals.

At least prison inmates understand the idea of consequences, unlike these horses."

"Just wondering, but how often did you come to the ranch before you moved in here?" I asked.

"Sometimes, but not often. Jessie's dad ... man, he did not like me back in the day, given my crazy permed mullet down my back and all." Scott now had short blondish hair and looked nothing like someone who was a hair metal musician two decades earlier.

"I only met the man once," I replied. "I've never forgotten that day."

"Come on, let's drive the Ram back to the house," Scott said, with a sly smile.

Scott wanted me to hold Pug, which I tried to do, but the dog squirmed and touched the new leather seats of the Dodge. Scott mildly freaked.

"Oh, man. Jessie will be pissed. I hope that damn dog didn't do any damage to the seats." I bristled. We settled down Pug and made the short trip back to the house in the truck.

Shortly after lunch, Scott informed me of a used car dealer who was supposed to stop by and finalize a deal for some old junker he and Jessie wanted to buy for driving around the ranch and nearby. Until then, we chilled and continued to talk.

"Want a beer?" he asked.

"Sure," I said, even though I didn't usually drink during the afternoon.

Scott handed me a cold Budweiser, then proceeded to take our conversation in a highly political direction as we downed the beers. As I would learn, Scott was (and likely still is) a mad dog conservative. I'm talking about wild Bircher level lunacy. Add in his would-be rock star background, and he was a poor man's Ted Nugent.

"So ... when is the primary in Kentucky?" he asked. "Oh, Kentucky sucks when it comes to primary scheduling," I said.

"The primary isn't until May 20. McCain has the Republican nomination sewn up, but I'm not sure about Hillary and Obama. I don't care about the Dem primary. Probably won't vote in it at all, since Hillary is obviously winning Kentucky, but not likely to catch Obama, nationally."

"I can't wait for the Democratic convention in Denver," he replied. "If Obama doesn't have this thing locked down, I can see them trying to screw the black man out of the nomination. That would be so glorious. I'll grab my popcorn and everything."

"I doubt that will happen. He'll have the nomination clinched by then."

By this point I felt slightly tipsy from having one beer. I wasn't used to drinking. Scott opened another and kept going. I started to see what Rochelle meant by her "drunken father."

"I don't understand why anyone votes Democrat," he said, emphatically, while taking a swig. "Case in point. I know a girl whose parents were trying to get her into a quality college here in the state. FSU? Anyway, they were jacking her around on admissions, to the point where her dad contacted a local Democratic politician for help. Did he do anything? No! You know who did? The Republican rep from the area! He helped her out!"

In my tipsy state, I had no idea what the hell he was talking about, so I let him rant. We may have differed politically, but I was used to having these discussions with Chad in similar roles. I may not have known who or what he ranted about, but he was certainly passionate.

"I don't know much about it," I replied.

"Here, let me show you a book by Glenn Beck. Great author, love that guy."

Scott handed me his copy of Beck's *An Inconvenient Book*. I knew little about Beck circa 2008 but would hear his name more in the following years. Before Obama became President, Beck was mainly known in right wing circles, but Obama gave Beck a punching bag.

"Look at how he expertly skewers the idea of global warming!" Scott exclaimed. "The world heating up slightly every year isn't a huge problem. You know what would be? Another ice age!"

Mercifully, the phone rang before I had to sift through more of Glenn Beck's works. The car dealer was on his way. Scott signed the papers this guy brought, and I had a respite from talk radio talking points as the two mumbled to each other by the door. After the salesman left, Scott informed me of something curious.

"Okay, listen to this. I'm supposed to take delivery on Sunday, but he doesn't have a plate yet. You may need to come with me before you leave for the show and drive that car back to the ranch."

I said nothing, neither agreeing nor disagreeing. Instead, I fixated on the dog poop on the rug near the dining room table. Finally, I had to say something.

"Um, Scott. I think the dog left something on the carpet."

"Yeah, well it's not my dog," he said, walking away.

Sometime later, Rochelle came home from school and immediately cleaned the feces riddled section of the floor.

In the back of my mind, I was still concerned about Dory. I hadn't encountered him yet but considered that outcome inevitable. Around 5:00 p.m. he pulled up to the house, and he certainly made an impression. Dory drove a massive black monster truck with huge mega wheels and a skull and crossbones on the back. He chewed tobacco and wore a cowboy hat, his face adorned by a semi beard, which seemed like he couldn't make up his mind whether he wanted a full beard or not.

Thankfully, Jessie returned soon after. There was no big family style meal here, but instead we all found something to eat out of the fridge on their own time. Jessie pulled me aside to discuss the sleeping arrangements going forward.

"Why don't you move your stuff into my brother's room? I doubt he shows up this weekend, but if he does move your stuff out. Okay?"

"That's fine by me. A real bed beats the couch any day."

Jessie and Scott retired to their room and left Rochelle, Dory, and me in the living room. We mainly watched *Smackdown* and flipped back and forth to the NCAA tournament games. I sat on the couch distinctly ill at ease, while Rochelle sat in Dory's lap, or they exchanged kisses. Their displays of affection couldn't help but upset me, though I tried not to register dismay. Dory sat in Grandpa John's old recliner, almost as if he were now the ruler of the ranch.

"So, what match do you think about main events on Sunday?" I asked Dory.

"Maybe the three way with Cena, Orton, and Triple H?" Dory didn't have any particular accent, being from a small town outside Toledo. Dare I say he came off like a faux redneck? Believe me, I'm from Kentucky. I know the difference.

"Could be. Maybe Edge and Taker," I responded.

"I'm excited, though," Rochelle said. "I've never been to a huge stadium with 70,000 people."

"Hey, I played high school football at a major stadium," Dory noted. "Not in front of that many people, but at least in a big pro type stadium. Before I tore my knee up, anyway."

After *Smackdown*, Rochelle and Dory retired to their bedroom. I stayed up a while longer watching another game on CBS but soon turned the TV off and went to my room. Ah, my room at the ranch. Sounds odd to say. Around midnight, I couldn't help but hear Rochelle and Dory arguing in the next room over from me. I couldn't make out what precisely was being said, but I could easily infer Dory's frustration. He did not seem happy with me being there. I can't blame him, but if he had a problem he should have said something to my face and not taken it out on Rochelle.

I realized on Saturday I needed to do something to get away from the ranch, even if for a couple of hours. I was bored, truth be told. The hectic nature of a weekend there when John was still alive seemed a distant memory, with few guests or workers milling about the property. I had been talking to my uncle Monty's wife Merrie on Facebook in the weeks leading up to the trip, so we agreed to meet up and have dinner. I hadn't seen Monty since Christmas 1994, when he had briefly moved back to Henderson from Florida to evade local authorities investigating his marijuana dealing.

Until then I would make do at the ranch. Rochelle spent part of the afternoon riding Sonny in the arena, while I mostly stood around looking at the other horses. Jessie joined me as I watched one of the horses unleash a pile of dung while standing a few feet from me.

"What is up with that horse?" I asked. "Stomach trouble?"

Jessie proceeded to give me the horse's entire life story, and by this, I mean his sire, mare, previous lineage, and quarter mile run time. I was amazed at her attention to detail, even if I can't remember any of it today. I stood bewildered by the time she finished.

"And that's the story of this particular horse," she said.

"Yeah, uh … that was quite a dump." This trip had its share of scatological moments.

"Can you hold Pug for a minute while I go see what Rochelle is doing with Sonny? Be careful not to let him slip because he will run and spook the horses."

"I guess so."

Jessie handed me Pug by the collar. He squirmed like crazy once I had him, and my hand quickly lost its grip on his collar. Pug raced away and right into the horse arena, where several horses immediately freaked out. Rochelle dismounted Sonny and quickly grabbed her dog. Once again, I took the L at the Morgan Ranch and felt like a moron. I could have gotten someone hurt, or some of the horses hurt.

Dory's family was in town from Ohio, so at least he didn't skulk around the ranch on Saturday. After Rochelle finished riding, she finally decided to spend some time with me. We spent the afternoon playing Monopoly, of all things. I heard her say "Do not pass go, do not collect two hundred dollars" more times than I care to admit. Somehow, when I envisioned this trip in my mind, sitting around playing Monopoly on a Saturday afternoon wasn't part of the plan.

Around 5:00 p.m., Monty and Merrie arrived at the ranch in Merrie's weathered and beaten Cadillac. Rochelle bid me adieu at the gate, while I shook Monty's hand and jumped in the car. I noticed a small girl in the back seat.

"Brian, this is Nicole," Merrie said. "Our granddaughter." More precisely, Nicole was technically their adopted daughter, as well. Monty's daughter Jennifer was a drug addict lunatic, who lost custody of Nicole to them in court. I remembered Jennifer the last time I saw Monty, around Christmas in 1994. She asked me if my dad's keys were in the ignition, wanting to go joy riding in the car.

"Nice to meet you, Nicole," I said.

We drove about a half hour away to the nearest Cracker Barrel in Spring Hill. This particular Cracker Barrel had a TV, which surprised me, since most I've been to did not. While we were eating, I tried to keep an eye on the score of UCLA and Xavier in the Elite 8, but the game quickly became a squash.

"I can't understand why anyone would travel all this way for a wrestling match," Monty said, wiping the food away from his mustache.

"Well, I'm also here visiting some people I haven't seen in a while," I replied. Monty, having seen Rochelle at the gate earlier, knew what I meant, even if he likely had the wrong idea about what had been happening. I couldn't help but think, in another time and place, Monty and Jessie might have made an amusing couple, even if he would have been yet another pothead in a long line for Jessie.

"So, the Citrus Bowl is going to be like Woodstock tomorrow?" he asked.

"Not that many people, but I would say sixty or seventy thousand."

"I was barely a teen when Woodstock happened, so I didn't go. I missed out on a lot of other things over the years. I've been bartending lately, when I can get to the bar. Sometimes we go out on my small boat. New Port Richey is solid. We like it."

"You see, Monty doesn't have an active driver's license," Merrie said. "I drive us everywhere."

Monty and Merrie smiled at each other. From there, we ate up and left. From there we made the trek back to the ranch. Monty and I had some parting words by the gate, while Merrie and Nicole waited in the car.

"Hey, you all are always welcome if you ever find yourselves in Louisville," I said. "I'm sure my dad would be glad to see you again, after all these years."

"I can't bear to see him in a wheelchair like that," he replied.

"He's hardly a vegetable. He'd be glad to see you and talk to you."

"We'll have to make it up there sometime."

From there, we shook hands, and Monty got back in the Cadillac. I waved as they drove off.

The time was here for the evening's main event: U of L vs. North Carolina. Winner headed to the Final 4. I raced back to the house, hopeful of watching the game. Instead, I found Jessie, Scott, and Rochelle set in the living room, ready to watch a movie.

"I've been wanting to see *Saw IV* for months!" Jessie said. "We're even buying the movie on pay per view. That's how much I want to see it."

"Oh," I said. "Can I watch the U of L game on another TV, at least?"

"Sure, I'll turn it on back in our bedroom."

Jessie and I walked to the bedroom. She turned on the TV, and USA replayed a ten-year-old *WrestleMania* match between Steve Austin and Shawn Michaels.

"Wow, Shawn was a stud back then, huh?" Jessie said.

"Wait, you've never seen this match?"

"No," Jessie shrugged.

"This is where Austin won the title from HBK for the first time," I said. Mike Tyson as guest ref. This sent the WWF back to the stratosphere."

After we watched the ending of the *WrestleMania XIV* main event, Jessie turned over to CBS. The game was about to start.

"Should be set now," she said. "See you after the movie."

I sat and watched the first half of U of L vs. UNC. The game did not go well in the first half. I knew the Cards faced an uphill battle against North Carolina in Charlotte, but this was still disappointing. Tyler Hansbrough and Company were the better team. At the half, the score was 44-32. I turned off the TV. I walked back to the living room to overhear Jessie's comments on *Saw IV*.

"I dunno, man. So, this main guy is doing all of these tests because these other men were his buddies? I'm not feeling it. Too confusing." Sometime later, the movie was over.

"We're stepping out now," Jessie said. "You and Rochelle can have the main TV for the rest of the game." Jessie and Scott left the house and headed to a local bar.

"How is the game going?" Rochelle said.

"Not great," I replied. "Down twelve at the half."

"The game will tighten up in the second half."

Oddly enough, the game did tighten. Even though we were sitting several feet apart, this was the first time Rochelle acted invested in being around me since I came down. We sat glued to the screen as U of L made a comeback, cutting the lead to two points late in the second half. She rooted for U of L, even though the Cardinals were hardly her team. U of L had a chance to tie or take the lead, but in a key moment Earl Clark missed what should have been an easy layup.

"Ughhhhhh!" Rochelle and I both groaned, simultaneously. With the air now out of the room, the Tar Heels went on a 7-0 run and that was the ball game. Final score: 83-73. I sat on the couch, dejected.

"Want to watch *EuroTrip*?" Rochelle asked. I nodded as if to say, "Whatever." She put on the DVD, and we watched this forgettable teen comedy. After the movie ended, Rochelle and I stood. She gave me a hug, while I couldn't help but notice her leopard style underwear under her shorts. Rochelle retreated to her bedroom. I walked in sullen fashion back to the guest room.

Chapter 16

WrestleMania XXIV Sunday

The big day had arrived. *WrestleMania XXIV*. The first time any of us had been to a wrestling show this big. Previously, the biggest PPV I had been to was Judgment Day 2000 at Freedom Hall, which featured The Rock vs. Triple H in an Iron Man match. While I held no illusion this show would match that one, I had my hopes up.

This being the Morgan Ranch, the day got off to a bizarre start, as I walked into the kitchen to overhear Rochelle and Jessie bantering at each other. They weren't arguing or angry, but I could tell Rochelle wasn't necessarily pleased with her mom.

"God, mom. You and dad need to quit smoking weed."

"See, this is what you 'straight' kids don't understand," Jessie replied. "The idea of having a good time without anything *too* illegal happening."

I grabbed a bowl of cereal and some milk, amused at the idea of the teen lecturing the parent on not smoking marijuana. Jessie addressed me.

"Remember, this morning you and Scott need to head to Tractor Supply," she said. "We need some hay and fertilizer. Also, while you are out, pick up the car Scott bought the other day."

I had been dreading this situation. I didn't fully understand this car deal, or why this car wouldn't have a valid plate or temporary tag if Scott was taking delivery. Regardless, after finishing breakfast, Scott and I hopped in the Ram and headed out for the Tractor Supply Co. in Bushnell.

As we hit County Road 469, Scott once again started a conversation, which lasted until we arrived at our destination. I mostly stared out the window at the beautiful scenery of rural Florida. It was rather like Kentucky with palm trees.

"I hate Florida," he said.

"Why?" I asked.

"I'm from upstate New York. There's good people up there. But here? Go south to Miami, and it's nothing but Cubans, and no one speaks any English. At least the signs are in English in Fort Lauderdale. Then you go north and inland, like we are here, and are surrounded by rednecks."

We passed a road sign with a mention of X amount of miles to The Villages, among other locations.

"See, The Villages," he continued. "There's the place I want to retire to someday." I had no idea what The Villages is, later learning it is an ultra-conservative retirement community.

"Wish I had my other daughter's record demo," he continued. "I'd play it for you. Except the company we submitted to has screwed her over and won't release it officially and won't give us the master disc back."

"That sucks," I said. "Sounds like she's talented. But then, you were a musician, right?"

"Back in the '80s, yeah. I played in a hair metal band and also had a business running the lighting equipment for other bands to use for their shows. We may not have had the income of top bands of the day, but we lived the lifestyle! It was really something. I think *Appetite For Destruction* is my favorite album from that era."

"I'm more of a '90s alternative rock fan, myself."

"Yeah, given your age, I figured as much. But that trash wrecked my music career. Also killed off my lighting and pyro biz. Instead of actual professionals who had a serious stage setup, all clubs wanted were these kids with no presentation who just *played*."

"That's the point," I said. Scott shrugged.

We reached Tractor Supply before any further music discussion. The two of us grabbed bales of hay, fertilizer, and a couple of horse bits. As we checked out, the woman behind the register couldn't help but notice how out of place I looked in my shorts and Punisher t-shirt.

"So, is he your horse business partner?" she asked Scott.

"Well, he is today," Scott replied.

Once we loaded these goods into the back of the Ram, we headed over to a random parking lot a few miles down the road. I didn't know the roads well, so I had no clear idea where we were. The lot was empty, other than what appeared to be a creaky, fifteen-year-old Chevy Malibu. I saw no license plate. Scott gave me the keys to this jalopy.

"Remember, this car has no plates, and we are driving past the police station in Center Hill on the way back to the ranch. Follow closely behind me."

"Are the cops going to pull me over?" I asked. "I'd say there is a forty percent chance. But it's Sunday."

Against my better judgment, I started this old sled. Few cars were out on the road on a Sunday morning, so the trip proved uneventful. My heart skipped a beat upon seeing the police station Scott warned me about, but there were no signs of cops around. I followed him back to the ranch without incident. Once we pulled up to the house, avoiding Dory's monster truck, I exhaled. Why did I feel as though we had gotten away with something?

"Man, that was beautiful!" Scott exclaimed, shaking my hand.

As the afternoon progressed, Rochelle once again rode Sonny in the arena, while Jessie and I watched from the porch. I couldn't help but think we needed to leave for Orlando and grab a bite to eat before going near the madness of the Citrus Bowl. Jessie had other ideas.

"I figure we will slip out a little later and hopefully avoid the traffic as it dies down closer to the time the show starts," she said.

This was a horrendous idea. I knew deep down if we left too late all the decent parking near the venue would be taken, so we would be a mile away. No use arguing the point, though. I realized by now not to argue with Jessie.

"Okay," I said. "I hope we don't miss any of the matches."

"Nah, we'll be fine," she said. "So, how did the game go last night?"

"We lost," I replied, dejectedly. "But I knew Carolina was the better team. In a Best of Seven we might win one game. We'll have to settle for being the fifth best team in the country this year. By the way, can I use your cell phone to call home?"

"Sure, here you go," she said, handing me her cell.

I dialed my mom, and she answered. I didn't stay on the phone long, just confirming my flight details with mom for the following day. I neared the point where I couldn't hold off on buying a cell phone of my own for much longer. This one brief conversation was the only time in the three trips to Florida I ever called home.

Feeling restless, I wandered back inside and sat down on the couch to watch the ending of the Memphis vs. Texas regional final with Dory. I never inquired about the argument between Rochelle and him the other night, figuring it was none of my business.

"What's the score?" I asked.

"I dunno," he said, lethargically. "I think Memphis is up eighty to sixty something."

"Ugh. U of L goes home, and Memphis goes to the Final 4. What fresh hell is this?"

"I don't care who wins this game. I'm an Ohio State fan."

"Hey, they almost won it all last year. Ran into the one team they couldn't beat. I couldn't believe the second-round game against Xavier, though."

"That one had me sweating, no doubt."

"I had no rooting interest," I said. "But after a point I gradually pulled for the upset. I remember when Xavier was up three in the waning seconds yelling at the TV 'Just foul them!' But they didn't. OSU made a three, won in overtime, and advanced all the way to the title game."

"Maybe we'll win the title in a couple of years," he said.

"Maybe U of L will, too," I replied, in an unusual bonding moment.

We finally headed out belatedly around 6:00 p.m. for a PPV which started around 7:30 for pre-show matches, 8:00 for the main card. But on the way we also stopped at a McDonald's for food, eating in the car as we meandered into Orlando. Rochelle drove her

Malibu, with Dory in the passenger seat. Jessie and I were in the back seat.

"I'm looking forward to the Money in the Bank match," I noted. "Jeff Hardy has been pulled from the match due to a failed drug test or something. I think CM Punk wins, instead. We know he's not on drugs."

"What a dope!" Jessie said.

As I figured, we had no chance of us making the show on time. The entire area around the Citrus Bowl was a madhouse by the time we arrived. The venue is in a fairly ghetto area of Orlando, with run down apartments and public housing scattered nearby. Once you leave the Disney tourist areas of Orlando, the city is a dump. I much prefer the Tampa/St. Pete area.

"Rochelle, we need to ask someone for parking directions," I said.

"I *really* don't want to talk to these people, though," she said.

Finally, she relented and rolled down the windows, and I asked some random black guy where we could find some available parking. We wound up outside one of these projects nearly a mile from the stadium. By this point the show had already started.

Our seats were in the nosebleed section right next to the luxury suites, rather amusing, since we watched the bulk of the show with Shane McMahon literally one row up. We banged on the glass a few times to get his attention, but he didn't care. The weather was overcast and barely holding off rain. From these cheap seats, I also had an eerie view of Orlando's dubious areas, and the curious number of small lakes populating the region. Since Dory and Rochelle sat together, I sat next to Jessie the entire show.

We had already missed the Money in the Bank match, which I wanted to see, and later did, after buying the DVD. We later heard CM Punk won. We arrived in time to see Batista defeat Umaga in a marginal seven-minute match. Kane followed by squashing Chavo Guerrero in eleven seconds for the ECW title. So far, this show wasn't rocking my world.

Fans perked up for the next contest, one of the feature bouts of the evening: Shawn Michaels vs. Ric Flair, with Flair's career on the line. This match was later voted Match of the Decade by Pro Wrestling Illustrated readers, but being there live the experience felt almost funereal. The fans in the building knew Flair was losing, the crowd being somber regardless of the emotion in the match. Near the end, a saddened HBK tuned up the band for Sweet Chin Music but before hitting his super-kick said something we even picked up in the cheat seats.

I love you. I'm sorry.

Soon after, the match was over, along with Flair's career. People sat quietly, pondering the moment they had just seen. Sometimes wrestling can wreck one's emotions. I recall watching the DVD later with my dad, and he was practically in tears by the end of this match.

Dory's anticipated three-way with Cena, Orton, and Triple H produced fifteen minutes of routine action. Orton retained his WWE title. This was not the main event, which I could tell irritated Rochelle slightly, since she remained a huge Triple H fan.

Jessie was amused by the bizarre Big Show vs. Floyd Mayweather "boxer vs. wrestler" match, which featured the seven-foot, 500 lb. Big Show against the famous boxer, all of 5'8" and 150 lbs. As Show tossed the small boxer around the ring with ease, Jessie was greatly amused.

"See, this goes to show you what happens when a boxer is out of his element. Domination."

"You do realize there's no way Mayweather would agree to lose here?" I asked.

Shenanigans ensued, Mayweather's cornerman got involved and passed him some brass knucks, which he used to K-O Big Show. I recognized the mystery corner man as Charles "The Hammer" Evans, a local OVW guy who never amounted to anything on the WWE main roster.

The main event was next: Edge vs. The Undertaker. The entrance setup for The Undertaker was one of his all-time coolest, with druids holding torches populating the staging area as he entered. The match? It bored the hell out of the entire building. I saw people leaving during the middle of the main event, since the match was slow and plodding. Perhaps it meant more to the TV audience at home, who could see the more subtle heel stuff Edge did? In the building, however, no one thought Edge had a prayer of ending The Undertaker's WM win streak, so the match had little heat or suspense. Once the ref was bumped about twenty minutes in, things perked up.

"Oh no, it's time for Edge's twin lackeys!" Rochelle yelled. Zack Ryder and Curt Hawkins arrived for their mandated run in. Justice prevailed as Taker stomped all three of them, the ref regained consciousness, and Taker applied his new Hell's Gate submission to win the World title. Overall, an enjoyable show, but one which I needed to see again to check out what I missed.

As we left the venue, I couldn't help but notice Rochelle and Dory holding hands the entire way down to the street. Jessie wondered if she could still buy a shirt to commemorate the event, but once we left the building all we could find were sketchy guys selling bootleg merchandise on the street. I approached one of these "vendors," but someone else pulled him aside first and they skulked off whispering to each other, mysteriously.

"Wait, were they conducting a drug deal?" Jessie asked. I shrugged. We left the vicinity empty handed and headed back to Rochelle's car. Thankfully, it was still there and undamaged.

As we drove along the lonely Florida Turnpike and state roads back to the ranch, Rochelle turned on the radio. She and Dory were still holding hands and schmoozing in the front seat when "Amarillo by Morning" started playing on a local country station. Rochelle turned up the volume. In that moment, listening to George Strait croon about a down on his luck rodeo cowboy, I felt a great emotional crash, one building inside me for years. I didn't cry or make a fool of myself. I am unsure if Jessie saw my reaction, since I looked out the window at the darkness and streetlights.

In that two minutes and fifty-two seconds, I realized I had spent several years of my life thinking of Rochelle, even pining for her. I sometimes wondered if she thought about me as often as I thought about her. I visited Florida again because I wanted to know where I stood with Rochelle. Now I knew the answer. Clearly, she didn't feel the same way. I don't think she spent much time worrying about me at all. I was now in my late 20s, my life going nowhere. I hadn't attained a full-time job, gone back to grad school, or committed myself to Amanda on a truly meaningful level. Eventually, the song ended, but my melancholy feeling of sadness did not. Life certainly can come into focus at midnight on a lonely country road.

CHAPTER 17

OPENING DAY

I was set to leave Florida the afternoon after *WrestleMania*. Jessie had to head back to St. Pete for work, so her taking me to the airport was out of the question. Rochelle had school, though I'm still baffled as to when Sumter County dismissed for spring break. Dory was already at work, not that I wanted to be seen in his monster truck monstrosity. Scott was the only one left who could drive me to Orlando.

I quickly ate another bowl of cereal for breakfast as Jessie ran around the kitchen and living room like a chicken with its head cut off, bewildering Scott. She also had her nose taped up, which I immediately noticed.

"Okay, Scott," she said. "I'm heading to work, but you take Brian to the airport! Rochelle! Here's the key to the house for the realtor! Take it with you to school and drop it off on the way back! Speaking of keys, where are my keys?!"

"Jesus, Jessie," Scott said. "Will you calm down? You act like you've snorted five lines of coke or something."

"What happened to your nose?" I asked. "Are you selling the ranch?"

"I had a recent nasal procedure," she replied. "Bit of a nosebleed from it. The ranch is on the market, but I'm unsure if I want to sell it yet. We'll see. By the way, if you finish breakfast, you can probably catch Rochelle before she leaves."

I left the house and saw Rochelle on the front porch, about to head over to the stable to check on Sonny before she left. The sun was rising at the Morgan Ranch on the last day of March, starting to burn away the dew on the grass. While the weather felt slightly chilly in shorts, the fields were beautiful, with a slightly ethereal, hazy quality at that time of morning.

"Walk with me," she said. We headed towards the stable and barn. We engaged in some routine chit chat about the show the previous night, as she checked on Sonny and a few of the other horses. The initial conversation was trivial, but our talk during the walk back has stayed with me ever since.

"We'll probably head to Ohio to visit Dory's family soon," Rochelle said. "You are welcome to visit us there, if you'd like."

A strange invitation to be sure, one which I had no desire to accept. I kept quiet for a few seconds as we walked towards the house, then finally stopped by her car and gave my response.

"Rochelle, this is the last time we will ever see each other."

I wasn't overwrought, angry, or intending to be hurtful, but almost immediately I saw a profound change in her expression. Her eyes nearly watered up, but not quite. My eyes were watering up slightly, and my nose was about to run. Neither of us said a word, but instead we embraced for a few seconds. I thought about kissing her and moved my head towards hers, resting the right side of my nose against her nose. I came close to doing so, but in the end, I pulled away. We stayed that way, heads resting against each other for a while. One of the few times in my life where time stood still.

"Goodbye," I said. I typically don't say goodbye to anyone. I figure I will see them again sometime.

"Goodbye," she replied, voice slightly breaking.

From there, Rochelle unlocked her Malibu and drove away into the rising sun, seemingly out of my life forever. I walked back into the house, making sure neither Jessie nor Scott saw me in such an emotional state. I sat down on the bed in the guest room and stared at my suitcase for a long time before packing.

I walked back to the kitchen as Jessie left for work. She gave me a goodbye hug, which I found curious because she had never done so before. I almost wonder if she knew how crestfallen I felt. Perhaps I hadn't masked my reaction entirely. After the hug, Jessie left. I haven't seen her since.

Monday was Opening Day in MLB. I watched a few minutes of baseball action on ESPN before Scott and I left for the Orlando airport. Opening Day in baseball brings a sense of renewed hope for teams and their fans. In a different way, I felt a sense of moving on with my life. I couldn't be sure if the feeling was hopeful, but definitely a feeling of turning a page.

I had to endure Scott listening to Rush Limbaugh and other right wing talk radio hacks all the way to Orlando. Limbaugh blathered on about the movie *Mars Attacks* as a metaphor for illegal immigrants, or some such nonsense. Scott nodded along with all of these pundits, while I tried to tune them out. I didn't protest, however. His car, his radio. Upon pulling into the airport parking garage, I shook his hand and headed out. In spite of considering him a lunatic, politically speaking, I rather enjoyed Scott's company. I understood that much like me, he was an outsider at the ranch, someone trying his best to fit into a foreign world. A world which didn't come naturally to him.

The trip back to Louisville brought no new insights, aside from a brief stopover in Birmingham, where I became enthralled at the oddball nature of the restroom toilets. They have rotating plastic sheets on all the toilets, so when you are done you flush, and the used plastic rotates out and is replaced by a clean version. Fascinating.

I used the flight home as time to think. There would be time to plan my next move, once I returned home. But from Birmingham to Louisville, I mostly thought about the previous six years, and a girl who meant so much to me. In the end, I had to let Rochelle go because through no fault of her own, she was having a detrimental effect on my life. Reflecting back now, I can't help but think I had a detrimental effect on hers as well, given the tension my presence caused to her friendship with Callie in 2003, or Dory on this trip. There has always been a bond between the two of us and distance can't change that. But as of March 31, 2008, I was ready to begin a new chapter in my life.

CHAPTER 18

THE INTERVENING YEARS

Rochelle and I kept chatting online occasionally in the years following my last trip to Florida. My intent was never along the lines of, "I never want to see you again!" or anything so dramatic. During my time in grad school with the U of L debate team, we talked less and less. AIM went the way of the dodo bird, replaced by Facebook for our chats.

The most memorable chat we had during that time period occurred while I was stranded at the Syracuse airport with the U of L debate team after the 2011 CEDA tournament. While getting drunk on warm Natural Ice, I hopped on Facebook messenger and Rochelle and I chatted about the insanity of the entire trip. As she headed off to bed, I signed off with "I love you, Rochelle Morgan." She responded in kind.

As I prepared to graduate with my masters in 2011, I talked to Rochelle on the phone a few times. She was now working on her nursing degree, with a concentration on helping cancer patients.

"Isn't that a bit ... depressing?" I asked.

"Some people may feel that way, but I find it rewarding," she said.

When I started applying for PhD programs, I found the University of South Florida a perfect choice to go, alongside closer schools such as UK, Purdue, and IU. USF specialized in qualitative research, which interested me. Besides, I already knew people in Florida, although the ranch was a decent distance from Tampa. I'd be lying if I hadn't considered USF in order to be around Rochelle, though I had no idea what such a scenario might entail. I even traded emails with Jessie, asking about her time at USF.

Regardless, Amanda became pregnant that summer, and we were married in December 2011. Once I got married, I decided to make a clean break with anything Florida related. We didn't especially feel like moving down there with an infant, so I decided to pass on USF. Of the schools I applied to, USF was the only one interested. And I ended up passing on their offer. Life is full of ironies. I sometimes ponder what may have been if I had applied earlier and been ready to leave in late 2011, instead of waiting to apply until after I had graduated from U of L with my master's. What, if anything, would have happened with Rochelle? Probably nothing, but I do think about it from time to time.

But once Amanda and I were married, I threw away most of the outdated floppy disks containing pics from my Florida trips. Anything else was lost when we moved to our current house. The only pics I still have were ones from 2008 that were already developed, scattered in between Myrtle Beach pics from the same year.

Over the years, Rochelle and I spoke less and less. She became another friend on Facebook to go along with random people from high school I barely knew. Sometimes we might exchange an email or two, or an occasional text. I know little about her life from 2012-18. I know Dory moved back to his hometown in Ohio, but I know nothing of the circumstances surrounding their breakup. I'm fairly certain Scott moved out later as well, but I have heard nothing about him in years.

A couple of years later, I noticed Rochelle posting pictures with another woman on Facebook, so I surmised she was in a same sex relationship. She mentioned feeling as though she might be bisexual years earlier, which I never saw any particular signs of in the times I traveled down there, but who knows? I rarely spoke to Rochelle during those years. I had no idea what to say.

Curiously, one day, all of those pictures ceased, and she now seemed to be in a relationship with a man, Kristopher, who is now her husband. We've never spoken about any of the circumstances involved there. If she wants to open up and discuss this with me, fine, but I don't consider it my place to pry.

When my dad died in 2018, Rochelle was the first person to reach out. "Give me a call. I am here if you need me." We had our first serious conversation in years, echoing the time in 2004 when her grandfather died, and I tried to be there for her in somewhat clueless fashion. That's the fascinating aspect of talking to Rochelle. We can always pick things up and riff about any subject.

Rochelle has two kids of her own now, though I have to admit we have never talked about her husband and children much at all. I never raise the topic, and she doesn't raise it with me. I typically don't click "like" on her family pics on Facebook. I just ... can't. We did spend a rather memorable Christmas during the pandemic texting back and forth about absurdities such as sucking boob fat out of someone to use as natural breast augmentations in someone else. I might not be the ideal person to discuss family matters, but who else is going to discuss boob fat on Christmas? I vowed to send her a detailed email, which I did.

In the email, I mentioned feeling lost, with no particular job prospects during the pandemic, and unemployment being cut off, as well. I even dropped the bombshell on her about the potential reasons I turned down USF, one being I didn't want to put myself in an awkward position of looking her up now that I was married. She didn't respond to this aspect and mainly focused on the job prospects in her reply. She also mentioned she wishes Andrew could play with her son, so we could continue our friendship. I've come to realize Rochelle often says a great deal with a few words.

Even after all this time, I'm not sure I have ever quite known Rochelle. As of now we are amiable with each other. Are we destined to have surface level communication and little else? I mostly have surface level communication with some of my closest friends, such as Chad and Isaac. Do I truly know them, either, or are we merely people who have patchwork discussions of U of L sports, wrestling, and the occasional life event? What does it truly mean to know someone?

But at least when talking to guys like Chad and Isaac, I feel as though I know what makes them tick, on a basic level. Rochelle? Hell, who knows. I can't read females very well, nor communicate at a high level. Perhaps the *idea* of Rochelle and what she represented was more intriguing than the reality. Breaking away from Louisville, new opportunities, new people. Trying to understand Rochelle was akin to working a 1,000-piece puzzle, with half the pieces missing. Sometimes people drift in and out of your life, no conclusion in sight, leaving only memories created in time.

Her November 16, 2023, text crept into my mind for days after the fact.

"Coming to Louisville in May."

The House at Morgan Ranch, 2008.

A view of the barn and stable at Morgan Ranch.

Rochelle's horse, Sonny, in 2008.

Other horses around the corral at Morgan Ranch.

Another view of horses at Morgan Ranch.

The vast fields of the Morgan Ranch.

PART THREE

JANET

CHAPTER 19

THE DOROTHY LEE GAL

Life since the pandemic hasn't exactly been thrilling for me. My departure from Jefferson County Public Schools was a long, drawn-out affair, lasting nearly a year. I found myself having to drop off Andrew at school and pick him up in the afternoons, which made subbing high school more or less impossible for most of the 2021-22 school year. Since I wasn't getting anywhere, in terms of full-time employment, I decided to cut my losses.

I have been locked into a prolonged dispute with the Kentucky Unemployment Department over pandemic era payments made to me (as well as other subs) during June and July of 2020. Apparently, since school was not in session, these payments shouldn't have occurred, but no one knew this at the time, and as a result, I now owed $3,600.00 in pandemic assistance money. Now I felt beyond worthless. Now I felt as if I had anti value. I spent day after day applying for jobs on Indeed, with no meaningful results.

As 2023 dawned, I felt a great strain in my home life. Every day seemed to turn into little more than Amanda and me arguing over anything imaginable. Silly nicknames she doesn't like? Check. Talking too much about her prosthetic leg and stump? Check. My rants about desperately wanting to move and get away from where we live? Definitely. People driving like idiots on the Gene Snyder Freeway? Of course. Amanda's daily tirades about the awful students and admins at Rutherford Elementary? I was sick of hearing about all of them.

Amanda had become increasingly frustrated with my crypto fiascos and Nigerian arbitrage attempts, feeling I had done nothing but waste time and money. *"None of these wild ideas of yours ever work out."* Her disdain for *Sonic Screamer* was clear: *"Next time we do spring cleaning, that box of CDs should be the first to go."* She wasn't impressed by my writing, either, offering little encouragement when I published *Salvaged From the Flood*, dismissing it as yet another frivolous pursuit. *"Who wants to read a memoir of someone that isn't famous?"* I'm not saying she was *wrong* about any of these criticisms. Still, I longed to talk to someone who might better understand my creative endeavors.

Enter Janet Billingham. I first became aware of Janet as far back as May of 1995, or at least an inkling someone like her existed. In Dorothy Lee's introduction to Edward Watz's book *Wheeler and Woolsey: The Vaudeville Comic Duo and Their Films,* she mentioned having "fifteen-year-old kids who write me fan letters." Since I, too, was a fifteen-year-old W & W fan, I wondered about this line for years, wondering who else might be like me. Who else my age was also interested in such an obscure comedy duo?

When I first had home internet access via WebTV, circa 2000, one of the first orders of business involved searching for W & W related websites or articles. The first search results included a Dorothy Lee/W & W fan site containing various articles, mainly about the duo's frequent co-star, Dorothy Lee. The main thing I remember was the auto music on the site I had to turn off, especially while surfing the net on campus at U of L. The song choice was "Button Up Your Overcoat" from the 1929 Broadway musical *Follow Thru*. I always found the song selection curious. Why not a song from a W & W movie?

At the time I sent an email or two to the address on the site, but the response must not have thrilled me, since I never kept in touch with Janet. I knew nothing about her back then - age, or any pertinent information beyond an email address. I recall being baffled at someone being *this* obsessed with Dorothy Lee, since the site was more about her than W & W themselves. I used to chat with various W & W fans on AIM in subsequent years, but I never bothered talking to Janet.

Over time, I forgot about the site, and it faded into oblivion. Fast forward to 2013. I found out in the W & W Facebook group about an upcoming book about Dorothy Lee, written by Ned Kuroda and Janet Billingham. I quickly added Ned as a friend on Facebook but saw no signs of Janet. I enjoyed the book very much, though part of me couldn't help but wonder what personal connections existed between the authors and the subject. I also took note of the book's credits, and saw 1978 as Janet's birth year, which finally crystallized for me that Janet was the teenage girl corresponding with Dorothy Lee in the 1990s, which Lee alluded to in the Watz book. However, since Janet had no particular online presence, I lost interest in contacting her, and the book took its place with several other film books on my bookshelf.

SEPTEMBER 20, 2023

While looking through Facebook, I noticed a few unread posts in the W & W group, including one by the recently added member Janet Billing-ham. I immediately clicked on the profile and sent a friend request. Janet looked to be an attractive brunette, but otherwise her profile featured little info. A few other pics, but no personal details at all.

I sent a message asking if she was who Dorothy mentioned in the Watz book, while introducing myself as a fellow W & W fan. She accepted and wrote back the next day, clarifying that she was, in fact, who Dorothy referred to years earlier.

"We are so like-minded to be of a similar age and interested in them!" she said. "Please tell me more about your experiences as a fan, and how you became interested. Dorothy always joked that I was four-teen going on forty. I definitely want to talk more, but my life is hectic. I recently had a medical procedure, so please bear with me."

"Nothing too serious I hope?" I asked.

"I had an infected cyst wound on my shoulder, plus other hectic duties I will share as we talk."

I related how I saw my first W & W movie on March 1, 1991. I know this because I found the first *AMC Magazine* I used to own on eBay, with Roy Rogers on the cover, and retraced my initial fandom. I already knew W & W were a comedy team somewhat similar to the Marx Bros., so I circled two of their films to record, *High Flyers* and *Cockeyed Cavaliers*.

"*Cockeyed Cavaliers* was my first one. I believe the same showing you mentioned in March 1991," she observed. "I laughed my butt off! I had to know more about the charming leading lady in the film, so I spent a solid year trying to contact Dorothy."

"Cavs aired on March 5, so I beat you by four days!" I joked.

During this initial messaging, I also mentioned my upcoming book being re-edited and the W & W related chapter from 2001. I left my phone number, and she gave me her email address to send the chapter in question, namely the "Diamond Horseshoe" chapter from the book. She still used her old AOL email address, which I found endearing, so I made sure to send responses via mine, as well. I took notice of the time of her reply, 2:44 a.m. As I would come to realize, these ultra late-night messages from Janet were hardly rare.

She loved the chapter. "Arianne didn't deserve you! I feel like we grew up living and liking the same things, which is wild because my friends didn't understand me." I sent "The Yearbook" chapter as well, and she enjoyed it, too. I also shared some scans of the March 1991 *AMC Magazine*, but by then Amanda, Andrew, and I were busy packing to head out on fall break to Asheville and then Gatlinburg.

The topic of Arianne, the ill-fated L.A. trip, and the early 2000s time period haunted me the more I talked to Janet. *If I only knew more about Janet back then*, I thought to myself. Would I have bothered with Arianne at all? Why did I not attempt to keep in touch? What about those email replies on WebTV that didn't interest me? Janet lived two hours away in Cincinnati, certainly closer than traveling cross country to Los Angeles.

I noticed I hadn't heard anything back from Janet during the entire week we were gone. Odd. After all the years of wanting to talk to her, she seemed to be gone again at the drop of a hat. I finally heard back from her the afternoon we returned from Gatlinburg. Apparently, the cyst acted up again, festering to the point of nearly becoming septic, so she had to have it lanced and drained. She even shared some grisly pictures of the before and after, with puss leaking out of this golf ball sized infection on her back shoulder. I could sympathize. My mom had a freak cyst on her back shoulder as well, though it never became as infected as this one. I later sent Janet a pic of a mass amount of puss I squeezed out of a painful bump behind my ear, as if to stand in solidarity.

As October moved on, I became more and more enamored with Janet. How often does one meet someone who has such similar interests? Beyond Wheeler and Woolsey, she was also a huge fan of *Masters of the Universe* and *She-Ra* as a kid, though I will admit to never much watching the latter. She even remembered the Hordak slime pit set, where you could drown the heroes in green goo, almost as if you were a guest star on *You Can't Do That on Television* and decided to torture your toys.

During this period of time, I began to understand more about Janet. Since the publication of her Dorothy Lee book, I hadn't seen any other books or pieces by her, and I wondered why. I also wondered whether or not she would find me to be a prick after reading these chapters of my book.

"Well, you see, I am a full-time caregiver, and I have little time to myself. But trust me, I'll never think any less of you." I wish she hadn't said the last part. Hell, I almost took it as a challenge.

As she revealed, Janet cared for her elderly grandparents, both of whom are over ninety and not in good health. Her grandmother is an Italian woman her grandfather met while serving as a G.I. overseas in Europe. I saw in her the same noble dedication that my own mother possessed when dealing with my dad for so many years after his stroke. In Janet's case, the end result saw her own writing career suffer, and she now wanted to get back on track while caring for her grandparents. I made a mental note of her writer's block she mentioned, wanting to help her if I could.

Janet also spoke in passing of having to essentially raise her younger male cousin for a solid decade, since his unreliable mom lived "on the wild side." He had long since moved back, and Janet rarely mentioned him, other than to express concern over whether he might be drafted someday, if the draft was ever reinstated.

These messages were quickly becoming the highlight of my day. I debated over the course of a weekend whether I wanted to tell Janet "I love you" or not, since I hadn't told another woman that since Amanda and I had been married. I finally threw a random "Love you" in at the end of a message about her overall health, fearing she might not respond, but she seemed fine with those words and started ending her own messages "Love you, too." I wasn't sure how I meant those words, but I certainly felt closer to Janet than anyone in a long time. Who else obsessively looked at the TV Guide for W & W showings, or stayed up until 3 a.m. for a TNT showing of *Silly Billies*? I couldn't shake the thought, as it ran through my head on a daily basis ...

Where has she been all of my life?

Talking to Janet was a bright spot in my life for much of October 2023. I asked if I could read some of her previous pieces, so she sent me an article on Lynda Carter and Wonder Woman she wrote some years earlier. She even dug up her old Dorothy Lee/W & W fan site, and I had fun reliving the articles posted therein. I even watched the 1939 version of *Wuthering Heights,* since she mentioned loving the film as a teen. At long last, someone understood my love of classic cinema. A fellow writer who I could share ideas, thoughts, and help reduce stress in life. In turn, I gladly did the same.

I even shared the YouTube link to the entire *Sonic Screamer* album. Amanda detests my album, finding it unlistenable screechy noise. My mom is terrified of it. Shockingly enough, Janet seemed to enjoy the parts she listened to, and felt I had musical talent (!). I have no idea if she truly enjoyed *Sonic Screamer* or was merely being nice.

The topic of my soon to be released book, *Salvaged From the Flood*, often became a subject of discussion, as well as the hassles of trying to self-publish. Janet even offered to do a review or interview with me about the book for future publication, but this offer never led to anything. She had a difficult time caregiving and maintaining her writing career, even relating feelings of anxiety and writer's block.

"I'm trying to find a delicate way to say this," I said. "Your grand-mother is over ninety. She's had a long and full life. Are you prepared to let her go when the time comes? If you need someone, don't hesitate to give me a call. You can vent and I'll listen. I know how stressful dealing with ailing family members can be, but you don't deserve to be abused, even by close relatives. I'll be your proverbial shoulder to cry on if you'd like. I don't know if I'm the right person or not. I'm not a family member and I'm not your husband. But I can try."

"I want my grandma to be here as long as she can," she said. "All I can do is help. I try to be prepared, but can one really be? I may need your shoulder to cry on. Thank you. You're one of the kindest, most understanding people I've met. Why couldn't I have met you twenty years ago?"

"We might have exchanged one or two nothing emails," I replied. "But I think we met at the exact time we were supposed to."

I can't express how desperately I needed this validation. All I heard at home was how useless I acted, or how selfish. I never felt the latter to be true, given how I had deep-sixed my PhD pursuits to stay in Louisville and get married once Amanda became pregnant with Andrew. Indeed, from Janet I received positive affirmation. To her I was an excel- lent writer, a talented musician (not sure about that one), and the most wonderful guy she'd ever met. In real life I felt like an unemployed fail- ure. When talking to Janet I felt like I could conquer the world. Who wouldn't want more of this?

As the month ended, I asked Janet if she wanted to hear some of these absurd nicknames, the wacky names which drive Amanda crazy. When she responded affirmatively, I reeled off some of my usual nicknames: Kroger, Hoss, Beef or Beefette, or in her case Wounded Beef, due to the cyst.

"LOL!" she responded. "Those are great. I laughed out loud. You're so much fun. Since you are Cabbageboy, I could always be Cabbagegirl, since we evolved from the same cabbage patch."

"I have many more nicknames for thee. Crouton, Bacon Bit, Ham N Eggs, Stinky ..."

"Okay, Stinky is a riot. Or Gouda Cheese? My feet are sweaty quite often. Even had minor frostbite during the winter due to excessive sweat from thick socks. They are okay now, though."

"That's a relief to know. See, my feet are constantly freezing cold. I need to rub my cold feet against your hot, stinky feet and balance the universe."

"You are too silly," she said.

"Remember the old commercials with the man drinking champagne out of a woman's slipper only to spit it out?" I asked. "'What is it, my feet?' 'No, the champagne's not Korbel!'"

"Oh my, yes, I remember that."

"In your case, it's the feet, after all!"

"You are killing me here, haha."

"How about these: Dumpling? Dewdrop? Buttmeat? Lambchop? Tenderloin?"

"I'm laughing so hard at these. Tenderloin is a hoot. I do think Stinky is best though, so let's go with that."

"There's always Stinkor, the old He-Man villain. Used to have the toy. He smelled awful, though."

"Would that make me Stinkra? How about Cysta? Incidentally, I think you should do one final edit on your book before publication."

"Yeah, I have a self-imposed release date of November 1. I can still tinker until then, though."

During the barrage of nicknames, the subject of various toxic Wheeler and Woolsey fans arose. One thing I have realized over the years is that while W & W have a small fanbase, these people are wildly obsessed and will be glad to argue over the smallest classic comedy trivia. Janet had an on again/off again friendship with writer William Drew, an avid W & W supporter.

I usually avoided Drew on the W & W Facebook group. One Christmas I recall him going off on another fan for daring to enjoy *Mummy's Boys* more than *Silly Billies*, which frankly are both among W & W's weakest works. "*Silly Billies* has the ethos and magnificence of the Old West, or classic westerns, of Americana!" he ranted. "*Mummy's Boys*? All that film could aspire to be is a B horror movie spoof. Bah!"

My one clash with Drew was over his off-topic waxing poetic on D.W. Griffith's *Birth of a Nation*. I couldn't let his comments slide, so I replied that I found Griffith's film as inherently evil as *Triumph of the Will*, and certainly more overt in its messaging. He then targeted me and ranted, but I tuned him out. I never blocked him, but I don't engage him in conversation, either.

I also discussed a major falling out I had with W & W biographer Ed Watz, who used to be a Facebook friend of mine until he moved to Germany and closed his profile.

Here's what happened with Watz. I recall in his book a mention of a battered 16mm reel of deleted footage from *Rio Rita*. I asked him where he found it, and he pointed me in the direction of the William K. Everson collection at the Eastman House. I gave these people a call, emailed, and they finally got back to me and said, "Yes, we have something on that title. Let us screen it and we'll get back to you." A couple of days later they wrote back detailing the trivial details of the reel. A couple of *Rio Rita* deleted scenes, but hardly a discovery of all the deleted footage.

"What happened?" she asked.

"I took to the Nitrateville message board on *Rio Rita* and discussed my findings, basically skewering Watz. He responded by attacking me there. 'How dare you call me a liar. I saw the footage years ago. I couldn't copy it to VHS at the time, yada, yada.' Anyway, I tried to smooth things over. I couldn't know for sure what he saw compared to what Eastman House had now, and I apologized for the mix-up. I thought the whole thing blew over, then a few days later he came after me again, this time sending me a Facebook message, once again ranting at me for trying to besmirch his reputation. He closed his account anyway, but if he hadn't, I was done with the guy."

"Do you think anyone will ever find the missing *Rio Rita* footage?" she asked. "Besides the clips that have surfaced online, I mean."

"Who knows? Finding the missing *Rio Rita* reels is a lifelong goal of mine. Shall we make a pack to find those reels? I'd say a blood oath, but I don't want to smear the computer screen."

"You are too much," she replied. "But yes, it's a deal. As far as Watz goes, there are some curious people in the W & W sphere, no doubt. I never had a problem with Watz, but Ned clashed with him over a Three Stooges book they co-authored some years ago."

"I haven't mentioned Tim and Linda Eleniak, but you read about my encounters with them when I visited L.A. in 2001. I tend to think

Linda does W & W no favors writing some of these Facebook group posts. Why crap on other actors like Gene Wilder, Humphrey Bogart, and Lauren Bacall? Those people are a whole lot more popular than W & W."

"I've had my run-ins with Linda over the years, but we're at peace now," Janet said. "Are you acquainted with Vic Santo? We have also been hot and cold over the years."

Vic was a Facebook friend, but not much else. I hadn't had a negative experience with him, and mainly knew him as a fan of W & W. He also wrote the foreword to Janet's book on Dorothy Lee. There seemed to be a hint of "We used to be close but aren't anymore" when Janet spoke of Vic, but I never understood their deal. Janet alluded to being unhappy with Vic's Introduction to her Dorothy Lee book, feeling he made it all about himself. I re-read the Introduction and didn't see what bothered her about Vic's intro. I did notice Vic had alienated the W & W group on Facebook by dissing Robert Woolsey as a performer. He now focused more on promoting his Abbott and Costello book.

All of this talk made me think about what could be done about this toxic fandom. Wheeler and Woolsey needed some new spokespeople. Janet and I were the ones who needed to positively promote the forgotten duo. We could truly bring in new fans.

Before anything else, I had a book to publish on November 1. On the 30th, however, Janet sent a brief message, mentioning her aunt broke her ankle and to bear with her. Oh, no. This was rotten timing. On Halloween, I finally received the treasury check reimbursing me for the entire BitConnect disaster, and I wanted to share this news with Janet, as well as the big day of publication. I became concerned as the days passed by without a message. Is something else wrong? How's her aunt doing? Is her cyst wound acting up again?

Sensing that she desperately needed to get out of the house, I invited Janet to join Eric, Isaac, and me in going to the *AEW Dynamite* taping at the KFC Yum Center. Janet had professed to enjoying wrestling in the past, and even though she knew nothing about AEW, I figured why not invite her? "I can't vouch for anyone else's body odor, though," I joked. "Aside from my own." I never received a reply.

After no new messages for several days, I sent Janet's co-author Ned Kuroda a brief message on Facebook, little more than asking if he had heard from Janet lately. He responded that he hadn't, but thanks for mentioning her, and he would give her a call. This routine message marked my first major mistake in communicating with Janet. Others would follow.

CHAPTER 20

THE LORD AND LADY BEEF SHOW

Janet finally emailed me over the weekend. If she was upset at me for contacting Ned, she certainly didn't mention anything at the time. Her reaction was the opposite, her reply in the vein of "Sorry to not be online this week, things have been hectic. Lots of appointments, doctors, and so on. I have been under the weather as well. The cyst is flaring up again."

Even though I didn't entirely understand Janet's reaction, I wrote back saying I did. During these emails she also gave me her cell phone number, which in hindsight was probably a bad idea. "I don't want to text much out of respect for your wife and son," she said.

"Eh, no one reads my texts anyway," I replied. "But if you like we can keep things on Facebook." This arrangement would prove short-lived. I did promise I wouldn't contact anyone else asking about her going forward.

As November rolled along, I started understanding more about Janet's situation. These long breaks in communication were part of her norm, as she noted sometimes losing contact with people for weeks on end before responding. I will admit to feeling slightly weary at times when hearing about what a nightmarish day she had dealing with her grandmother yelling for her every five seconds. Regardless, I strove to be as kind to her as I possibly could be.

"Janet, you are a wonderful person. Far better than me at dealing with ailing relatives. People have a couple of options in cases like yours, or me with my dad some years back. One, you fully commit to helping like you are doing. Two, get as far away from the situation as possible. I never did either one. I had my own apartment, so I had time to myself, but always visited at my mom's house. I never escaped the situation, but never truly committed to help."

"I would never want to put them in a nursing home. Doctors say it's a death sentence for the elderly to be in those places. I'd rather have a clear conscience."

As we talked more, I detected a certain melancholy in Janet. She seemed like someone who had grand ideas for where she wanted to be in life, yet life got in the way of those plans, and she was now in her mid-40s with no answers. I may not have understood the stop/start communication, but I understood her predicament because it echoed my predicament.

NOVEMBER 11, 2023

Veteran's Day. Or Armistice Day, if you like. I had a wonderful time chatting with Janet, bouncing from Facebook to texts and back again, riffing on classic movies, life, and shared experiences. She finally sent me another picture of herself, a more recent one than the profile pic on Facebook. Her hair looked a shade auburn in the newer pic, so I asked about it.

"Yes, I try different shades from time to time. My real hair is going gray now."

"Hey, that's nothing to be ashamed of. Mine is going gray as well. As far as pictures go, I wish I still had the picture of myself from a hot tub at Myrtle Beach from 2001. I tried recreating it in Branson a few months back, but not as good. Too old and fat now."

I ran the picture she sent through Picwish and fixed the blurriness. This became a running gag between the two of us. Whenever she sent pics, I would unblur them on Picwish. I even sent her some of my ghastly 2000 era pics, such as one standing by my old 1986 Oldsmobile, or one standing in front of mounds of VHS tapes while wearing my RVD shirt. Janet responded by sending me a cryptic recent picture of herself holding William Drew's biography of Pearl White. I responded by sending her a picture of myself holding up her Dorothy Lee book.

"You are a strong and handsome man, a very good-looking guy," she said. "Almost like a well-built actor. Haven't aged much at all in twenty years."

"Yeah, well you haven't seen me up close. All the acne scarring ... not a pretty sight."

"Hey, I had trouble with acne, too, but those scars have faded over time."

More positive affirmation. I sent some other pics I found from 2004: silly pics of me waking Eric up, as well as Kitty, the cat my mom took in that winter, not destined to live out the year.

Janet felt for Eric the more I discussed him. I sensed some similarities between them, as both have been through the mill and experienced trauma due to family dealings. Eric was different. He never had a choice in the matter. Ever since he was seven years old, he had to deal with my dad being at home in a wheelchair, and then once my dad left for the nursing home, he had to deal with my mom being in a wheelchair.

Amanda views Eric as nothing but a lazy bum, someone incapable of doing anything in life, or even keeping up decent grooming. Eric may go a week without a shower. Never wants to shave, so he has a chaotic beard. His only haircuts are when I get fed up with his caveman look and give him one myself. What she has never understood is Eric has never had a life of his own to live. Some people are so shattered inside that you can't begin to know how to help them. I sensed Janet understood this about Eric in a way Amanda did not.

As those November days passed, Janet sent more and more pictures, as if to stitch together a highlight reel of previous years. Some were of her at the Cincinnati Film Festival, wearing a flowing white dress. Some were from a nearby park. I detected a distance or detachment in these pictures, almost as if they were taken slightly far away, like she didn't want anyone getting too close. She appeared in these photos, no doubt, but I had trouble *seeing* her. I told her she looked better now.

"Stinky is looking better than ever," I said. "I might also reserve the right to alter the name to Stanky. But given your fondness for soaps and perfumes, I'm not sure either is accurate as a nickname."

"I think you are right," she said. "We'll have to keep searching for a better one."

During this seemingly lighthearted exchange of pictures and banter, Janet once again drifted into an emotionally charged rant about her grandmother's health problems. "She has so many ailments these days. She broke her hip last year and now is like Jekyll and Hyde, one minute being sweet and the next she yells at me, calls for me incessantly. I never get decent sleep, but I can't bear the thought of putting her in a home. So, I live in a mini hell day and night. I'm glad you are okay with hearing all this. I love you, Brian."

I was overwhelmed to the point of tears. The heartbreaking nature of her situation, also the loving connection we had made in such a short amount of time. I didn't know how to handle this. On one hand she claimed to be busy caring for her grandmother, yet during various days another relative might spell her and we had these long discussions. I was flattered when Janet spent this free time talking to me. I never felt comfortable talking to her on the phone, but did propose a Zoom meeting where we could talk face to face, if she had time. She never seemed to.

I wanted to do something for Janet. Even though I lived a hundred miles away, I searched for Cincy area dermatologists for her cyst, searched online for various automobile suggestions once she mentioned she still drove a 1999 Volkswagen bug. I felt like someone needed to help her out. Lord knows my mom could have used more help when she felt overwhelmed. By this point I was head over heels for Janet.

"You have a historic vehicle," I said in slight terror. "What brand and make are you looking for?"

"A jeep!" she exclaimed.

"As in something made by Jeep the company or an actual jeep?"

"I've always wanted an actual jeep."

"That may take some looking into. I'll keep an eye out. I'm scared of you driving such an old sled, though. And a jeep might be cold in Cincinnati, come winter."

A more feasible short-term idea involving buying Janet a Christmas present to cheer her up. During one of our texting marathons the topic of W & W related books came up, to which I mentioned the Henry Jenkins work *What Made Pistachio Nuts?* I practically had ownership of the book in college and kept it checked out of the U of L library before finally purchasing my own copy. I checked online, and this book's prices were now insanely expensive, going for nearly $100.00 on all the sites I perused. Finally, I found a quality copy on eBay for about $20.00 and bought it quickly. Since she mentioned liking Pears soap, I figured I could also throw in a bar of Pears as a gag gift along with the book.

"I don't want you to feel obligated to buy me anything," she said. "If you want to, okay? I'll think of something for you, too."

"Janet, I don't often pray, but last night before I went to bed, I said one for you." She sent back a heart shaped emoji in response.

In the following days, we also discussed what her future plans might be whenever she was free of caregiving. I asked if her associates degree in Audio/Video from Southern Ohio College might not be valid anymore, since the college later became part of the now defunct Brown Mackie group of colleges. Such a question would be best left to a college advisor in the event she decided to go back to finish a bachelor's degree.

"What about you?" she asked. "Do you ever think about going back for your PhD?"

"Sometimes, but I can't fathom how. My GRE score is long outdated."

She raised a valid point. For the past few years, I have been haunted by my decision to reject the offer from the University of South Florida. In retrospect, I consider this decision a poor choice, given how little I have accomplished since. Out of sheer curiosity, I looked at the PhD options for the University of Cincinnati. UC had a PhD program in Communication, which must be fairly new, since it never crossed my radar back in 2011 when researching doctoral programs.

I had a renewed sense of motivation, so I sent an email to the department asking for further information. To my surprise, the program didn't require a GRE score. On the surface, the UC doctoral program sounded like the wokiest thing that ever woked, so I had no idea how a white male in his mid-40s would fit in. I focused the application essay on my time with the U of L debate team, figuring the team's social protest bent would fit well with UC's program. I raised the idea of helping their debate program if they had one, or I could help start one.

I contacted four of my professors from U of L for recommendations, at least the ones still actively teaching in the department. They were all supportive, though one did ask me how this would logistically work if I did gain acceptance. A legit question to be sure. Regardless, I now had four letters of recommendation secured, and my end of the application went easy enough.

Amanda obviously had to be told of this news. She was befuddled at my decision to apply.

"You did what?! How on earth is that going to work?"

"Well, you hate Rutherford, and I have wanted to move for a long time now. If I get in, we'll have some major decisions to make."

"You already have two degrees in communications, but you are the worst communicator ever. How is adding another degree going to help?"

"U of L's program always prided itself on being more theoretical than practical."

"You've been known to grunt like a caveman through entire phone conversations."

"Most academics I've met in the communications field are terrible at communicating. I'm deconstructing what I learned in Interpersonal Comm. I got an A in the class."

"How?!" Amanda asked.

Once again, I had zero coherent plan. I wasn't sure why exactly I applied, or my end game for doing so. Was I applying to fulfill some unfinished goal? Hoping to escape from my dreary life? Or was I hoping to gain admission in order to be in the Cincinnati area to be around Janet? Some combination of all of these. I kept this news from Janet for the time being. I couldn't be sure how she would react, and besides, I had no idea if I would gain admission.

149

On the Janet front, we resumed having wonderful conversations on a daily (and nightly) basis. The concerns over texting went by the wayside and now we were texting each other past midnight. Around 10:00 at night I would slip my cell phone into the living room around the time Amanda headed to bed. I felt the need to hide these conversations. Something felt wrong somehow. We weren't sexting each other or anything, but our connection had grown deeper, to the point where I needed to figure out how to process it.

One particular conversation offered up a hint of promise for the future. I had long considered starting a podcast, but didn't know how or what to talk about. I raised the topic with Janet one evening.

"Have you ever given any thought to starting a podcast?" I asked.

"Yes! I have wanted to for years!"

"What should we call it?"

"Hmm ... I don't know. Any ideas?"

"I've been toying with the silly beef concept mentioned in some of these nicknames. We could call it *The Lord and Lady Beef Show*. The amusing aspect is we should never explain the name to any of the guests or the viewers and listeners. We would be a power couple in Olde England, or something wild."

"How on earth could you have known I liked to do medieval cosplay?" she asked, somewhat amazed. "This is such a great idea. We can get so many great guests. I bet Vic would be on the show. But the beef part reminds me of the old Wendy's TV ads with 'Where's the Beef?' Remember those?"

"Oh, of course. But I wouldn't want to use the slogan. Copyrights and all."

"Yeah, we won't use it. How about 'You want the best? Do you want the best?! *The Lord and Lady Beef Show*!'"

"Or at first, 'Do you want the best? Go somewhere else. But we'll try and we'll get better!' We could start by having some of these W & W types. I'm iffy about Linda. Who knows what she is likely to say, given some of these Facebook posts, but controversy could create buzz. We can do absurd special episodes designed for different audiences, using different names. Ma and Pa Beef for rural American themed episodes, or Herr and Frau Beef for Germany."

"We will have to develop this idea. But thank you so much. You've given me something to look forward to."

"What if we suck?" I asked. "What if we have zero chemistry? I have all the charisma of a plank of wood."

"No way. Not a chance!"

The question now became thus: What were we going to talk about on a podcast? We could talk about Wheeler and Woolsey movies first, with guests such as Vic or Linda, but such a premise presented problems. The biggest problem is that the public at large doesn't care about W & W, so the show would garner few YouTube clicks. Second, the duo provided a finite amount to discuss. But what else could we talk about? Several ideas came to mind.

"I was a big fan of the *Lord of the Rings* movies when they came out," she said. "We could discuss those."

"See, now you're talking. *LOTR* is at least something everyone knows, so I would bet a podcast reviewing those movies or our personal connection to them could draw some viewers. I wish we had known each other back when those movies were out. I would have loved to take you to the old Showcase Cinemas on Bardstown Road, preferably theaters four or five, with the biggest screens. I didn't see the first one at the theater, but *Fellowship* was the first DVD my parents ever bought. By the time the third one came out I was so excited I rushed to the midnight showing of *Return of the King*."

"How interesting," she said. "I, too, missed the first one in theaters, but caught it on DVD later. By the time the sequels came out I was obsessed."

"So *LOTR* is a definite yes. What other movies could we discuss?"

"Tell me, what would you think of an aunt who took a four-year-old to see *Death Wish 2*?" she asked.

Another wild coincidence, much like having the same Smith-Corona typewriter. Two months earlier Eric petitioned me to watch the entire *Death Wish* series, so Amanda and I watched as many as possible on HBO Max. *Death Wish 3* was especially amazing, worthy of a standing ovation at its sheer lunacy.

"That's hilarious," I said. "My dad took me to see the fourth one when I was a kid. Oxmoor showed all those crappy Cannon flicks. I recently watched the entire series, and the second one may have upset me the most. The original is classic '70s vigilante fare, but by the third and fourth ones the series became crazed '80s action movies. But the second? Neither fish nor fowl, made during the odd early '80s era, where goofy action movies hadn't taken hold yet, but passe for the vigilante genre."

"Either way, that film made quite the impression on me as a young child. Good movie. Always liked Charles Bronson."

"We can review it if you like," I said. "Any particular eras you want to cover?"

"Instead of 1930s cinema, why not do '80s and '90s movies? The good times." She may as well have quoted Obi-Wan and finished by saying, "Before the dark times."

"I noticed something about you I like," I said. "You never curse. I'm an old-fashioned square in that regard. I dislike hearing females cuss. I don't often cuss, either. I have to be extremely upset."

"Glad you noticed," she said. "I am nothing if not a lady. I don't usually care for movies with a lot of cussing in them, either."

We discussed other potential guest ideas, including the disgraced writer- director James Toback, whom Janet had met at a Cincinnati film festival some years earlier. He asked her to come up to his hotel room, to which Janet agreed, and the next day came with her mom and grandma in tow. I hadn't heard of him much before this, so I took a look online for info. Yikes! This guy has been accused of sexual misconduct by 395 women!

"I looked up Toback. You knew that guy? I have to say if we had known each other circa 2003, there's no way I would ever want you to go up to his hotel room."

"Yeah, I know. But he never bothered me. Oddly enough, he said I reminded him of his own mother. I found that a nice compliment. If you can get him to talk about film, he's a brilliant mentor. But obviously he has a darker side. I walked out on his film at the Cincinnati festival in 2004, *When Will I Be Loved*. Seeing the movie made me realize he cared about nothing but sex."

"I'm unsure if I want him on our show. Maybe if we're desperate. I can set up a new Gmail address for this show and post these clips on

YouTube. I have no idea if we can get monetized or not, but if we do I will PayPal you any money we make on a 50/50 basis. I would never cheat you on money."

Thanksgiving arrived soon after. I chatted with Janet during the holiday weekend, but not as much as we had been. I sent her a wacky picture of myself wearing a turkey hat while at my mom's house waiting for Thanksgiving dinner. We had an enjoyable enough talk on Friday, and then another amiable talk on Sunday. She cut that chat short because she expected a call from out of town, which I found unusual.

I heard nothing from her on the Monday after Thanksgiving, at least not until late at night. My phone chimed over a Facebook update, noting Janet had changed her profile pic to a curious, blurry pic of her smiling ear to ear. She also changed the spelling of her last name to a baffling abbreviation. I had zero idea what to make of this. I ran the pic through Picwish as I had before and sent her the clearer version. I also asked about the baffling last name change, which she didn't address.

"Thanks for fixing the pic," she replied. "Please forgive me, I'm down tonight. Very tired. Today has been a bad day and tomorrow will be another one."

"I'm here for the next twenty minutes or so if you need to talk. I'll try to cheer you up."

"I'm not helpable. Too sad. I'll be okay. Don't tell anyone. This is private."

Okay, now *this* was truly bizarre. I had no idea what this out-of-town phone call entailed, or who called. Apparently, the call left her an emotional wreck. I heard nothing from Janet on Tuesday, so on Wednesday I decided to send her a text to cheer her up.

"Hey, I was wondering if you would like me to send a DVD of *So This Is Africa* in with the book?" The film being W & W's lone Columbia outing, not available on any form of home video. Her response astonished me.

"Excuse me, but we cannot keep going on this way! I'm going through too much right now and I can't do this today. I'm having boyfriend problems at the moment, so I will talk to you later."

I felt bewildered, baffled. I stared at my phone screen for several minutes in a shocked state. Finally, I typed something lame like, "Okay,

I'm here for you." What in the world happened to her in the past forty-eight hours? What were we doing which must cease immediately? What kind of answer was that to a simple question about a movie? Was she unwinding, mentally and emotionally, at a rapid pace? And besides ... wait a minute ...

What fucking boyfriend?!

CHAPTER 21

THE RETURN OF LADY BEEF

I spent four sleepless nights worried sick about Janet. Whatever happened certainly didn't seem like anything normal. I had no clue what emotionally wrecked her to such a degree, and at one point I seriously feared she might be capable of self-harm. I didn't *know* this per se, but her behavior was so jarring and sudden, so erratic, that I couldn't help but worry about her well-being. I also had no idea what to make of this boyfriend revelation. We had been talking for over two months without nary a mention of this guy, nor did she have any Facebook pics of the two of them out and about. As far as I knew she was a lonely, put upon, middle-aged woman, caring for her nonagenarian grandparents. This being the side of herself she chose to show me.

I started to have a sinking feeling about the entire situation. I already bought her a Christmas present, which she seemed fine accepting. More alarming, I already applied to the PhD program at UC, but this revelation caused second thoughts.

A week after Thanksgiving, Amanda and I had a bizarre text conversation while she toiled away at school. I pondered some big picture thoughts, hoping for some reassurance or clarity. I hadn't shaken the feeling we had been out of sync for months now.

"Why do you put up with me? What do you see in me?"

"Well, on account of my leg there weren't many boys interested in me. Also, my back. As far as your questions, well, we have our vows. Andrew needs you as his dad. I'm not sure what else you want me to say."

This wasn't the reconnection I hoped for. Amanda then discussed all of the things I had been doing wrong, from harping on her stump to driving her crazy 90% of the time with a veritable laundry list of ludicrous nicknames too numerous to mention. These were meant to be silly, yet she doesn't see them the same way. Ah well, back to the drawing board.

In typical Janet fashion, I finally received a text early Sunday morning around 3:00 a.m. Apparently, she had walked back off the ledge. "I am doing better now. Thank you for being there for me, my wonderful friend." I was relieved to hear from her. We sporadically texted each other and I tried my best to lighten the mood, noting she needed some "merciless tickling," to which she howled with laughter.

That night produced a fateful conversation. I had to know more about this situation and what caused her bizarre meltdown.

"I'm glad to see you are okay. Do you want to talk?"

"As you might have gathered by now, my boyfriend works out of town and called me long distance the other night. The conversation didn't go well and let's leave it at that."

"Okay, I don't want to pry. I swear, hearing this reminds me of the frustrating phone calls my dad would get from my aunt Carolyn back in the day. She always used to call ranting about her ex-husband, and my dad would blow a gasket. She, too, lived in Cincinnati all those years ago, before moving to Pigeon Forge."

"Why, what did he say to her?"

"He used to implore her to get rid of the stressful people in her life, including her ex. I can give you the same advice, to rid yourself of bad actors who harm you. But I do have something more delicate to discuss."

"What would that be?"

I hemmed and hawed around the topic of conversation, as she guessed a series of mental issues until I finally came out with the thought in my head.

"Janet, is it possible you are bipolar?"

"Nah, I'm not bipolar," she said, without a hint of serious anger. "I have moments of feeling down or depressed on occasion, but nothing bipolar."

I am hardly a mental health expert or practitioner. I merely pondered her odd behavior, from the random days of ghosting and being out of contact, to being wildly upbeat one day with grand ideas about inviting any number of famous people on our podcast (Joe Burrow, Billy Ray Cyrus, Lynda Carter among them). Then the next day, crashing emotionally, and refusing any attempt to console her.

"Okay, I was worried about you, though."

"Don't be. No matter how awful things get, I would never kill myself."

"Would you like to hear more about my dad's crazy side of the family?" I asked, changing the subject.

"Sure, it's compelling."

"My cousin Chris has spent his teen years and adult life in and out of jail and prison. The biggest incident I can recall involved my aunt Retta calling around Thanksgiving 2000. Apparently, he carjacked a local Evansville minister and led the police in a high-speed chase across the Kentucky border into Henderson. He ditched the car downtown, stripped naked, and tried to swim away in the Ohio River before the cops arrested him."

"Oh my God!" she replied. "Where is he now?"

"I'll look him up and find out." I did a brief online search and reported back. "Okay, he's apparently in jail yet again in Evansville for, guess what, another carjacking attempt. The article says he also had a fight with a fellow inmate and tried throwing hot coffee at the guy."

"Keep Andrew far away from him."

"Thankfully he doesn't know our address. But what is with him and futile carjackings? He used to try to hold up convenience stores with water guns. At least change tactics. Wear a mask or something."

"I know, right? This is all wild to hear, and oddly comforting. Thank you for sharing all this with me tonight."

So, were we back in business? If anything, our bond seemed stronger now than before. If we were texting each other often before, now we were doing so until past midnight. Amanda never noticed or cared much about all this late-night texting. She usually fell asleep by then, same as Andrew.

I reviewed the acknowledgments page of her book for ideas on potential podcast guests. I knew a few of these names, including known people such as Nick Clooney.

"Would Nick Clooney be interested in our show?"

"Probably not," she said. "I used to talk to him some years ago, but somehow, I think he got fed up with me after a point. We could try, but I don't know if he would agree. I bet William Drew would be interested if I asked him."

"I can imagine him talking about D.W. Griffith. I can see the intro to the episode now. 'This week on *Lord and Lady Beef* we will have three white people discussing *Birth of a Nation*! What could possibly go wrong?'"

"LOL! He's obsessed with that movie."

"Hmm ... I also saw Sean Kimble mentioned. I haven't talked to him in about fifteen years."

Sean was a Detroit based punk musician I used to chat with back in the AIM days. As a fellow W & W fan, I found him to be a fairly cool guy.

"Well, let me tell you about him," she said, ominously. I waited for several minutes as she typed the response, fearing something unpleasant happened between the two of them. Finally, she continued. "Sean and I talked for several years online. He always expressed hurt over his girlfriend dumping him for a drug dealer, since they used to watch W & W movies together. We reconnected on Facebook during the pandemic, and he suddenly pronounced his undying love for me, saying he had felt this way for years. He wanted me to come visit and take care of him, since he's been in poor health. He's about twenty years older than me. I told him his request was impossible, not interested. He threw a fit and said he never wanted to talk to me again, that we couldn't be friends anymore. I haven't heard from him since."

"Poor guy," I said. "I lost touch with him years ago after AIM shut down. But hearing this he's off the list. A shame. I used to like his band, The Zanies."

"I still have some of their CDs."

Hearing about Sean's unrequited love for Janet intrigued me. I wondered what she said to him over the years to prompt such feelings? Were those conversations similar to the ones she had with me? I couldn't say, but I tracked him down on Twitter (or X) and followed him for a while. I never talked to him and soon became fed up with his bizarre conspiracy theory posts and unfollowed him. Another sad shell of a W & W fan, a fandom which seemed to deal in broken souls.

I still wanted to cheer Janet up, so I sent her a link to the unearthed footage of Isaac's epic audition as Brad from my botched *Welcome to Paradise* scene. One night she had a look at the hilarity, and she absolutely died laughing.

"Wait, is he dead at the end there?" she asked, while cracking up.

"No, just passed out."

"This is hysterical. The way the mistakes build, I am howling. I almost peed my pants watching this! You were doing a solid job, though. You tried to direct him."

"Oh no, I did a horrible job! I'm going to send this to Isaac, too. I asked if he was okay with me posting this on YouTube, and he said, 'go for it.'"

For his part, Isaac told me later, "I watched this three times the day you sent the link. Kate and I needed popcorn. We hadn't seen the footage in years."

One of the most distinct memories I have of chatting with Janet occurred a few days later. We were increasingly comfortable discussing all manner of topics. She jested, "You can tell me about bumps, skin tags, rashes. I'm your old war nurse." I remembered this line when discussing a growing problem, one I noticed as I got further into my 40s.

"I may need to ask War Nurse Beef about something sensitive in nature."

"That's fine, go ahead," she replied.

"Well, I've had trouble urinating more and more lately. Sometimes I stand at the toilet waiting for a long time. Other times I notice a minor yellow stain on my underwear. Think I'm starting to have prostate troubles?"

"My grandpa has had a bad prostate for years, but he's far older than you. What might help is to take some pumpkin seed oil. Would you like some of those pills for Christmas?"

"So sweet of you. Don't spend a bunch though. Buy whatever is cheap on Amazon."

"I'll have a look online tomorrow." She paused for a moment before saying something astounding. "I've had to insert a catheter in my grandma in the past. I've never done that for a man, but I would be willing to do it for you. I will make sure you don't explode."

I was stunned. I had to ask myself the question: *Would Amanda be willing to do that?* I thought about this for a moment and decided she probably wouldn't, but then again, she would hardly know how. I decided to quote the title of one of the best Bert Wheeler/Dorothy Lee duets from *The Cuckoos*.

"I love you so much."

She responded in the affirmative.

"But I wouldn't want to be a burden on you, Amanda, or anyone else," I said. "I saw what that was like for years with my dad."

The next day I sent her another routine selfie, to which she reacted, "You look amazing. Seriously, I mean it." These statements seemed like more than a compliment.

I figured I would send Janet's Christmas gift two weeks before Christmas in case of mail delays during the holidays, wanting the package to arrive with plenty of time to spare. I hid the package in the bottom of a dresser, not wanting Amanda to know I sent a gift to another woman. I wasn't sure how to explain such an arrangement. Along with the book, *What Made Pistachio Nuts?* and the bar of Pears soap, I included a brief note:

"To a soulmate I met twenty years too late. I hope you enjoy the book, as well as the soap. Thee needs, Stinky! I can smell you a hundred miles away! Love, Brian."

We kept texting every night until midnight for the next few days, until finally the long-awaited package arrived. I distinctly remember eating at Cheddar's with Amanda and Andrew when Janet's text popped up saying she received the package.

"I got your present today. Thank you for the book and the soap!

The letter was an unexpected gift. I laughed, so funny and sweet. I love you!"

Texting Janet back during the middle of dinner became a regular occurrence. I enjoyed these conversations, yet I felt as if I were doing something wrong. This was uncharted territory for me. Since Amanda and I got married, I hadn't ever messed around with other women. But what *was* this? We weren't planning a clandestine rendezvous in a sleazy motel. We'd never even met. Hadn't even talked on the phone. The only times I heard Janet's voice were a couple of token voice to text messages she sent lasting all of fifteen seconds. Her voice is fairly mundane, an average sounding Midwestern female with an ever so slight southern drawl. Perhaps an ancestor snuck across the Ohio River from Newport?

Some of our conversations didn't click the way I would have liked. My attempt at giving her a crash course in the various scandals plaguing U of L basketball since 2009 didn't go over well. She stayed alert through the Karen Sypher mess and then the eventual Katina Powell fiasco, but she quit responding around the time I ranted on Chris Mack and Dino Gaudio's extortion scandal. When I woke up the next morning, I found another text from 3:00 a.m. saying, "I'm sorry, but I was tired and fell asleep. I just now saw all of this." I always like to keep my audience riveted.

Maybe she's not a college basketball fan, but I will try again some other time, I thought. I wished she would tell me if she's crashing and needed to go to sleep, or had to tend to her grandma, instead of talking to me. I would have understood.

The next day we had a seemingly innocuous conversation which became one of lasting relevance. For the past month I wanted to check on the idea of whether caregivers could receive federal or state money for tending to an elderly family member. I managed to find a site with info on organizations in Ohio, as well as Kentucky, since I wanted to share this with my mom and Eric. I mentioned the news to Janet.

"I found an informative website with links to government programs or private groups who pay money to caregivers. Would you like me to send it your way?"

"That would be great," she said. "Nice of you. I've looked into those programs in the past but never got anywhere. By the way, I've been meaning to ask you about something."

"Yes, Lady Beef?"

"Are you looking at writing something else anytime soon?"

"I have. I've considered writing an entire history of my Wheeler and Woolsey fandom, explaining why I cared about the team, and also the frustrations of collecting rare and out of print movies from 1991-95."

"Sounds amazing. Would you want this published in *Classic Images*? I've written articles for them in the past and can contact the editor. They would probably publish this piece. It would be right up their alley."

"Does it pay anything?"

"Unfortunately, no," she replied.

"Would you like to co-author this with me? I can type out my entire thoughts but leave openings for you to chime in with anything related to their fandom you'd like. Your own personal stories, interactions with Dorothy, anything that comes to mind. I think this could work, and help you ease back into the groove of writing again. Get another credit to your name."

"Yes, I'd love to. Might take me a little time, though."

The next day I hammered out this W & W fanboy piece in a couple of hours. Writing about this topic came easy to me. I spent the weekend going over this piece. On Monday, I texted Janet, asking if I could go ahead and send it her way. Her response was curt, to say the least.

"Excuse me, I don't want to be rude, but I am so busy right now. I can't do this."

"Hey, I understand. Christmas is a week away and this is a stressful time of year. I will go ahead and email you this piece, as well as the Medicaid caregiver site I found. You can check both of those out when the holidays are over."

"You are a true friend. Thank you."

I sent her the email attaching the W & W draft, as well as the caregiver info. I didn't hear from her the rest of the week, which in this case didn't alarm me, since Amanda and I were headed to Nashville for our yearly anniversary trip. When we roamed around Opryland, my thoughts drifted to Janet. When we saw *Aquaman 2* at the theater, my thoughts drifted to Janet. When we ate dinner at the Caney Fork next to Opryland, I couldn't help but think of Janet. What was going on with her?

Upon returning to Louisville, I wanted to send Janet a Christmas greeting, which I filmed on my phone. Amanda and Andrew left for Grayson County to spend a few hours on Christmas Eve with her mom, so I filmed this brief video while they were away. I sent the video on Christmas, in addition to other routine Christmas texts to Chad, Isaac, and Rochelle. Everyone else wrote back quickly with "Merry Christmas!" greetings of their own. Everyone but Janet. She didn't respond. I checked my phone intently over the next few days, but no reply.

When Janet ghosted me on Christmas, I figured she was never going to talk to me again. Who doesn't bother responding to a thoughtful Christmas video message with not so much as a "Merry Christmas back at you" message? To tally the total amount of vanishing acts: We talked initially for about ten days, then she disappeared for a week due to the cyst and other health matters. We then talked for the rest of October until she vanished again around Halloween, leading to me sending the ill-advised Facebook message to Ned. We talked for most of November, but then after Thanksgiving that phone call sent her spiraling into a funk for a solid week. Then another enjoyable two weeks before Christmas.

The week after Christmas passed. No messages from Janet. Eric and I did our usual New Year's Eve drunken antics, downing multiple craft beers, and the usual bottle of Andre, much to Amanda's chagrin. Amanda never drinks any form of alcohol. I don't drink much these days, but on New Year's I make an exception. Two weeks had passed since I last heard from Janet. When I checked my email late on New Year's evening, I saw an email from her. The contents of this email saddened me considerably.

"Clearly, we have gotten carried away the past few months. You have a wife and son. I have a boyfriend. We practically live on each other's phones, and over Christmas he saw all of these texts I received from another man, and he was not happy. 'This is not cool.' From now on I do not want you to text me, but you can send me emails here. Further, I know you are highly motivated to write and do a podcast, but I am not in a place right now to do those things. Maybe there will be a time. I've had my say when it comes to W & W. You can have yours. I wouldn't want to hurt you for anything in the world. Love, Janet."

So much to unpack here. First off, I was mortified that this guy read all of my texts. I felt before this our conversations were exactly that: Our conversations. Frankly, the tone of the email felt like a kiss off. Given how infrequently she checked her email and wrote back, I figured this was her way of gently pushing me aside. She dictated the means of communication on her terms, with me being allowed zero input. I wrote back what I figured might be one final email.

"I've had an ominous feeling over these past two weeks. I felt like I said or did something wrong, and you never wanted to speak to me again. Yes, it's been bizarre texting until after midnight, but we never crossed a certain line. I'm saddened that you now don't want to collaborate on anything with me. Understand, I don't want you as an illicit mistress. I think too highly of you and love you too much to treat you that way. Kinda sucks though. I got a new webcam for Christmas for the podcast.

"You have quickly become one of my favorite people. I would like to explain the note I sent with the present. When I mentioned you being a soulmate I met twenty years too late, this is what I mean. If we had started talking two decades ago the way we have been the past few months, I would have flat out said, 'Look, we need to get married right now because there isn't anyone I could possibly meet that is better than you.' I hope you don't find this emotionally overwhelming and continue to write back. I don't regret anything I've said, and you don't need to regret anything, either. I meant every word. I may never get a chance to sign your copy of my book, but I will go ahead and share what I wanted to say:

"*To Janet, 'The Should Have Been' Mrs. Paige. There is no greater nickname I can give you than that. Love, Brian.*"

Then I pressed send.

CHAPTER 22

LORD AND LADY BEEF RULE THE WAVES

I couldn't sleep after writing such a draining email. Around 1 a.m. I saw my phone light up on the desk, so I dragged myself out of bed to see who had texted me at this late hour. It was Janet. She had already seen my email and in the past hour written an impassioned response. After issuing this edict not to text any further and only email, she violated her own framework literally an hour later. Good. I hated the idea.

"Um, wow. I'm stunned. Yeah. You really care for me, huh? Believe me, we'll talk. We'll talk. I will think of a wonderful reply for all you had to say."

She rambled like this for a while in a clearly rattled text. I was half asleep, so I typed a brief response. "We'll discuss more in the morning." She quickly wrote back in agreement, and I attempted to go back to bed but again had a difficult time sleeping. I could cynically say my email included my best material, but I wasn't using such meaningful words casually enough to call it "material." In reality, I have never said those things to *anyone*, Amanda included.

I can't remember the next few days, still hungover from getting hammered with Eric on New Year's Eve. I do recall another text where I promised to send Janet another email discussing various frustrations in my home life, details I hadn't shared with anyone else, including friends like Chad and Isaac. I sent this email a couple of days later, to which Janet texted she would write back detailed responses to both of my emails. She never did. The fact that she texted me again spoke volumes.

Janet seemed in better spirits than she had been previously. She seemed happy, which was the goal. I wanted to make her happy. Apparently, she also felt gung-ho about the podcast, as well as my W & W article.

"You'll have to give me some time to think about what to write on the W & W piece, but we can go ahead and plan the podcast. I think it could be great! We need to get a following, some advertisers, and possibly some big-name guests."

"Who do you have in mind?" I asked.

"I met Priscilla Presley a few years back," she said. "I have some signed photos of her, and I felt we hit it off. I think she might be interested. I've been obsessed with seeing the new *Priscilla* movie by Sofia Coppola. I've heard it is similar to the older *Elvis and Me* miniseries, which I loved as a kid. I used to correspond with Dale Midkiff, who played Elvis in the film.

This idea started to show some real promise. I had my doubts as to whether we could get notable celebrities to show up on our unknown podcast. Realistically, I merely hoped for a few geeky W & W fans to show up and chat with us. We could do our own retrospective film reviews. While gaining a following and being monetized were major goals, I mostly wanted to record the show as a way to spend time with Janet. Still, I felt a few things needed clearing up.

"I understand your grandparents right now need to come first," I said. "I'm not trying to compete with them. If you have something to tend to, I will understand."

"Yes, I also realize Amanda and Andrew have to come first for you," she replied. "I don't want to do anything wrong. All that said, I wouldn't mind having my copy of your book signed with your inscription." She followed this statement with a loving happy face emoji.

"By the way, did you enjoy my Christmas video? You never said."

"Oh yes! Thank you so much! I didn't get around to sending those pumpkin seed pills, but you can expect those in a couple of days." The bottle of pumpkin seed pills arrived a few days later. I took the entire bottle but didn't notice any particular difference.

One major aspect I had been slacking on for some time was my physical fitness. I had been meaning to start another diet for a few years but never had the proper motivation to do so. My childhood friend Jeremy Stigler's untimely death from a heart attack in August 2023 was a wake-up call. Chad regaled me with his incredible weight loss (240 lbs. down to 175 in a year's time). Janet shed fifty lbs. she put on during the pandemic. Therefore, I made my New Year's resolution to lose weight. I desperately needed to do so. Once again, I had no stamina for physical activity, my clothes now tight and ill fitting. I was concerned that the extra weight might cause me to have sleep apnea. Amanda often complained about my snoring, which hadn't been a major problem in the past.

I spent the first few days of January drinking the rest of my Mountain Dew supply and eating the last pieces of lunchmeat and cheese before I truly began this journey. I had no idea if I could successfully diet the way I did in 2008, when I was much younger and had the motivating factor of the Orlando *WrestleMania* trip. The batteries on the scale were dead when I first started the diet and took two Hydroxycut pills, left over from a theoretical diet Amanda never attempted. As such, I am unsure where I started, but I would venture to say 217 lbs.

I made some modifications to the previous diet:

1. I ate two Eggo waffles for breakfast, using zero sugar, ten calorie Mrs. Butterworth syrup. I drank decaf zero calorie coffee, mainly because regular coffee gives me the jitters.
2. For lunch I ate the two dill pickle spears, but this time I disregarded milk, since there were too many calories. I typically eat a fair amount of baked cheddar and sour cream Ruffles. I started out drinking water or unsweetened tea but later dabbled in zero sugar soft drinks. I've tried Coke Zero, Mountain Dew Zero, and Pepsi Zero. The Mountain Dew Zero was awful, I could barely stomach it. Coke Zero is decent but something felt missing somehow, in terms of

taste. Pepsi Zero is terrific, so I kept drinking it long term. But to each their own.

3. Each day I made my way across the street to the patio home clubhouse exercise room. The room has a Nordic Track bike that keeps track of miles, and also calories, ideal for my purposes. The first time back trying to pedal five miles nearly killed me. My legs felt like they were trapped in cement. I started out needing almost twenty-seven minutes to pedal five miles but eventually could do five miles in under twenty-three minutes. Any speed faster and I noticed I burned fewer calories, and I wanted to keep the goal of burning 130 calories per five miles.

4. Dinner is where I would eat a solid meal. I tried to avoid any fattening, major calorie options. Steak and rice is fine, possibly steak fries on occasion. When eating Italian, ignore the alfredo-based options and go with marinara or meat sauce, since those have fewer calories. Pizza isn't necessarily fattening, as long as you don't overdo it. Again, I would drink unsweetened tea.

5. I started with Hydroxycut, taking four pills a day, but after a point my old right-side ailment started flaring up, so I cut down on the pills after finishing the bottle. Amanda cautioned against those, as did Janet. I moved on to Green Tea Fat Burner, which produced excellent results, taking two of the green tea at lunch and another at dinner.

6. I weighed every Monday morning once I had new batteries in the scale. I always took a picture of my scale progress, then texted the picture to both Amanda and Janet. I texted these pics to Chad and Rochelle as well.

As I started Beef Reduction 2024, Janet and I were back to being copacetic. The Monday after winter break turned into a fascinating day, one where we spent most of the afternoon discussing the podcast as well as her sending me a barrage of old pictures of herself. She also sent some newer ones for me to compare and contrast. These were typical daily photos, but I was surprised at how many notable names she had come across over the years. One featured her in a slightly uncomfortable facial expression with Bebe Neuwirth of *Cheers* and *Frasier* fame. Another had Janet looking semi drunk at a party with Lynda Carter.

"I can seriously take an ugly picture," she jested.

"I wouldn't say ugly, but you aren't looking at the camera. Look at Lynda. She's clear eyed and owns the camera, looking straight ahead. You have pretty green eyes in the newer pics, yet in these older photos you never seem to make quality eye contact with the camera. Just curious, but do you have a pic from before you lost weight?"

"Oh, why bring down the mood?" she said. "Here, wait. I might have one."

She sent me a pic taken during the pandemic. She was clearly heavier and seemed miserable, wearing a floppy hat on a summer day. Fishy pale.

"You looked miserable here. Glad you are healthier now. Brave of you to send, though."

"I weighed around 180 lbs. in that picture. About 134 now. I need to lose a bit more."

"You look fine now. Looking at a BMI chart as we speak. If you want to meet a goal, you could lose another five lbs. to get under 130."

"My goal is to go as far as 115 lbs."

"Eh, why? At 115 you would be nothing but a bone and a hank of hair. Need some meat on those bones."

We continued sharing pictures into the evening. I vividly recall eating gator meat at Storming Crab, one of my last fattening meals before committing to the diet. As Amanda, Andrew, and I were leaving the restaurant, Janet sent an eyebrow raising text.

"I could send you some sexy pics if you'd like. These are rarely seen twenty-year-old pics, but I could send them out of friendship."

"Uh, I'm not sure about that," I replied. "What sort of pics are these? Are they nudes? I'm not sure I want those on my phone."

"No, they aren't nudes. More like lingerie, dress up, some bikini pics."

"Can you wait until I'm back home and in the bedroom on the computer before sending those? Email the most questionable ones?"

I felt anxious the entire way home. Until this point, I felt we had kept things on a relatively high moral level, with loving declarations but nothing in the realm of dubious pictures or sexually charged discussions. Once I arrived home, I readied myself for these pictures she wanted to send.

"Okay, I sent them," she said. "Those were self-taken on a timer. Blush."

I checked my email once Amanda settled on the couch in the living room. My first reaction to these lingerie pics is they were so blurry I could barely tell who was in the pics, so once again I ran them through Picwish. She also sent another curious picture of herself dressed up like a French courtesan passed out near a couch, reenacting a Toulouse-Lautrec painting. I later reenacted this for a joke picture of my own, being exhausted after my initial five miles on the bike.

The purpose of taking these pictures eluded me, or her purpose in sending them. Were they meant to be titillating? Was she trying to get me off? They were too artsy for such a purpose. I knew one thing for certain, however. These were taken during the time when she was ultra-thin, to the point of being scrawny.

"I'm sending back improved versions. Then I will delete these emails if you want me to. I enjoyed the pics, but I must say you are significantly better looking now." I deleted the more sensitive pics a week later. When I told her, she seemed to have no recollection of ever having sent them. Weird.

"I have heard that before, that I look better now," she said. "Wait, here's one more from 2006."

She sent another pic to my phone, which I wasn't expecting. This one featured her in Jennifer Beals *Flashdance* style black leggings, doing a variation on the famous Betty Grable pinup pose. Now this one was a turn on.

"Why were you keeping this one from me? Whoa! I feel like you took that picture in 2006 for me to see all these years later. By far your best picture. You have nothing to be ashamed of. Everyone has the right to feel sensual."

"Do you think I'm pretty?"

Oh, no. I wondered if she was messing with me. She has my book. Clearly, she read the chapter where I was asked this exact question and replied with a boneheaded remark about this girl "looking better five years ago." Could this be a trap?

"Yes, you are quite pretty. Given you now have some curves and filled out in the right places I'd say you are far better than in these older pics." This was exactly what she needed to hear, with no lies on my part.

"You were right," she said. "We *are* soulmates. We should have met and gotten married years ago!"

I smiled from ear to ear. I responded with a smiley emoji, but I had no response to respond adequately to such a declaration. After deliberating, I followed by saying, "I don't have any pics of this sort, but I did find one from when I weighed 170." I sent her my old 2009 era Facebook profile pic, merely me wearing a baggy U of L shirt while sitting in a chair over at my mom's.

"You were wrong, this is a sexy pic," she responded. It isn't a sexy pic at all, merely a routine profile picture.

I decided to use the new 1080p webcam for a test run of how the back bedroom looked for our podcast. There was nothing to this clip. Three minutes of me rambling in a monotone voice and pointing out items such as the wall posters of *Cockeyed Cavaliers* and *Hips, Hips, Hooray!* I posted the clip on YouTube, set it to private, and sent Janet the link. I also created a *Lord and Lady Beef* title card on Canva, which may not have been great, but would do for a first attempt.

"Great video," she said. "You will make for a good podcast host."

"You think so? I need to not be so monotone, but I have a deep, low voice, so sometimes I have trouble projecting. I found some of your old articles online with Gloria Jones and Deana Martin, trying to gauge how you interview guests. Those were printed interviews, whereas we'll be doing a video show. When you have a chance, could you test out your webcam, so I can see its quality?"

"Right now, I look like a mess, but I will try to record a video later." I wasn't worried about how she looked. I was interested in the video quality of the webcam.

One of our most meaningful late-night conversations involved the subject who brought us together in the first place, Dorothy Lee. Janet found some old photos of Dorothy's home in Galena, Illinois, dubbed "The Little Ponderosa." She shared these pics. I became curious and

Googled Galena and realized the town is located on the Mississippi River, across from the Iowa border. A quick online search revealed Dorothy was buried in Prospect Hill Cemetery on the outskirts of Galena.

"Did you go to her funeral?" I asked.

"No, we mainly talked on the phone or wrote letters," Janet said. "I never met Dottie in person."

"Really? You seemed so close, almost like a granddaughter. Seeing your pictures and looking up her gravesite online has given me an idea. I have no idea when or how this will happen, but I'll run an idea past you. Someday we should go on a road trip to Galena to Dorothy's grave and pay our respects. What do you think?"

"I'm not sure. I can't get away right now for anything like that."

"This could be a decade from now. No set time. Since you've never been, I feel like this would be an emotionally gratifying trip."

"You know what? You are a wonderful man. Deal."

As I lay in bed that night, I thought back to when this trip would have been perfect, namely the time period circa 2001-04. A time in which I felt painfully lost after college, aimlessly selling bootleg movies online. Why did I not reach out to Janet back then? I wasn't kidding about those words in the New Year's email and this hypothetical Galena trip would have been the perfect time.

This scenario came to mind around the time we were discussing the road trip to Galena. The Chestnut Mountain Resort is a ski resort overlooking the Mississippi River between Illinois and Iowa (and not hugely expensive, about $71.00 a night on Hotwire). We could get some flowers for Prospect Hill Cemetery, pay our respects to Dottie, then grab some dinner at a decent restaurant in town. (Cucina Bella sounded decent). Back at the resort, we could walk along the scenic hills overlooking the river, and as the sun started to set, I'd drop to one knee, bust out the engagement ring, and hope for the best.

Hey, that scenario certainly beats clumsily proposing in Eric's bedroom and discussing the warranty information from Shane Co.

As January progressed, I finally took her up on a previous suggestion and watched the European made two-part series of *Anna Karenina* on YouTube. I decided to watch this epic one afternoon after biking and texted Janet thoughts as I viewed it.

"Whoa, I saw a boob in the opening scene! Interesting beginning."

"LOL! Yeah, it grabs you right off the bat."

We had this entire running dialogue about the film to the point where she jumped on YouTube and watched along with me, riffing along during the second half.

"I think this guy playing Vronsky is the same guy who played Captain Rios on those first two awful seasons of *Picard*."

"Wow," she replied. "I had no idea he was on *Star Trek*."

"The South American guy playing a Russian officer. This casting, I swear ..."

"Karenin himself isn't such a bad guy," she said. "If I were Anna, I probably would have stayed with him."

"But isn't he supposed to be a dick?" I asked. "I know Basil Rathbone likely played him that way in the 1935 version. I'll watch it next to compare. I think too much like a 1930s mogul for this modern stuff. 'We need to have Anna and Vronsky as the focus! They need chemistry! Karenin has to be a heel, otherwise no one will care!' By the way, who are the Russians fighting in this?"

"Good question. Let me see." Janet paused for a minute and came back with a result. "Could it be the Franco-Prussian War in 1870?"

"Was Russia involved? Were they allies with France yet? I know they were by WW1. Stuff like this bothers me." (Later I watched the 1935 film and in that film Vronsky and Company were gearing up to fight as mercenaries in the Serbian-Turkish War of 1876.)

After Anna threw himself in front of the train (spoilers from 1878), Janet wanted to know my overall thoughts.

"You know ... I dug it. I certainly enjoyed our riffing."

"You don't know how much it means to me," she said. "I've had so much trouble sleeping. That's why I have watched all of these. I like anything with true love."

"Should we tackle this topic on our show? The concept of true love. Does it exist? How do you know when it happens?"

"I bet that one would get some views," she said.

In the following weeks, I watched more of these Euro-made adaptations of famous works. I had no idea why I watched these adaptations, other than to please Janet. The worst one was probably the snowy adaptation of *Romeo and Juliet*, utilizing entirely new dialogue, Romeo killing a guy in the opening scene, and the duo having siblings who weren't in the original Shakespeare.

"Did these fools think they were going to improve on Shakespeare?" I asked. "Everyone now has to be a bad boy archetype. The whole point of Romeo killing Tybalt later is this was the first blood he ever spilled. Why should I care if he killed some random geek in the first scene?! Also, the idea of them having siblings is insane. The tragedy of the play is due to their deaths the Capulet and Montague lines may well end."

"Eh, not one of my favorites either," she said.

"The girl playing Juliet could have been hot if not for the jarring mole on her shoulder during the love scenes."

"OMG, I was going to mention that. She should get it removed. Could be cancerous. Poor Juliette." Yes, she always misspelled the name, even after I repeatedly used the correct version.

I followed by watching more of these bizarre, reimagined works, going through a 1950s Rome set *Cinderella*, which featured a male lead who reminded both of us of accused Idaho killer Bryan Kohberger. Janet had an unhealthy interest in the case, complete with conspiracy theories. I looked at one picture online and thought, "Yeah, that guy looks psychotic."

Other outings included an unfaithful adaptation of *Beauty and the Beast*, with a guy who looked like wrestler PCO and never donned any beast makeup. I followed up by viewing the 1946 French version on HBO Max as a palette cleanser. Lastly, I checked out a version of *1,001 Arabian Nights*, which also featured the same girl, Vanessa Hessler, who played Cinderella, except with dark hair. Apparently, Hessler had a romance with Gaddafi's son before he was killed in the same attack which eliminated the dictator himself.

Janet still hadn't sent me even a brief clip to show her webcam quality, and we were no closer to putting together the podcast. No guests were lined up. She hadn't touched the W & W piece. I didn't press the matter, and I enjoyed our conversations, but I was somewhat puzzled as to what we were doing.

Even as she implored to me, "You can always trust me," I had a nagging feeling. I debated sharing some of my streaming accounts with Janet so she could watch certain movies we might review for the show. I definitely wanted her take on the recent *Barbie* movie. Eric and I both had plenty of thoughts on why my mom and Amanda didn't care at all.

Yet I never shared these accounts. I didn't feel sure about doing so. I couldn't shake the nagging feeling our conversations weren't our own, especially if this supposed boyfriend of hers could see login info and passwords. As much as I felt a great sense of love for Janet, could I truly trust her?

CHAPTER 23

I MISS SEEING THE SUNRISE

As January closed, I felt closer to Janet than I did my own wife. I acted as a better "husband" to someone I'd never technically met than as an actual husband to Amanda. In prior months, Janet would occasionally mention Amanda to rein me back in, but for much of January these mentions of Amanda ceased. Amanda was dealing with a persistent case of fibroids during the first half of 2024. She started having longer menstrual periods in late 2023, starting a day or two early and ending a day or two later than normal. Finally, a doctor put her on some meds, which were horrible. She was bleeding every day as a side effect. I pleaded with her to stop taking these Myfembree pills, since she became low on iron, and even anemic. She finally did in early March. But in January and February the strained home situation became even more stressful.

In late January, the wrestling world was shocked by the Janel Grant lawsuit against Vince McMahon and WWE. The details of Grant's complaint were shocking and can be found online, but the aspect of her as a former caregiver for her now deceased parents reminded me so much of Janet. I sent her a link to the complaint on Facebook, and we had an entire discussion.

"I am shocked and disgusted by this entire situation," she said. "It says here he pooped in her hair! I'm reading more of this. I never thought Vince was capable of anything like this. That he only played this role on TV."

"I knew this woman was his mistress and he hired her for a phony job, before passing her on to Laurinaitis. But these details are so sordid. Promise me you would never be taken in like her, no matter how down-trodden you feel."

"No poopy on the head for me."

"Protect Frau Beef."

"Love Herr Beef."

The McMahon news broke the weekend of the Royal Rumble. Eric and Isaac came over for the show, which admittedly I had a hard time getting into after the twisted McMahon allegations, which forced his resignation from the company on the eve of the event. I live texted updates on who won the matches to her.

"*I* don't think wrestling is stupid," she said, referencing my email on Amanda's various issues with me. Once again, setting herself up as a preferable alternative.

On Monday, Janet sent me a cryptic text, which had me somewhat worried.

"Lady Beef has a gift for you. Expect it to arrive in a couple of days via Amazon."

"Thank you, so much. I wonder what it is?"

"Think back to a previous conversation, heh."

I worried about what this gift might be. A bottle of pills was one thing, but I had no idea what she sent in this case. I definitely needed to be home by myself when this arrived.

A couple of days later the Amazon package arrived. Thankfully, I was alone, Amanda and Andrew both being at school. I opened it to find a pair of Utopia pillows, which are fairly pricey on Amazon. In a previous conversation, Janet and I both lamented that neither of us could find a decent quality pillow. I was stunned at the gesture. But how would I explain these new pillows? An awkward position to be sure, so I quasi lied to Amanda. Not a total lie, but more along the lines of not saying who bought them, texting her, "Some new pillows arrived, I will give these a shot."

"You and the pillows," Amanda replied. She never asked much about them again. Crisis averted, thankfully. I could explain a Christmas present, but these arrived the first few days of February.

I sent Janet a pic of the pillows to confirm their arrival and thanked her for them.

"Hope you like them," she said. "One for you, and one for Amanda." I found this a peculiar sentiment. Amanda didn't have trouble with her pillow, so I never bothered having her take one of the Utopia pillows. Something about having Amanda sleep on a pillow sent by another woman felt ... wrong.

Isaac and Kate held a birthday party for their son Gabriel on the first Saturday in February. They were holding the party at the last remaining Chuck E. Cheese in Louisville, way out on Hurstbourne Parkway a half hour from our house. There used to be one near my old apartment on Preston Highway, but it closed years ago.

Amanda, Andrew, and I all attended. I hadn't seen Chad since before the pandemic and was shocked at how thin he had gotten. I ate one slice of pizza due to my diet. We were heading to Shogun for hibachi Japanese shortly after. Pizza and a hibachi grill on the same day were making my diet more difficult, though I dropped down to 209 by early February.

Isaac and Kate were mostly concerned with other kids in attendance, but Amanda managed to take a pic of Chad, Isaac, and me for posterity. Looking at the pic later, I was in the middle of the three weight wise, less than Isaac, but now considerably more than Chad. I set a goal to go lower than Chad's 175, at least down to the 170 I reached in 2008.

Chad and I had a few minutes to talk while his daughter Jacqueline played with the other kids. Harley did not come, though. I discussed my application with UC.

"We will see how this goes, but I applied for the Communications PhD program at the University of Cincinnati. I need to do something. Right now, this seems like an option."

"Good luck getting in, man. Harley and I discuss leaving Louisville for Cincy sometimes, since her mom and stepdad live there. Find a house in the right area and Cincy could work. Louisville has become a cesspool in recent years. Cincy, oddly enough, has gone in the opposite direction, from what I've seen. I'd probably move there myself if I could get a new job there."

"How's your job search going?" I asked.

"Applying on Indeed, same as you. Getting nowhere."

I didn't reveal one of my possible reasons for going, namely Janet. Even though Chad was one of my oldest friends, I couldn't confide those details. Surely a decision will be made in another month or so. I wanted to debut *The Lord and Lady Beef Show* and sign off by surprising Janet with the news I had been accepted to the University of Cincinnati for doctoral studies.

Amanda later joined the two of us and the topic shifted to Chad's incredible weight loss.

"How have you done all this?" Amanda asked.

"I eat lots of fruit, cut out carbs, fatty foods. Harley and I have taken time to reconnect since her hysterectomy, if you know what I mean. Fifteen minutes a day of sexual activity burns calories."

"Right now, that's somewhat of a problem with my fibroids," Amanda said. "This medicine I'm taking causes bleeding." I sat beside her, cringing at this discussion.

"Well, once you get those under control you should be good to go," Chad said.

Andrew soon cashed out his tickets for lame prizes and we headed out. We had plenty of time, so we headed over to the nearby Half Price Books. I wanted to check the place out, since I considered asking about doing a book signing there, but in the end the idea went nowhere. I figured no one would show. While there I took a few pics of some silly items. One joke pic featured several DVDs, such as the recent M. Night Shyamalan movie, *Old*. I sent this pic to Janet, continuing a running joke about us both not being as young as we used to be. Then I added a brief voice text riffing on the fun. song, except now I said "Toniiiggghh-htttt ... we are ... *old*!"

"LOL! You are killing me with this old thing," she replied. "Hilarious. We're young!"

I also took a picture of a Vince McMahon action figure. Why they had this I have no idea, but I couldn't resist. I sent this one to both Janet and Rochelle. Rochelle didn't react to the pic, having heard scant details of the Grant suit. Janet was tickled.

"Does his action figure come with poop on command features?"

"No, this toy was made well before the lawsuit news," I cracked. And no, I did not buy the Vince toy.

By early February, Janet and I also started engaging in a truly scandalous activity. We started playing online checkers late at night. She randomly asked if I wanted to play one night, and I found an online game site, then sent her the link. I never especially liked this site, since it forced you to take jumps when you didn't necessarily want to, since your own pieces would be taken in the next move. I was amazed at how awful Janet was at checkers. Perhaps due to playing late at night when she may well have been exhausted, but she would miss obvious and easy moves to take my pieces on a regular basis. During the times we played, she never came close to a single victory, to the point where I felt bad about playing. We typically signed in with our wacky nicknames, either Lord and Lady Beef or Herr and Frau Beef. One time her phone's autocorrect misnamed her "Fraud Beef," which became an instant inside joke. After losing yet again she messaged, "Maybe I *am* Fraud Beef!" The next day I sent her a joking voice message saying, "Frauddd Beeef" in dramatic fashion, and we both laughed.

We also tried chess once or twice, but neither of us understood much about how to play and quickly gave it up and returned to checkers. The only experience I had with chess was in Mr. Orwick's class during my senior year of high school. I sucked then, too.

Otherwise, some of our discussions were becoming questionable. Obviously, the Grant lawsuit talk required discussing the sordid sexual nature of the allegations against McMahon and Laurinaitis. But we veered off in some sleazier directions otherwise, such as an entire late-night discussion of *Fifty Shades of Grey*. Neither of us ever wanted to engage in the activities in the film, but more to take the piss out of it.

"The one device he used to spread her legs apart, then flip her over cracked me up," I said.

"How do people even maneuver into positions like that?" she reacted. "I know I'm not personally into that sort of thing."

Other curious discussions involved the various boob sizes of famous actresses. She might petition me to look up someone in particular in an incognito browser or discuss Jane Russell's boobs and how they may well have been a detriment to her career.

"I don't think the big breasts helped her in the long run," I said. "Once an actress is known for nothing but boobs, no one takes her seriously. A shame, since I found Jane Russell to be a solid enough actress."

"I've never had this trouble. My aunt jokes about me being flat-chested. She has big boobs, though."

"I hadn't noticed yours. Wait, that came out wrong. Lady Lack of Boobfat? I thought about calling you the Noblest of Boobfats. Too weird. Noblest of Beefs."

"Let's go with the beef one! Amanda has better boobs than me. Pretty lady."

In retrospect, I can see these occasional mentions of Amanda may well have been Janet trying to get my focus back on Amanda and away from her. At the time I acted too 'in the moment' to think about that. There was a definite sense of mixed signals going on here. One moment she might mention Amanda, then later mention something about meeting her at the Eiffel Tower replica at Kings Island during a discussion of *Sleepless in Seattle*. Or a chat about meeting up for lunch in Carrollton, which is a small town halfway between Louisville and Lexington primarily known for being the site of the worst bus crash in U.S. history back in May 1988.

"Have you ever filled out an NCAA tournament bracket?" I asked one day in early February.

"No, I have no idea. I think my grandpa used to, though."

"That's wild. I'll tell you what. Come March I will help you fill one out. You'll probably do better than me. I never heed my own advice."

"I have no idea what I'm doing, though. I would be blind guessing the winners."

"And I bet you'd still do better than me!"

I figured things were going well between the two of us. Sometimes Janet mentioned wanting to cook me a pasta dinner, or other frustrations such as an ill-tempered groundhog who terrorized her porch. I recommended a Cincy area animal control specialist I found online. Anything I could do to help.

While watching these various cheesy Euro miniseries, the topic of true love came up often, as depicted in these movies, and also in our conversations. One night I decided to bring the subject up, with some hesitation.

"Speaking of true love, do you think what we have is a form of true love? Could it be considered as such?"

"I don't know," she said. "My brain is fried this late at night. I might need to think about that when I'm more alert." She showed no anger at the question, nor did she dismiss the idea entirely. As a lark I typed "signs of true love" on Google and jotted down some of the results: Mutual respect and support, wanting to protect, discussing the future, ease of communication, making an effort, and others.

Given Janet's surprise pillow gift, I felt the need to up my game and get her something decent in return. I would send something nice in time for Valentine's Day. Given her love of soap, I figured some bars of soap from Buff City Soap would be a decent gift. I managed to go during a 4 for $24.00 sale and bought The Narcissist (Buff City's premier offering) as well as a lavender bar and a couple of others.

I also included a more detailed note than the first time. Besides hoping she would enjoy the soap, I mentioned we should meet in person for the first time after the bracket reveal in March. Carrollton would be an ideal location for such a meeting, ideally at one of the restaurants overlooking the Ohio River. There we could at long last discuss what we were going to do with the podcast over lunch, as well as fill out the NCAA tournament bracket. I suggested nothing inappropriate, no "Meet me at a sleazy motel and bring lube" talk. A "get to know you in person" deal. I held onto the package for a few days, waiting until closer to Valentine's Day to mail it.

In the meantime, I tried to introduce Janet to *Top Secret*, since she professed to like Val Kilmer in the past. She never mentioned if she ever watched all of the film. However, she did go out of her way to pay for *Priscilla* once the Coppola film became available on Amazon Prime. A few weeks earlier, Janet pondered going to Corbin, Kentucky for a Priscilla Presley town hall meeting to promote the film.

"Can your jalopy make the trip from Cincy to Corbin, anyway?"

"Oh, not remotely. I can't get away to go, but I do have questions for her. A shame."

She texted me while watching *Priscilla*, relating how crushing her disappointment was as the film progressed. I had a faint interest in the film but refused to pay money for it by any means. I would wait until the film hit HBO Max.

"This girl playing Priscilla is a complete nothing," she railed. "No personality. No chemistry with the guy playing Elvis. Speaking of him, this guy doesn't seem like Elvis. He doesn't capture what made Elvis special. This movie is a lot of boring downtime of her sitting around Graceland. Oh, now she's having Lisa Marie. This movie is rotten."

"So, you weren't thrilled?"

"Oh, I want my money back. Give me *Elvis and Me* any day over this mess."

"I'll have to watch *Elvis and Me* after I'm done with *1,001 Arabian Nights*."

"You look somewhat like Elvis, you handsome Lord Beef, you."

"Thanks for the compliment, but I have no idea what you mean. Elvis was much more of a greaser than me."

"LOL!"

"Question. Are you actually laughing this much? Or are you just typing 'LOL?'"

"Oh, I am usually laughing that much."

I sent the package a few days before Valentine's Day, and Janet received the soap bars in plenty of time. I noticed she had scaled back some of these conversations. I wasn't necessarily upset about not spending entire afternoons talking to her, since I figured she was busy with her grandma. I mostly hoped she would enjoy the soaps.

"Thank you for the wonderful soap," she said, upon delivery. "Such a thoughtful gift. I may not be able to talk as much though, since I have hurt my back. Bone spurs acting up, and I've been in pain."

"Sorry to hear about that. I should have sent some Ben Gay or Absorbine Junior instead. Rub on ailing beef."

"Thank you. More like ground chuck tonight."

In the back of my head I wondered if Janet did have this mysterious boyfriend, why was he not in town to do anything with her on Valentine's Day? I didn't touch the subject, but I found the notion curious that she talked to me so late that night.

The next day I sent another video wishing her a speedy recovery from the back ailment, as well as some helpful tips for her aches and pains. I also raised the question of what she thought of the letter I sent with the soaps. How about my meet up idea?

"Thank you, sound advice about my back. As far as the meeting goes, I may have to give you a rain check on that one. I can't get away, and even if I did, I would probably spend the time there a nervous wreck, worried sick about something going wrong back home."

"Okay, but I will still send the bracket in a few weeks, and we'll fill it out."

I felt her slipping away again, but didn't know why. Sure, she mentioned some cryptic comments about her back and may have been slightly miffed when I mentioned something about her back being pitiful. I noticed after Valentine's Day Janet talked to me less and less. What messages she did send were strange to say the least:

"I feel so far behind. I promised an older friend to review his WW2 book, but I've been sitting on it for months. He's getting frustrated with me."

"A friend of mine told me I needed some 'you do you' time. That's exactly what I need, some 'me' time."

"We've been lucky I've had some other relatives around of late so we can talk about movies and other things. But it's just movies."

"I may not be around as much, but you don't have to worry about me. I'm all right."

"I used to wake up early in the morning and drink coffee. I miss seeing the sunrise."

These statements felt like a roundabout way of phasing me down in her life, but sometimes I am incapable of taking a hint. Perhaps due to my own selfishness, but I felt if I could keep her talking to me and upbeat then I could keep her spirits up. I could keep her happy. I was running out of ideas to keep her engaged in conversation, however.

The Sunday before Presidents Day, I received only one text from Janet, with cryptic verbiage. I responded by going for broke. I had one card to play - the absurd true love list I found on Google.

"I find it curious you would downplay our talks as 'just movie talk.' To me, we also have had discussions of love, family, being there for each other, so many things."

I also threw in a mention of the Medicaid caregiver program, wondering if she had applied. Eric had little luck with the Kentucky version of the program. My mom didn't understand why he would apply in the first place, questioning in heartbreaking fashion, "Why would Eric be considered my caregiver? If anything, I'm his."

I followed this text with another, where I reeled off the list of true love signs. I shared the ones I felt might apply to the two of us. I mentioned mutual respect, quality communication, willingness to protect, all of these flowery sentiments. I figured saying these things might be a risk. If I had only known how much of a disaster sending that text would be.

CHAPTER 24

PRESIDENTS DAY

Monday was Presidents Day, not especially notable aside from Amanda having to spend all day at Rutherford for Gold Day, which consisted of a series of boring meetings with teachers and admins. As such, I had Andrew all day, since students were off. I'm not sure why Amanda made an orthodontist appointment for Andrew if she couldn't go as well, but I ended up taking him instead. The whole appointment meant nothing once the orthodontist mentioned braces would be over $6,000.00 unless we had the right dental insurance. I had zero interest, seeing as I have never had braces and don't find them necessary.

Andrew and I ventured over to my mom's house in the afternoon. Andrew and Eric spent the afternoon playing video games on the Nintendo Switch, while I sat bored out of my skull surfing the internet back in Eric's bedroom. Around 1:00 I decided to send the same true love checklist to Amanda, since she, too, sat around bored in meetings all day.

"Would you like me to send you some criteria for true love I found online?" I asked.

"I'm in someone's room right now. Give me a minute."

A few minutes later she responded. I sent the list of items one by one, and we discussed them like two grown adults, going over the things we needed to improve on. Mainly, Amanda was frustrated with my lack of mutual respect when due to constantly harping on her stump. Mind you, I never said anything *mean* about her handicap, but the constant goofing around saying "Stuuuummmmppp" all the time drove her crazy. Oddly enough, I think she appreciated my effort.

While Amanda and I were finishing this conversation before her next meeting, I noticed a long text from Janet pop up on my phone as well. I bid Amanda adieu and pulled up Janet's text. To say I was mortified by its contents would be understating the matter.

"Your text from last night distresses me greatly. I've had an awful night and morning, and this has added more stress, though my mom felt the brunt of grandma's wrath. Look, you contacted me originally as a fellow film buff and potential collaborator. That's all. I'm not cheap. How would my boyfriend react if he realized someone else was constantly coming after me? A married man, no less. When I told you about the argument, did you ask about what happened? No! You accused me of being bipolar. I was upset because he told me, 'You need to work on yourself.' Here you are pounding away at me with these texts day and night! I noticed when I talk about the things I'm going through with grandma, you go silent and don't respond. I never did anything to lead you on. True love is a screenwriter's invention. It's not real. I watched those movies due to sleep deprivation. I don't care if you watch them or not. Also, while I found the beef thing amusing due to the 'Where's the beef?' ads, I am *not* beef. I don't want to be beef, and I can see why Amanda doesn't like it. After today, texting is off limits. Email only. Texts are for my family members and boyfriend, but lately I've given yours top priority. You are a waste of my time, constantly talking to me about nothing, pulling me away from my duties. It's almost cruel. How am I supposed to collect caregiver money if you are bothering me all day? I feel like this complete loser who can't figure out anything in life. You've got your situation figured out. Now let me figure out mine!"

Nothing could have prepared me for this onslaught. She raised so many points in such quick fashion that I had no idea how to respond to them all. Shellshocked, I finally mustered up little more than, "Oh my God, I am so sorry." Like a broken record, I wasn't sure why I felt the need to apologize to her. If I owed anyone an apology for my questionable behavior, it would be Amanda.

"That's okay, you and I are still friends," she replied.

I told her I would still watch *Elvis and Me* and give her my thoughts on the movie, as well as hopefully try to make sense out of what had happened between the two of us. I wanted to explain my position better, but did note she was wrong in saying I didn't care about what she went through with her grandma. I figured my lack of affirming responses shows the drawbacks of texting. I listened with great intent to her tales of woe, but how does one convey that while texting? She agreed at first and I hoped the entire meltdown would simmer down. Eric and I headed to McDonald's to pick up dinner. As I ate dinner, my phone vibrated again with another long text from Janet. I quickly finished eating, trying not to appear rattled, then excused myself and headed to the bathroom. I shut the door and sat on the toilet to read this second rant.

"I've changed my mind. I don't want to think about what happened today ever again, nor do I want to talk about it at all. We're done talking about anything personal in nature, so I'll save you the trouble of writing an email. If you want, send me an email here and there with thoughts on films, but that's all. But to address this true love silliness ... let's say you were right. What would you do then? Leave your physically handicapped wife? How would Andrew look at you if you did something like that? Anyway, email me if you want, but otherwise we are done here."

By this point I was practically hyperventilating on the commode. These rants presented such a wild overreaction, I couldn't begin to process any of it. I sent back one final text saying something insipid like, "Well, I see you are having a bad day, and I've added to it. I will email you later." This was the last text message I sent Janet. She never responded and I adhered to her wishes and never texted her again.

Even though I couldn't possibly care less, I fulfilled my promise to watch *Elvis and Me*. I couldn't focus clearly, being distracted and highly upset. I spent two days on and off watching this two-part miniseries, and when finished I sent Janet an email discussing various thoughts on the film. I mentioned one lone allusion to the previous unpleasantry, a mention of "needing to rebuild trust between the two of us." In truth, she could always trust me. But after the emotional terrorism she unleashed on Presidents Day, how on earth could I ever trust her again?

I didn't know where Facebook messaging figured into our lines of communication, so I sent a trivial message saying nothing more than, "Hey, I watched *Elvis and Me* and sent you an email." No reply. Later that night I opened up Facebook Messenger to find a message on the Janet chat saying, "This person is no longer available on Messenger." I could no longer find her on the platform. She had either blocked me or deactivated her entire profile. I was in complete shock. I had said nothing controversial, merely a routine message. What in the world?

On Friday, Janet finally emailed, at this stage trying to perform damage control on this outburst. She apologized for upsetting me, but said she never came from a place other than friendship, which I wasn't remotely buying. Further, all the texting had become detrimental to her. "I was way too open. I'm a private person who doesn't like discussing my family's personal issues, which is a violation." Apparently, now I had been violating her by showing empathy and concern for her family situation, which she had mentioned in the first place. If I asked too few questions, she found me uncaring. If I asked for details, I pried too much. What a framework. As far as Facebook goes, she was now under doctor's orders to stay away from social media to avoid distractions. Odd, considering she rarely posted or interacted with anyone on the site.

She finished this baffling email by mentioning this mysterious boyfriend had given up his out-of-town job to return home and be of assistance. Also, she hoped I would work things out with Amanda, since she was hardly the answer to any of my problems. By now I had already come to realize as much. The ultimate irony of this entire email is after dictating "No more personal stuff," she spent an entire email discussing personal matters.

I tried to be civil in my reply, even though I fumed inside. She finally took some ownership of her role in this mess, but I brought up her own words such as, "We are soulmates" or "We should have gotten married years ago." Clearly those were more than friendly in nature. I might have deserved a portion of her rancor, but she took it too far. She offered no explanation for those statements other than "I acted childish."

I also, at long last, discussed this boyfriend, even though I knew nothing about him. I felt none of this was any of my business. Also, hearing the part in her text rant about "You need to work on yourself" upset me greatly. I've never told a woman something like that, not even Arianne when the situation cratered. I was glad to hear he finally stepped up, however, and ended with a laundry list of problems she had mentioned, everything from the groundhog to being as loving as I attempted to be. Frankly, I felt relieved to no longer text her, as if I had been doing something wrong. Maybe I was?

Janet wrote back one more long winded, rambling email, beginning ominously with "This email has been a long time coming." In it she expressed shock at the idea of me, a married man, becoming so emotionally interested in her. She never dreamed such a thing would happen. She thought she was safe talking to me, and now it will be difficult to ever trust me fully again. She mentioned some mumbo jumbo about how soulmates can be a variety of things, but no mention of the part about getting married years ago.

Much more disturbing, she excoriated me for sending one brief message to Ned Kuroda back in early November. She found this a breach of trust and said I should have tried harder to contact her before contacting him. (which I did - I sent multiple Facebook messages and an email). She was so upset, yet she did not have a problem at the time. On the contrary, she seemed touched at my concern and gave me her cell phone number. Now she feigned being retroactively pissed over a non-issue? Even more bizarre, she was mortified that I looked into her friends or people mentioned in her book. "Should I rape the contacts in your book or try to contact them one by one?" she pondered. I had no idea what she was talking about. I merely looked for possible guests for our podcast. I hadn't contacted anyone about anything. In truly cryptic fashion, she threatened to tell Vic about all of these horrible things I had apparently done to her. "Vic and I are relatively close, and he would be irate!"

She ranted like this for several paragraphs, also accusing me of bullying her into all of these texts, despite repeatedly trying to get away from me (!). I assumed this was her idea of some major "Gotcha!" style email, or a final kiss off, except I became so glossy eyed midway through that I could barely finish reading it. She mentioned something about a project she worked on with someone else that had gone to hell, and I was uncaring, since I never inquired. Again, I had no idea about this project in the first place. She even dissed the lone fart joke I told her some three months earlier (Hey, not all my material can be great.) She talked about "I guess it's true, men and women can't be friends," before feigning naivety over her role in this train wreck. These arguments were all over the place emotionally and conceptually. I felt as if I were back with the U of L debate team, having to listen to teams spread three dozen pieces of evidence in a nine-minute speech. There was no way to keep track.

Looking back, this hallucinatory email was a masterclass in gaslighting and emotional manipulation. It was designed to make me doubt myself, feel guilty, and ultimately accept blame, even though she clearly played a major part in how things escalated. Especially bewildering were her attempts at moral superiority, positioning herself as a paragon of virtue and ethical behavior, yet her actions contradicted this assertion every step of the way.

Further, I had no idea what to make of the boyfriend. Suddenly, he's back in the picture 100%, despite barely being mentioned at all, previously. She had never remotely defined him as a human being to me. I had no concept of him, none of the pictures she sent featured him whatsoever. She never even mentioned his *name*. So, why would I possibly care about him? He seemed like an irrelevant nothing, a blocking device. To me, he was the equivalent of "Mark" on *Star Trek: Voyager*, Captain Janeway's unseen and irrelevant fiancé back on Earth. A non- character invoked whenever Janeway became too close with any potential love interest on the show. That's who this guy became to me: " Mark."

By now I was sick of hearing this drivel. I had already apologized and started feeling weary of being told what a terrible, awful human being I had been. And yet ... she stopped short of a total kiss off. In truly baffling fashion, she ended the email on a relatively upbeat note, wishing we could still be friends, and wishing she could be friends with Amanda, as well. "Good luck with the diet." A perplexing final line, as I finished scratching my head.

I wrote back one more email. I still tried to salvage this situation, even though I felt any of my words were bound to be twisted against me, since lord knows enough of them had been already. I tried to allay her concerns about people such as Ned and Vic, noting they had been Facebook friends of mine for years, and I hadn't mentioned her to them beyond the lone message to Ned. Further, I certainly never attempted to bully her into texting. If she told me she was busy, or running errands, I would gladly let her go and talk later. If anything, she picked back up texting me after long intervals. I left her alone after the meltdown with the out-of-town boyfriend. I left her alone around Christmas when she mentioned being busy. I can't read the room if I'm not in the room though, so if she texted back, I assumed she was free to do so. I gladly would listen about any project she worked on.

I felt 85% of our communication had been ethical and terrific, but the other 15% is where the lines became blurred. Now we had much clearer and established boundaries so there shouldn't be a problem going forward. I wasn't going to say or do anything that could be deemed inappropriate.

"All I can do is try and be a better husband to Amanda and a better friend to you. We can argue about 'You said this and hurt me,' or 'This upset me,' and get nowhere. I want to look forward to hearing from you, not dread it. Let's work this out and move forward. I still love you as a friend, even after the past week. Shouldn't that say something?"

How did we get to this point? How did the situation escalate to vicious accusations of betrayals, of lost trust, and emotional abuse? I hadn't knowingly done any of these things, nor would I have wanted to. Someone I deeply cared about had spent the previous eight days unleashing emotional terror on me, and I had no way of being able to process the situation. This vitriol went beyond the pale of anything I had experienced. At various points we discussed the whole falling out I had with Arianne all those years before. Arianne was a foolish twenty-one-year-old, who deep down I knew wasn't worth a damn. I thought Janet was better than that. I really did.

I desperately needed someone to confide in. But who? Anyone here in town may well discuss these events with Amanda. I didn't want Chad or Isaac to hear about these embarrassing messages and emails. Few of my Facebook friends were close enough to discuss this level of emotional angst. I needed to think. Who could I rely on?

CHAPTER 25

ADVICE FOR THE CONFUSED

After analyzing the situation, I decided to confide in two people I felt I could trust. They needed to be out of town and also had to keep what I said to themselves. I may have texted Rochelle in recent years, but we hadn't had a serious phone conversation since my dad died in 2018. I gauged her interest in discussing the entire Janet debacle.

"Rochelle, can we talk? I don't mean text. An actual phone conversation. Something has been bothering me of late, and I need someone I can trust."

"Yes, in a day or two when I have time. Friday around 2:00 p.m. sound okay?"

"As long as we are done by the time Andrew's bus arrives, around 5:00 p.m. these days. I have screwed up and become emotionally compromised by someone."

"I won't judge. Believe me, I have skeletons in my closet, too." A strange statement, but I never pressed for details.

"Rochelle, what would you say to a man who said, 'You need to work on yourself?'"

"I would probably tell him to pound sand."

Rochelle and I discussed the entire situation about Janet on Friday. I was concerned about Rochelle calling me from work, but she seemed to have enough down time. She mostly listened as I described my interactions with Janet. I didn't sugarcoat anything, but I wouldn't say I vilified her, either. I told her my version of the truth, complete with multiple ghostings, confusing mixed signals, and the recent meltdown. Rochelle had the same reactions I did as the events were unfolding, such as asking "Wait, what boyfriend?" when I mentioned Janet's post-Thanksgiving behavior.

"I'm an RN and not a mental health expert, but yeah, there's some mental and emotional issues going on here," Rochelle said.

"I tried to be sensitive, gently asking about whether she'd ever been diagnosed as bipolar or anything else. I am not at ease discussing mental health, but I felt enough signs were there. One day she seemed ready to start a podcast, bring in famous guests, and conquer the world. The next she moped around and acted like her world was ending. She never threatened any self-harm, so I never panicked and called her local 9-1-1."

"I have to ask," Rochelle said. "What are you trying to accomplish with her? Because I think you need to ask yourself that question."

"I have no idea. She already blocked me on Facebook or deactivated her entire profile. But why deactivate? Hell, block me and move on. I didn't do anything to be blocked there. Who knows? A relationship can't work between two crazy people."

"What about you and Amanda?"

"I'm the crazy one. Amanda is eminently sane. The current dilemma is this, however. I still have this University of Cincinnati PhD application decision pending. These people take forever."

"Oh, you are finally going back for your PhD? How would that work? Would you move there? What about Amanda's teaching job?"

"I haven't formulated a coherent plan. As of now, I'm hoping they send me a letter of rejection, and I'll move on. I don't want the same situation as what happened with USF, when I felt as if I had to turn them down."

"I'm not sure whether or not to tell you good luck with the application or not," Rochelle chuckled.

The conversation veered into more pleasant matters, namely Rochelle's upcoming trip to Louisville in May. Her hospital was sending a delegation to a National Nursing Convention at the Galt House.

"So, when exactly will you be in town?" I asked. "Looking forward to seeing you again."

"My mom and I will be in Louisville from May 16-20. Bear in mind I will be at the convention either listening or presenting for most of those days, but we'll get together. I've been working on my poster today, as a matter of fact."

"I'm trying to figure out how to go about this with Amanda. She vaguely knows who you are, and I would definitely bring her along. Otherwise, I would be saying, 'Why yes, I am going to meet up with another woman. See you later.'"

"To be sure, bring Amanda with you."

"I started worrying about your mom recently. She posted a Facebook rant while waiting for a tow truck, something about twenty years of broken dreams in Sumter County. She seemed upset, so I sent her a message asking if she was okay. We wound up having a decent chat."

"Oh, God. I saw the message as well. She's a force of nature, to be sure."

"She went into several details I never knew, such as the circumstances surrounding your grandfather's divorce from wife number two, and how she deep-sixed the ranch's government cattle contract. I had no idea."

"That's why my mom has to breed horses. We lost most of the cattle due to the divorce and the aftermath."

"Well, I hope you enjoy the Galt House more than Amanda and I did. We stayed there back in 2016 for our anniversary for one night before heading to Indy for a Colts game. Not impressed. Our main bedroom area didn't have a garbage can. They do have a massive breakfast buffet, but it's costly."

"Where is the hotel, exactly?"

"You will be right by the Ohio River downtown. Should have a view of southern Indiana. Next door is the KFC Yum Center, home of the national disgrace known as the University of Louisville Cardinals. Well, the men anyway. The women aren't awful."

"I've seen how bad they've gotten. I feel for you."

"4-28! This year we will be 8-24! We are so shockingly terrible. Kenny Payne should have never been hired in the first place. His hiring was the uniquely disastrous blend of an Affirmative Action-DEI hire mixed with alumni cronyism. I wanted to give him a chance, but he has to be gone."

"I swear, down in Florida we don't follow college basketball to the same degree. I never filled out a bracket before you had me fill one out."

"Well, you'll get to see firsthand the lunacy. But given all that's happened I'm not sure Louisville is as basketball crazy as it used to be. I should think the NCAA is at fault for deliberately destroying the number one market for the entire sport."

What started as a sullen conversation about my angst over Janet turned into so many other topics, typical of my talks with Rochelle back in the day. I enjoyed talking to her now as an equal adult, though she was always mature in demeanor, and capable of having serious discussions. We chatted most of the afternoon until Andrew's bus arrived. I eagerly awaited our reunion in May.

The other confidant, an older woman named Anastasia, I found uniquely positioned to hear this perplexing tale. I first met Anastasia circa 2008-09, the dying days of my Cabbageboy Movies website, when she became one of my steady W & W customers. She also moderated an online dating website. As such, she was used to hearing about this exact brand of nonsense.

I talked to Anastasia a few days later. Anastasia is quite the character, always saucy and funny to talk to, albeit at times borderline inappropriate. Though I have never been entirely sure of her age, I would say she is likely in Jessie's demographic.

"So ... are you ready to hear this tale?" I asked.

"Of course, Baby Bri-Bri. Lay it on me." Yes, she has called me that for years.

I proceeded to tell Anastasia the entire story up until Thanksgiving. She might throw an aside here and there, before finally having a full-blown point.

"So far, I'm not sure what is awful on your part. Right now, I've heard nothing but empathy and caring."

Once I mentioned the part about Janet showing this guy all of our text conversations, Anastasia cringed.

"Ewww, *not* cool. But here's what I can't understand. If she wants you to quit hassling her, why does she keep dragging you back in by sending texts and emails?"

"After all this she had the nerve to say she never tried to lead me on. She said she would insert a catheter into my penis in my old age!"

"Awww, a strange but sweet gesture."

"Saying things like that, or we are soulmates who should have gotten married years ago. This goes beyond leading someone on. Now I'm led! I'm yours! She had me at 'I recorded *Silly Billies* at 3:00 a.m. on TNT! God, I feel like such an idiot. I've never encountered anyone like her in my life. I'm still unsure of exactly why she is mad at me, and believe me, she has ranted and raved of late. But I can't make sense of her tirades."

"Bri-Bri, I have seen people like this countless times in moderating online disputes. This is typical narcissistic behavior of wanting to be adored and contacted but then feigned outrage when someone takes the bait. For people like that you can always expect a slow drip, drip, drip of information."

"She took over two months to even mention this boyfriend, then she's mostly mentioned how jealous he gets, he would go ballistic ..."

"If he exists ..."

"I have to admit the thought occurred to me. Ever since first hearing about 'Mark,' I knew nothing relevant about him. Never saw a picture. She makes no mention of him on her Facebook profile or at least hadn't before she removed it."

"I am looking her up now. Is this her? This girl with black hair? Blue sky with clouds as the background?"

"Sounds familiar," I replied. "But I see nothing on my end."

"Honey, I think you've been blocked. Anyway, I don't think this guy exists. No pictures of them together, no name, the signs are there."

"I can't say one way or the other. How demented is this situation where we could have this as a serious talking point? Amanda's existence is hardly a mystery, if you look me up on Facebook. Neither is Andrew's. But the line about 'You need to work on yourself' amazed me. A statement like that is man speak for, 'Okay, look. I don't want to be in this relationship anymore, but in the absence of a better alternative I reserve the right to show up whenever I want and bang this chick, but not fully commit to anything until I feel she has completed these undefined goals

I've set.' Anyway, I would rather you be right about this and he doesn't exist. The alternative is the idea of her sharing sensitive personal conversations with this mystery man, and I have a hard time dealing with that."

"Oh, it's ridiculous. As far as taking care of a relative, listen. Millions of people are caregivers for elderly family members. She's hardly unique. Den and I had to take care of his dad for years. I have a pinched nerve in my back now due to this (Den is Anastasia's longtime boyfriend/fiancé).

"I wonder about why and how he saw my texts. I wonder if she showed them to him to make him jealous, to get him to play ball and move back home. I can't say for sure. What do you think about the pillows? She later said they were for both Amanda and me."

"Laughable. Look, she bought those for *you*. To think anything else is silly."

"Bottom line this for me," I said. "What, if anything, can I do about this?"

"As of now? Nothing much. She's probably blocked your texts too, so I wouldn't bother. I'll keep an eye on her on Facebook though. I would imagine in a few weeks she will reach out to Linda or someone in the W & W group. I will let you know. There's something else I want to ask you, however."

"Yeah? What's that?"

"Den and I talked about this when you married Princess Amanda. 'Is our son being trapped?' We wondered." Anastasia considering me like a son to her stunned me. I didn't think we had such a close relationship.

"Well ... of course I was trapped," I said, wearily. "I hinted as much in the email to Janet. I told her to read my book but read between the lines. But yes, if Amanda hadn't gotten pregnant with Andrew I likely would have gone to Tampa for doctoral studies. I've been at a dead end and looking for a way out. I thought Janet could provide that. I was wrong. Now I feel more lost than ever."

"Incidentally, mentioning Andrew in her rant? Such a low blow, as though she could know how he would feel."

"Andrew would watch his usual gamer idiots on YouTube regardless of whether I was around or not. Keep in mind I have no plan to split with Amanda. If I get into UC, we'll figure something out. I'd rather not go now, but there's always a chance of acceptance. Anyway, I need to put this episode to rest and move forward. If you want to bother following Janet's Facebook actions, I can't stop you."

"So, what else for the time being?"

"I may still send her the NCAA tournament bracket the day after it is announced. I promised her I would. Beyond that, I have no ideas."

"Why bother? If she wanted to fill one out, she could find it online and print one out herself."

"I know. But I promised. I wish none of this had happened. Before this mess at least I could say I was a decent husband in terms of this sort of thing. Now I can't say that."

"Look, you never met her. Nothing physical happened."

"Why did Janet fly off the handle to such a degree? Maybe I said the wrong thing with the true love talk, but why not be an adult about it? 'I don't feel like true love applies to the two of us. You are married and I'm not comfortable with such a topic, so let's not go in that direction again, okay?' How hard would that have been? Instead of ranting and raving at me for a week on and off?"

"You'll be okay, Bri-Bri. You'll be okay. One last thing. Beware of any attempt by her to reach out to Amanda. Who knows what she's liable to say?"

"Yeah, I'm wary of her wanting to be friends with Amanda. I'm sure Amanda would be *thrilled* to hear her story. By the way, about this 'son' business. My mom is still here. I might be in the market for a wild and crazy aunt, though."

"Talk to you later then, nephew."

In the following weeks, Anastasia gave me minor updates on Janet. I became frustrated as to why she felt the need to tell me that Janet was back in the W & W group, or why Anastasia posted a question about the Dorothy Lee book under an alias. These antics weren't helping matters, nor were they helping me either reconnect with Janet or move on, so I told her to stop.

I sent Janet an email with the tournament bracket as promised. When the email went unanswered, I resigned myself to her being out of my life for good. I felt confused about how the situation crashed and burned. I wouldn't say I felt depressed, but I was deeply hurt inside and didn't know how to deal with this level of emotional wreckage. I had been rejected in the past, but trifles such as being denied someone's phone number, or being told I had an acne scarred face paled in comparison to this experience. Someone I cared deeply about had emotionally destroyed me, left me for dead on the side of a road, then ran me over two more times to make sure I wouldn't move again. Imagine finding someone of such unique similarities you can finish each other's sentences, someone so similar as to be that one special person in the universe. Then imagine being viciously rejected by that person, baselessly being called cruel, a violator, a bully, and a waste of time. I could try and argue the merits of those first three, but if I'm a waste of time then what else needs to be said?

To be sure, I had plenty of alone time during March, April, and May to brood while Amanda and Andrew were at school. I thought about Janet with seething anger some days, usually while riding my five miles over at the clubhouse. I typically exercised alone there, and while pedaling I could become lost in thought. *What in our conversations was real?* I thought to myself. I wasn't sure anymore. Other days I felt an aching sadness. One I found difficult to mask. I toyed with the idea of filming another Zoom video and posting it to YouTube in a private setting. I thought of ranting and raving for minutes on end, giving Janet a piece of my mind. Giving her one of my dad's "Who Shot John" style eviscerations. In the end, I decided against it. I had already made her mad enough trying to be sweet and loving, so what would a verbal filleting do to her? Going scorched earth seemed ill advised.

Another question I couldn't answer kept gnawing at me: *What if she was right?* Her criticisms echoed several of Amanda's in recent years. However, there is a significant difference. Amanda has earned the right to sound off on me in such personal fashion. She's my wife and has been in the trenches with me for years. Janet hasn't earned that right. We didn't have those years of basic emotional safety, the type of safety where no matter how bad the argument may be you know you can always go to sleep and in the morning, everything will be back to normal.

The University of Cincinnati rejection letter finally arrived in late April, which is incredibly late, even by the molasses standards of college admissions. The semester was nearly over, and I didn't have time to accept an offer if one came. In this case, the rejection brought relief. The wind left my sails, as far as PhD work was concerned. Given the way events unfolded, I never told Janet about my UC application.

One day I pondered something upsetting while analyzing what went wrong in this case. Am I incapable of change? Here I am a middle-aged man still chasing a PhD. I'm still obsessed with wrestling when most of my friends have moved on. Still obsessed with college basketball. Good grief, I messaged a chick I met online in retro 2000 era nonsense complete with AOL emails. If anything, I'm getting worse. At least back in 2000 I took scant interest in the few emails we exchanged. Midlife crisis? There was little doubt.

Having watched my mom wreck her own health caring for my dad for fourteen years, I know firsthand there was no positive outcome to be found for her. No pot of gold at the end of the rainbow, merely a wheelchair of her own a year after placing my dad in the nursing home. I feel haunted by my experiences talking to Janet, possibly because I sensed the toll caregiving has taken on her, both mentally and physically. By the time my mom was Janet's age, she had been married for twenty-four years, had two foolish sons, a disabled stroke victim of a husband, and on disability for multiple sclerosis. The difference is my mom never complained about her fate, never melted down on those rare people who cared, and knew how to handle her business. My mom is worth twenty Janets.

One comment stood out to me in all of Janet's ranting, the part about not finding any answers to my problems with her. That's probably true. The prospect of being around two elderly people in constant need of care, with one in particular crying out every five minutes in pain, hardly sounds enticing. But when someone feels serious unhappiness, even irrational change might sound appealing. Better? Hardly. But at least that scenario might be a different type of unhappiness I've been searching for, one which my dad never found.

Another comment of hers has stayed with me for months. I recall one message where she said, "I have to be vigilant at all times, otherwise something bad may happen to one of them." The statement crystallized for me the ultimately nihilistic and futile nature of what she's doing.

She's fighting basic nature. There is no positive endgame to her situation. She can be as dedicated to her grandparents as much as possible, but the end result will be the same. What is this absolution she seeks? Is caregiving a way to shield herself from making real changes in her own life? I'll never know.

The Lord and Lady Beef Show was canceled before it ever got off the ground. Would the podcast have been a success? Probably not. We might have garnered a few hundred fans across multiple platforms, but that didn't concern me. I mostly wanted an excuse to spend time chatting about movies with Janet, even though I had the creeping suspicion she wasn't much of a film buff. Both of us had dealt with failures in the past. The clock was ticking to accomplish something before we were both AARP members. She already started taking "old lady vitamins" for women over fifty.

A middle-aged feeling of failure was another reason I found Janet a kindred spirit. Ours is a generation who never had its moment in the sun. Within that generation exists a subset of people who felt life's problems would eventually go by the wayside, and then we would be unstoppable. If only we weren't burdened by family drama, or the petty minutiae of daily life, preventing us from achieving greatness. Then we could find that pot of gold at the end of the rainbow. But as time passes, we both realized the pot of gold is fleeting, if it exists at all. I have seen a few rainbows in my time. Most vanish within a few minutes.

PART FOUR

REUNIONS AND FAREWELLS

CHAPTER 26

REUNION IN MAY

MAY 18, 2024

"Where are you now?"

"I am riding through somewhere called Butchertown, which sounds kinda freaky."

"So, you aren't far. Amanda and I are waiting outside Impellizzeri's. We will see you soon."

I had a sense of hope seeing Rochelle again, but such a meeting had to occur at a down moment during the convention. Originally, I thought of having dinner at the Old Spaghetti Factory downtown near the Galt House and the KFC Yum Center but then remembered we would have to pay to park at a garage, and didn't want to be on the clock and rush through the meal. Instead, we decided to meet up at the Highlands location of local pizza chain Impellizzeri's, since the location is closer to the Galt House than sending her clear out to Brownsboro Road in an Uber.

"Okay, this Uber driver dropped me off down the road at Enterprise," she said. "Where am I?"

"You are close. We are right outside the restaurant."

"Ah, now I see you! I'll be right there."

Rochelle approached Amanda and me in a dark gray nurse's outfit, having not had time to change before meeting us. She immediately walked up and gave me a hug. Rochelle, now thirty-four, was a little heavier from having two kids, but otherwise looked the same as in 2008.

"Long time, no see, stranger," I said. "Let's go on in."

The Highlands location was ultra busy on Saturday, with plenty going on to draw a crowd. The PGA Championship took place at Valhalla that weekend, notable for the absurd arrest of #1 player Scottie Scheffler dominating the local news. In addition to the golf tournament, The Preakness was set to take place that evening. I knew the latter would interest Rochelle. After a wait we were finally seated.

"So, how did your presentation go today?" I asked.

"The poster part went okay, but few took notice of my PowerPoint presentation."

"What do you think of Louisville?" Amanda asked.

"It's been pretty great so far. Last night the group of us walked down to Fourth Street Live and ate dinner, hung out for a while."

"I would advise you to stay around the downtown entertainment district," I said. "Don't venture too far west of downtown, and I wouldn't head anywhere directly south of the hospitals downtown, either."

"Yeah, we stayed around the Galt House and Fourth Street. Also, I ventured out to Churchill Downs yesterday. I saw my first horse race there."

"I had nothing much happening. I would have been glad to meet up with you all. Believe it or not, I've never seen a race at Churchill Downs. Been to the Derby Museum a dozen times, though. Derby was two weeks ago, but there's no way you would have gotten a room at the Galt House then."

The waiter took our order after a decent amount of time. We ordered what we usually eat at Impellizzeri's, namely a twelve-inch pepperoni and beef pizza, with a double side of their epic breadsticks. I also asked if they could turn on The Preakness, since all the TVs were showing the golf tourney, but the race was about to start. He flipped a few of them over.

"I can't tell you that moving here would be a good idea," I said.

"This city is not what it used to be. The pandemic, all the unrest after the Breonna Taylor shooting, JCPS is also completely dysfunctional as a district."

"We have my son in a charter school in Orlando."

Amanda jumped on this. As a longtime public-school teacher, she was certainly no fan of charter schools.

"There's enough of a union here to where there's no place for charter schools," Amanda noted. "We don't want them."

"Technically, not true," I said. "They are now legal in Kentucky, but there's no particular place to put one here in Jefferson County. A failing school could be converted into one, but by and large charter schools aren't a thing here."

"So, what are you doing nowadays, Brian?" Rochelle asked. "Still subbing?"

"I haven't been doing much of anything lately," I replied. "Since the pandemic I've had to take Andrew to school and pick him up, which took subbing off the table. I've been applying for stuff with no particular success."

"How about your mom and Eric?"

"My mom is about the same. You do know she's mostly wheelchair bound now, right?"

Rochelle nodded.

"Eric is a complete bum who does *nothing*," Amanda said coldly. "He takes care of nothing, he does nothing, and the house is falling apart."

"Where do you live?" Rochelle asked.

"You may have heard of Waverly Hills Sanitarium. I used the creepy picture of the place in my CD gatefold."

"You live by *that* place?"

"Within walking distance," I said. "I can't get the same shot now, though. Houses have been built since then."

Rochelle didn't know how to react to all of this, so we sat in awkward silence until the breadsticks arrived. Rochelle took a bite.

"This is seriously the best breadstick I've ever had in my life."

"We think the breadsticks are better than the pizza," Amanda quipped.

Rochelle ordered a local 502 beer, noting she liked to try the local brews in different cities. She also raised her shirt sleeve to show us an arm tattoo of her now late horse Sonny, who had died mere months earlier.

"I know you always loved that horse," I said. I wondered if Rochelle noted my slight disapproval. As surprising as this may sound, I'm a square. I eschew all tattoos and piercings and am generally not a fan. Wild hair styles, too. I figure I would rather be weird than look weird. Regardless, Rochelle's sentiment towards Sonny was touching.

The pizza arrived right as the race started. We each grabbed a piece while watching the TV. Rochelle rooted for Derby winner Mystik Dan, because otherwise what's the point of the Belmont?

"Come on, Mystik Dan!" she said.

Alas, a Triple Crown was not to be. Underdog Seize the Grey pulled the upset, finishing 2 ½ lengths ahead of Mystik Dan.

"Ah well, maybe next year," I said. "Before Derby this year I found the 1973 Kentucky Derby on YouTube. As many times as I've seen the Greatest Race mini movie at the Derby Museum, I'd never watched the 1973 race."

"What did you think?"

"Awesome race. I knew Secretariat won and set the track record, then won the Triple Crown. But the Derby was a close race. Sham came very close to winning. I believe Sham also set a track record, except Secretariat was that much better."

"Greatest horse ever," Rochelle said. "On a different note, what do you think of the political situation in this election year?"

"Oh, God" I cringed. "I'm trying not to think about it. Not sure Biden will last until November at this rate. Did I ever tell you I have considered running for office?"

"No, that's a new one on me," Rochelle said.

"Something unopposed where I don't have to spend a bunch of money or engage in mudslinging. I saw the local Justice of the Peace position had no one running in 2022, but then it was too late to get on the ballot."

"You want to perform marriages then?" Rochelle asked.

"Hey, if I have to. By the way, where is your mom?" I asked.

"Oh, she couldn't come after all. The hospital only paid for the nurses, so my mom needed to buy her own ticket and hotel room, which she refused to do. I don't follow my mom on Facebook anymore. She's been so weird in recent years. Been on the ranch too long now. I wish she would sell the place and move on, but she won't let it go. I think she might have ADHD."

"That's strange, I never had a problem talking to her in normal fashion. I wouldn't find her any different than talking to me in normal conversation."

"No, I can have a basic conversation with you. Her? Not anymore."

"Do you think you want to visit here again?" Amanda asked.

"You bet," Rochelle said. "My mom and I will be sure to come back here at some point. I promised her."

Soon after, we finished eating and left Impellizzeri's. We walked back to Amanda's car, a 2010 Hyundai we took instead of my newer Kia Forte, since I didn't want to risk the Kia being stolen while parked on the street. Thankfully, we arrived after the meter was cut off.

"Why don't we take her on a tour of Bardstown Road to the Watterson Expressway and back downtown?" I asked Amanda.

Bardstown Road has changed over the years. I still love driving through the Highlands, but so many of the old indie record stores have either closed or moved elsewhere for cheaper rent. The old Ear-X-Tacy building is now a Mexican restaurant. Still, it's a glorious area for a newbie, and Rochelle seemed impressed.

"You have a cool little city here, Brian," she said.

"Possibly, but I also heard Bon Jovi's 'You Give Love a Bad Name' while we were waiting outside Impellizzeri's. Who in the world would be playing Bon Jovi in the Highlands? What's this world coming to?"

Rochelle chuckled. Even though she had scant familiarity with the area, she could tell the Highlands was a hipster/indie/punk/alt rock scene. We hit the Watterson Expressway and headed back to I-65. At 7:00 on a Saturday evening the roads weren't busy, so we had a stress-free ride. I made sure to point out U of L's campus and Manual High School from the interstate, if Rochelle hadn't seen those places already.

As we neared the Galt House, we drove past a local restaurant/bar called The Boiler House. Under her breath, Rochelle muttered, "Boiler

Room Brawl," in reference to the infamous *Summerslam 1996* bout between Mankind and The Undertaker. I couldn't help but crack a sly smile as if to say, "Atta girl."

We dropped Rochelle off outside the Galt House. I regret not taking a picture for posterity, though I don't think Rochelle wanted many people to know she was meeting me. Maybe that's why she didn't invite me to Churchill Downs the prior day, or to hang out on Fourth Street. I even inquired about meeting up for lunch at the El Nopal across the bridge from the Galt House before she left town on Monday, but she declined. I couldn't decide if she was too busy with the other nurses, or after all these years she didn't entirely trust me, or maybe didn't trust herself. Rochelle remains an enigma to this day. The circumstances and players may have changed, but there will always be a sense of tension when we meet. I'm resigned to it.

As Amanda and I drove into my mom's neighborhood to pick up Andrew before heading home, Amanda seemed slightly perplexed as to the nature of my relationship with Rochelle over the years.

"So, what is the deal between you and her?" Amanda asked. "Did you want her to be your girlfriend or something?"

I paused before answering. The previous two decades flashed through my mind in the seconds after Amanda asked this obvious question. I mapped out an elaborate answer but realized it would only invite further queries. I opted for the simplest answer possible.

"No."

CHAPTER 27

DÉJÀ VU ALL OVER AGAIN

Thirty-three years. That's how long it's been since my grandfather's death. Every August 5 I always think about him, even though I'm fairly certain I'm the only one left who does. My mom never committed the date to memory. She has long since moved on. Eric, not quite two years old at the time, has no recollection of Willard Aubrey Logsdon at all. Each August 5, I think back on him coming to my little league games, or how I used to throw couch pillows at him while he read the newspaper, and his response was always a laugh. I still place a newspaper on the table to read it because I don't want Andrew doing the same to me. I think back to the weekends spent out on the boat at Nolin Lake, or taking batting practice in the impractical woods adjacent to the lake house. That's where he died, you know, at the lake house. He had a heart attack in the night and never woke up. My grandma kept going down to the lake after his death, often sitting alone on the porch. She sold the house in 1994.

Yes, thirty-three years. There was so much he never got to see, from my team finally winning the league title at Beechmont in 1992 to the usual major events, such as high school and college graduation. I'm grateful I never had to see him decline in health the way I did with Mamaw, or both my parents. But what I wouldn't give to have had him around and healthy for another decade. I've often wondered if one of my main problems in life has been the lack of a quality mentor. My dad barely lived day to day himself and had no answers to give. I never became close enough to my professors at U of L to consider any of them a mentor. Mr. Orwick in high school? He was so burnt out and loony even then that I wouldn't consider him a mentor or role model. No, the man who should have been my mentor was taken from me before I turned twelve, and I've never been the same since.

Imagine my surprise, on this day of all days, when I checked my email to find a message from Janet, the first time she had written in over five months. I was flabbergasted. I couldn't help but be mystified by the title alone: *Apologies for a very late reply.* Late reply? Seriously? She trampled all over my tongue with muddy feet in the last week of February, blocked me on Facebook, and never replied to my follow-up emails. I assumed she had blocked my email address, too.

"I hope you are doing well. I apologize for not responding due to a long series of negative events, which I would rather not get into." Why mention this then? She continued. "I don't want you to hate me, but I took you on as a new friend at a time when I should have kept to myself. My correspondence has gone to pot, but I'm still here if you want to communicate."

She thanked me for the soaps, and once again wished me well on the diet. I could have ridiculed this absurdly timed email, but in reality, I was happy to hear from her. I hadn't been able to move on from the unfortunate way things went awry in late February. I found no closure, no catharsis, just a downbeat ending to what had been a magical relationship at its peak. I immediately wrote back.

"I have to admit I'm surprised to hear from you. Yes, I am now down to 164 lbs. but still have some stubborn belly fat which won't go away. Amanda had this uterine embolization procedure back in June to relieve her fibroid problem, in which the doctor released particles of sand into her uterine wall to block the blood supply to the fibroids. School is also set to begin, but Andrew no longer has a bus to Farnsley Middle due to the district cutting back on busing to magnet programs after the logistical nightmare of the past year. We are going to carpool with some other people. This was so much easier when I could drive him to Stonestreet, which was five minutes away. Anyway, I'm glad to hear from you. I think you are mistaken about wanting to keep to yourself when you are stressed. That's the time when you need someone to talk to. I'm hardly perfect, but I'm here and will listen to anything you have to say."

I immediately messaged Anastasia with this shocking news. "Guess who emailed me after five months?" I asked.

"Oh ... my ... God. Please tell me you didn't write back. Or at least make her wait a few days before you do."

"Sure," I wrote back. I return emails and calls promptly. I respond to texts as soon as I can.

"Honey, by immediately writing back she has you back on the hook. I wish that girl would take care of her grandparents and leave you alone."

"We'll see where this goes. I agree with you. I feel apprehensive about this. I will keep you updated on future developments."

In subsequent emails she expressed sympathy for Amanda's fibroid condition and wished her a speedy recovery, as well as once again thanking me for the soaps back in February. She asked about how I enjoyed the pillows, to which I mentioned they were still fairly solid, but I still have yet to find a perfect pillow for my head. I considered tossing the pillows in the trash back in March at my angriest but didn't. Why throw out perfectly good pillows?

I had been talking to Vic on Facebook, hoping to be a guest on his Abbott and Costello podcast. Janet seemed intrigued at this news, figuring I would be a solid guest with quality insight into A & C's films. She even kept alive the idea of one day doing the podcast with me. By this point I wasn't seriously considering a podcast with her, so I ignored her statement. On my upcoming birthday, Janet vowed not to forget me and promised me a gift, which I found curious, since she swore off sending or receiving any more gifts back in February.

"I wasn't sure whether I could lose all this weight again the way I did in 2008. I am older now, and my metabolism may not be what it used to be. I considered one of those weight loss betting sites, but who knows if

I could win the bets? Maybe I should regain all the weight and re-lose it again so I can make some money?"

"You are always funny!" she replied. "But no, don't risk your health for the challenge. I'm having health problems, as well. I know, I know. Old. Sciatica isn't for babies. My knee is down to the cartilage, as well."

Janet had a keen interest in Eric, or at least his behavior. I think she viewed him as a fellow caregiver and traumatized soul. "Don't give up on him, he can become something yet. Bear in mind he had to deal with your dad's stroke at age seven, so he might have something inside him hurting so badly he can't articulate it."

I attached a recent pic in one of these emails to illustrate my weight loss. She responded, "Wow, you look great!" I enjoyed the compliment but was more measured by now listening to her praise.

During one of these emails, I also remarked on the coincidence of her coming back into my life on the anniversary of my grandfather's death. Janet's Southern Ohio associate's degree graduation took place the same day as Mamaw's death, or the funeral.

She said, "Who knows? Perhaps there is some significance to these dates."

These emails were infrequent, but at least we were more or less back on the same page. I realized she finally had me where she wanted, namely someone she could email when the time suited her, while I had no choice but to adhere to those terms if I wanted to keep in touch.

I spent the week before my birthday sharing various pics from our family vacation to Niagara Falls and Cleveland from back in June. "I'd be glad to see these vacation pics you have," she said. "Might cheer me up." I sent several pics, explaining the trip over multiple emails.

A strange trip to be sure, which produced mixed emotions. We traveled through Cincinnati on a Sunday morning, and once we passed Kings Island in Mason, Ohio, I couldn't help but notice the Eiffel Tower replica and think back to the conversation I had with Janet, the one where she wanted to meet me there and recreate *Sleepless in Seattle* (which recreated *An Affair to Remember*, itself a remake of *Love Affair*). As we passed Waynesville, I noticed the sign for the Renaissance Festival which Janet had mentioned in a previous conversation. Even on vacation I couldn't escape thinking of her.

Janet informed me I should expect a present from Amazon on either my birthday or the day after. This time I proved no dummy, and I had nothing to hide, so I told Amanda I was expecting another gift.

"Another gift in the mail? Who is it from?"

"Janet Billingham."

"Who?"

"You know her, she wrote the Dorothy Lee book. I told her my birthday, and she is sending a gift to be nice."

"Oh, okay. Whatever."

Anastasia seemed antsy about this, as well as my plan to send Janet a gift for her own birthday a month later.

"See, now she has you wanting to send gifts again. Didn't she say no more gifts?"

"Who knows with her? Anyway, this is merely reciprocating birthday gifts. I missed her birthday last year. We started talking a couple of days after her birthday."

A few hours before my birthday, Janet sent me a "Happy Birthday" email. Its contents were worth remembering. "Happy Birthday in a few hours! Remember, you are *not* old! I like to say I'm old, but I mean we're old enough to get over ourselves and not take things too seriously. We're in a place mentally of being middle-aged, lost in the middle of being young and old, our minds reflecting back upon our younger years. I've been through those emotions already, and I'm over it."

The package arrived the day after my birthday. A red movie themed blanket, with reels and a popcorn bucket. A cuddly blanket to be sure, though not ideal for a bed. More useful for a couch on a cold winter night. Thus, now I had a pillow to sleep on that she provided, as well as a blanket on the couch.

In subsequent emails, Janet mentioned various ailments, which started to rival Amanda's. Bone spurs in back, also a bum knee in need of possible surgery, requiring a brace a few months earlier.

"I'm worried about you," I replied. "With all these injuries, you are starting to sound like the Revolutionary War soldier in the Spirit of '76 deal."

"LOL, you pictured me well enough. I'm about like one of those patched up war veterans in those paintings. Sciatica, walking with a limp for months, but at least the brace is off now, and I put ice on it an hour a day. We have this almost ESP type connection."

Janet being Janet vanished again for the next ten days or so in the week surrounding Labor Day. By this point I resigned myself to the fact that this was what she does. I still expressed empathy for her various ailments and wanted to piece together a decent birthday package for her.

Once she wrote back in early September, she mentioned more about this mystery boyfriend's family. "My boyfriend's sister, 'Jill,' is going to get me a Half Magic makeup kit like Priscilla wore." Perplexing. She deliberately mentioned what the sister was going to get her for her birthday, but not the boyfriend himself. Curiously, she immediately named "Jill," yet still hadn't bothered to name the boyfriend. Anastasia's words about the slow drip of info in situations like these came to mind.

Where was this going? As September progressed, I struggled to find topics of conversation. I discussed a mini Bette Davis festival I showed Amanda, starting with *Whatever Happened to Baby Jane* and ending with *Jezebel*. Or my recent trip to the doctor, alongside discussion of my various blood levels and Cologuard stool results (negative for colon cancer). I railed against Lipton for discontinuing the powdered tea mix, and asked Janet to keep an eye out if she saw any at the store. I shared the riveting story of Isaac helping me install a new Delta toilet when the old Mansfield went belly up. Okay, he mostly installed while I acted in an executive capacity. Several times I found myself staring at the computer screen trying to figure out what to write.

I had a decent idea of what I wanted to include in this birthday box. I figured soaps had been a winner, so I bought four Dr. Bronner soaps at Meijer, ranging from peppermint to almond. Since Janet had mentioned needing to drop a few pounds herself, having slacked on her own diet, I grabbed the last bottle of Green Tea Fat Burner off the shelf as well.

On my way out of the store, I ran into Isaac and Kate. I hadn't seen them in a few months. Kate was now pregnant with their second son. I was bewildered when Isaac told me the news when they were over for Andrew's birthday.

"Hey, guys. When's the due date?"

"November," Kate said. "Right around Thanksgiving, if all goes as planned."

"We need to get together at some point," I said. "I know Chad has been talking about doing something."

"You mean the dad diaper party I'm not supposed to know about?" Isaac cracked.

"Well, yeah. I'm waiting for him to give me the heads up."

Once I returned home, I couldn't help but feel these soaps were inadequate, that other gifts were needed to fill out the box. Since I always look for reasons to be rid of Sonic Screamer CDs, I tossed one in as a gag gift. I also included a copy of *So This Is Africa*, since I wanted to include the DVD for Christmas but never got a straight answer.

In my never-ending quest to do the most foolish option possible, I decided to write another in-depth letter, which I included in the package. I began this letter with a silly gag: "Give me an O! Give me an L! Give me a D! What's that spell?" Given our various age-related riffing, I didn't consider this a big deal. Then I had second thoughts. I fretted over sending the fat burner. What if she took offense to the implication of needing to lose weight? There were portions of the letter I felt were too dark and downbeat for a birthday letter, where I brooded in self-reflection on what happened between us back in February and the need for emotional safety.

Even though the package was ready to mail, I ripped it open and removed the offending letter, then wrote a second letter without those paragraphs. I left in the concluding paragraph, however. In it I once again brought up the W & W article for *Classic Images*, asking if she wanted to have a Zoom meeting to discuss it. This too shouldn't have been a big deal, but in reality, proved a huge mistake. I mailed the package, informing Janet of the tracking info. I mentioned rewriting the letter since I truly did not want to upset her. Believe me, the last thing I wanted to do was upset her again. I was overthinking at this point.

"Please don't feel uneasy about sharing your feelings with me," she said. "I promise I won't freak out again. I was in shock then, but I've come to terms with our friendship. I'm sincere in saying we'll be friends for life, if you wish. I want to hear your feelings and thoughts about me. Sometimes I wonder why you like me? I'm an ordinary gal from southwest Ohio living a regular but difficult existence. I'm not famous, beautiful, or have the greatest personality. I'm just me."

Such heartbreaking words. She didn't seem to understand why someone would have loving feelings for her. Also, near the end of the email, she tossed in a curious postscript about my attempts to convince Vic to be a guest on his podcast. "Good luck with Vic. Be careful. He's not always what he seems." What on earth did she mean? Neither Vic nor I had a diabolical plan requiring the utmost secrecy. Either the man wanted me on his podcast, or he didn't. I wasn't *that* concerned.

Janet occasionally mentioned other colleagues who wanted to work with her, or read their latest book, but how she never had time. I merely asked about this, inquiring about how she managed her time, and the response genuinely left me unnerved.

"I have a busy life and it's not all about caregiving. We've talked a lot, but I didn't tell you everything about myself. Technically, other than our similarities you don't really know me. If I formed an opinion based on the bits I know of you, that would be called judgment, so don't judge what you don't know. My boyfriend and I had some friction and he's the mega jealous type, but we're better now. I have a ton of family members and his family who are there for me, so don't worry. I'm not telling you what to do. You'd resent it. Leave out opinions of my caregiving if you want to tell me I'm wrong about anything. I don't need to get upset. If you think something will upset me, why would you want to do that? Don't worry about the letter. I wouldn't want my boyfriend to find it. As if we're more than friends. He'd go ballistic."

By now, I felt uncomfortable talking to her. She had become outright hostile. I hadn't mentioned her caregiving or passed judgment on her in these recent emails or in the letter I sent with the package, so I have no idea what she meant. Further, hearing about her "broad shouldered and strong boyfriend," how "jealous" he could be ... well, now I felt physically unsafe as *well* as emotionally unsafe. What did she mean by those statements? Was he physically violent towards her? A chance he might come after me over a birthday present? I hadn't signed up for this. Later that night she finally sent me a picture of this guy. I was creeped out. He wore a dark pinstriped suit with purple trim, a Satan style goatee, and stared at the camera in borderline psychotic fashion.

This guy gave me the creeps. He could have been one of Gavin Rossdale's minions in *Constantine*. She also finally named this fellow "Ryan." A shame, I was used to "Mark" by this point. Funny, I recall Janet saying she didn't care for facial hair. I sent Anastasia this picture for her comments.

"My God, is he auditioning for a horror movie? Are you sure this is him? This could be any random guy she is talking to online. Has she sent any pictures of the two of them together, out and about?"

"Nah, I'm 'lucky' to get this one. We are way past the point where I want to hear about this guy, though."

I debated writing another letter, a longer form one discussing the various aspects not mentioned in the birthday letter. I discussed where things stood between us, how I wanted to be there for her, but also the need for feeling safe. She took a wrecking ball to any feelings of emotional safety I had back in February and as September progressed, I felt ill at ease yet again. I concluded this six-page declaration by noting, "Whatever happens from here on, you have to own it. I was out of your life for months and made no attempts to contact you. You wanted me to be a part of your life again, and I'm still here. I'm still here."

Her birthday arrived on the 18th. She sent a brief email thanking me for the soaps and expressed interest in listening to my CD. "You're a musician, too? Interesting." Odd since I shared the YouTube clips of my album soon after we first started talking, yet she seemed to have no idea about *Sonic Screamer's* existence.

In what had become an ominous pattern, Janet vanished once again after receiving a gift from me. She ghosted me for two weeks after I sent the Christmas present. The entire Presidents Day meltdown occurred after I sent the soaps in February. Now she vanished for another nine days. When she returned, I realized how fed up I had become with this entire arrangement.

"I wanted to address the article you whipped up out of the blue on W & W. I wasn't in my element when I first scanned it. This is not something I wish to participate in, nor do I agree with the contents. I don't want to mess with my W & W/Dorothy Lee connection any longer. I'm finished and don't share your story or experiences."

She cherry picked certain Gen X vs. Baby Boomers lines from the opening paragraph as parts that offended her, which could easily be edited. The rest consisted of my reflections on becoming a fan. Overall, a routine and inoffensive piece.

"No hard feelings, but yours is an article I'd never do. I wrote my story and I'm done. Besides, second billing? Not appropriate, sorry. LOL!"

I was nearly at the end of my rope. She had yo-yoed me for months about this trivial article, first agreeing, then not agreeing, then agreeing again. Now she dismissed the quality of the entire piece, badmouthing the content. I doubt she even read much beyond the first paragraph. And even if she had been interested, she wanted top billing. In *my* article. To my way of thinking, if someone wants top billing, they need to bring something to the table. What did she bring to the table? Nothing, as far as I could tell.

"Are you mad at me again?" I wrote back. "I mainly think you have a fascinating story about Dorothy you could tell." Amanda and I were busy packing to head to Pigeon Forge for fall break early the next week. I wanted this lingering issue resolved before I left.

"No, but I never consented to be part of this so take my name off it. You should tell your own story. Mine is too personal. Someday when I'm ready, if ever. Enjoy your trip though. No, I'm not mad. I've had a few people in my professional life try to sway my opinions, so that's where this stems from."

I wrote one final email discussing a few minor tweaks I wanted to make before sending the piece off to *Classic Images*. At the end of the email, I figured I would lighten the mood with a silly joke, so I sent a Wikipedia link to the recent film *My Old Ass*, which features Aubrey Plaza as a near 40-year-old woman who encounters her eighteen-year-old self during a mushroom trip.

We spent Sunday afternoon at a luncheon hosted by some people from Amanda's Sunday school class. Once we were back home for a few minutes, I decided to check my email before heading out to eat dinner. I found a shocking email from Janet with the title "NO MORE PLEASE!" I immediately opened it.

"I'm writing one last time, but I'm upset and I'm serious. I thought your humor had softened, but now you are downright insulting to me as a lady. I dare you to talk to Vic, a male, this way. He'd rip you a new one. You seem to enjoy prying and upsetting me. Please do not contact me again. Vic told me to block you, but I didn't listen. I re-trusted you. My guy is here, and he's upset and ready to contact you. I thought we could still be friends but now feel brought down and hassled.

"P.S. A friend told me all you wanted to do was use me and my past. Going through Ned and the contacts in our book is unforgivable. Shows your character. Still can't get over it. PLEASE DO NOT RESPOND OR CONTACT ME!"

I barely had time to process this last email, since we went to eat immediately thereafter, then left for Pigeon Forge a couple of days later. I feel as if she looked for a reason to crush me emotionally once again, and the minor *My Old Ass* thing was her excuse for going off on me, this time for good. I wasn't as upset as I thought I might be. By this point there didn't seem to be much left between the two of us. I noticed as much when she went to the lengths of distancing herself from the W & W connection.

I didn't respond to the email. I figured she blocked me now, but what good would responding to these bizarre allegations have done? She had previously laughed at the silly "old" bits, so feigning outrage over this one seemed wildly over the top. Even if she was tired of these gags, a simple, "Can you lay off the old stuff?" would have sufficed.

In terms of using her "for her past," what exactly does that mean? My main intent with the W & W article was to help her get another credit to her name, and hopefully she would feel better about writing again. Somehow, I now schemed to get rich off Janet Billingham's past with Dorothy Lee? And the last part? This again? The only time I contacted Ned was a one-line message on Facebook asking him if he had heard from Janet lately. I hardly asked the man about her deepest, darkest secrets, nor did I contact anyone mentioned in the acknowledgments page of their book. If she wanted to be angry at me for being a dick, that's her prerogative. But at least be mad at things I actually did, instead of inventing offenses I never committed.

As far as "Ryan" goes, I have zero desire to hear from him. I wonder if such a conversation would go the way Janet thinks it would. I may never have verbally eviscerated her, because I cared for her too much, but I have no similar reservations about him. Or maybe not. Instead, we could have a serious conversation, and I would ask him why he gave up his out-of-town job for Janet, especially if he read all those text conversations we had.

I don't feel like watching W & W movies anytime soon. I still love those boys and their films, but there's too much heartache now, not to mention too much toxicity within the W & W fanbase, small as it may be. I'll need some time. Am I mad at Vic? Nah. I have no idea what nonsense she told him. In his place I would have told her the same thing, just block him and move on. I noticed he and Janet are no longer friends on Facebook, yet he's still friends with me. Take that for what it's worth. I submitted the W & W article to *Classic Images* after returning from Pigeon Forge. It was eventually published in June 2025.

Anastasia, for her part, tried to comfort me, after I informed her of what happened. "Honey, be glad she's out of your life and this is over." Rochelle also chimed in. "She didn't seem worth the hassle. No one who is a 'soulmate' would ever speak to the other person that way."

In the end, I found relief. I had become a bundle of nerves, living in fear of the exact outburst which inevitably occurred. I always found the whole "Only email me at this address" line of communication offensive. My friends are perfectly welcome to call or text me whenever they like. Such a setup wasn't sustainable. I have plenty of regrets in my dealings with Janet but caring and trying to help aren't among them. The six-page letter? I never had a chance to send it. Rochelle is the only person I entrusted with reading it. This experience has been difficult. I may never get over it. When someone shows you who they are, who they *really* are, the revelation can be shocking. Any harm I may have caused her was accidental. Can she say the same? Perhaps we never were as similar as I thought. She was right—I never knew the real her, only an idealized version she presented. Fraud Beef, indeed.

CHAPTER 28

THE TRIALS AND TRIBULATIONS
OF ISAAC LONG

NOVEMBER 15, 2024

I hadn't heard anything from Chad about the shindig he had planned for Isaac. Kate's due date fast approached around Thanksgiving. I started to wonder if we were going to meet up for this dad diaper party at all. Chad's original plan involved renting the clubhouse next to us, but since the cost is usually $100.00 for the day, Chad balked. I figured we could all meet up at my house to save the money, since we were expecting roughly six people. I thought of texting or calling Chad that afternoon, but before I could do so, Isaac's number popped up on my cell phone. *Is he calling about the get together?* I thought.

"My dad died."

"Wait ... what?" I said, completely stunned.

"He'd been under the weather the past few days, but hardly anything he thought serious. He had a heart attack, and now he's gone."

"Hey man, whatever you need," I said. "I'm in disbelief. I haven't seen your dad in years, so I hadn't heard of him being in declining health. When I saw your number on my phone, I figured you were calling about this party we're supposed to have."

"We'll still do something. But I'm having a hard time right now. In another two weeks he could have lived to meet his new grandson. Now he won't."

"That's rough. Let me talk to Chad and see what's going on, okay?"

I knew Isaac's mom, Bonnie, was in poor health, but I didn't know about Pat. Even though Isaac insisted I saw Bonnie at one of Gabriel's recent birthday parties I couldn't recall seeing her in such a dissipated state. All I knew were his descriptions of how sad her condition had become. Doctors weren't sure precisely what ailed her, but rather she stayed in a chair all day and didn't want to move, eat, or go to the bathroom. For all intents and purposes, she decided to stop living. Since she couldn't care for herself anymore. Isaac and Kate were set to have a second child in the home, so Isaac made the difficult decision to place Bonnie in a nursing home.

I never discussed this situation with Isaac, beyond relating to him my mom had to wave the white flag and put my dad in a nursing home back in 2010. "This doesn't make you a bad person." Isaac's dilemma consisted of losing Bonnie's social security, which helped pay some of the household bills. Isaac found a friend of his in need of a room, so this guy was moving in soon.

I finally talked to Chad late Sunday night. We discussed what we were going to do for Isaac in the wake of his father's death.

"The whole party idea never came together," Chad admitted. "I'll tell you what. Why don't we meet up at Isaac's house tomorrow and hang out for a while? Get some lunch. I need about thirty minutes to get there."

"Let me know the time. I thought about Isaac and Kate's wedding the other day. So hilarious."

"Oh, I'll never forget that day. I couldn't believe how late Kate was for her own wedding. I had to run off a group of Black people from the gazebo area, except I think they were at the right place, and we should have been further down by the lake!"

"I don't remember any of this at all," I said, laughing.

"Isaac also accused me of losing the ring, but I had it all along."

"See, I don't remember that either. But those were your experiences instead of mine. Everyone has their own truth, I suppose. I still think about Jeremy Stigler from time to time and he died over a year ago.

Heart attack at our age? I hadn't seen his dad in thirty years, so seeing him so grief stricken at the visitation has burned into my memory."

"Jeremy was definitely a frenemy of mine back at daycare, no doubt," he said. "But I hadn't talked to him in years." An odd choice of words, but I didn't feel like discussing the topic further. We ended the conversation soon after.

I trekked over to Isaac's house slightly after noon on Monday. As I arrived, I noticed Chad's SUV already parked in the driveway, so I did my best to park on the side of the road, which is tricky, since his house is right by the entrance to the neighborhood off Johnsontown Road, and cars are prevalent. I brought a couple of gifts that Amanda purchased for the baby, a bath rinse cup and a tummy time play mat. I also brought two copies of *Salvaged From the Flood* for Isaac and Chad, since neither had read the book.

"Did you at least autograph my copy?" Chad joked.

"Nah. Would it be worth more if I did?"

"You could write, 'Thanks for giving me all this material over the years.' Haha!"

As we entered, I was reminded of the chaotic mess in Isaac's house. I hadn't been inside there since they first moved in back in 2022, when Isaac and Kate were living downstairs in the basement. Kate runs a dog rescue service, so they typically had large Dobermans upstairs, which terrified me, given my lifelong fear of dogs. One immediately jumped at me.

"Down!" Kate yelled from the living room. "Sorry about that." Well, they were living upstairs now, I gathered. We exchanged greetings, and I handed over the baby gifts and the book.

"So, what do you all want to do about lunch?" Chad asked.

"Well, Gabriel's bus arrives around 2:00, given the Pre-K schedule he's on. Wherever we go needs to be around here."

"When in doubt, there's always El Nopal. There's one nearby on Dixie."

This seemed agreeable, even though I didn't want a huge lunch. I was still on my diet, after all, and ate my usual lame lunch of pickles, cheese, and baked Ruffles before I arrived. Kate and Isaac took off in their car, while I rode with Chad.

Once we arrived at El Nopal, Chad ordered an entire burrito lunch, while Isaac and Kate ordered their own split meal. I ordered one taco and a glass of tea. We had the same indifferent waiter I usually have when we have family meals on Sundays there.

"This waiter isn't exactly quick with our drinks," Chad said.

"That's probably because of me. We eat here all the time on weekends, and Andrew often buries this same server. Not quietly either. He's not wrong, given how slow he is, and the way he wanders off and never checks back, but I'm not sure Andrew is doing us any favors today."

"Excuse me, I need to use the restroom," Kate said. Isaac moved and let her out.

"I saw your Facebook post about the election," Chad noted. "Aren't you happy now to see your boy back in the White House?"

"If you saw the post, you know I don't want to discuss politics these days. The people who voted for Trump again now have to own their votes."

"Hey, I think he's a complete jackass, too," Chad, the usually reliable conservative, said. "But once he institutes these tariffs, all this crazy inflation should go down."

"That isn't how a tariff works," Isaac chimed in. "Tariffs are a tax paid by the consumers themselves for imported goods."

"All tariffs will do is cause inflation to increase," I said. "Frankly, the inflation over the past few years is not legit inflation. It's more like price gouging, since businesses lost out on so much money during the pandemic. Now they are screwing us all."

"I thought you didn't want to talk about politics?" Isaac asked.

"I didn't."

"Anyway, I probably won't be over for *Survivor Series* after Thanksgiving. Given Callum is due a couple of days earlier, I think Kate would divorce me."

"I figured as much. You all have Peacock anyway, so you can watch the show at home. I have never cared for WWE doing Wargames matches at *Survivor Series* though. Wargames is an NWA/WCW concept. This is not *Survivor Series*. Teams of five strive to survive, and all that."

"I'm not a huge fan of most Wargames matches," Isaac said. "Especially not the WWE version. Too long and drawn out."

"Why did they stop doing actual survivor matches?" Chad asked. "I haven't watched wrestling in forever."

"Triple H is an old NWA fanboy. Besides, the original survivor concept stopped drawing years ago. A shame, since the original 1987 event is an old favorite of mine."

"Oh yeah!" Chad exclaimed. "Hogan got counted out, Bigelow had to face Andre, King Kong Bundy, and One Man Gang, three on one."

"Yeah, he took out Gang and Bundy, but had nothing left for Andre," I said. "That's awesome booking. Bigelow got over huge, even in a loss, since he nearly did the impossible. Andre claimed victory and laid claim to number one contender to Hogan coming out of the pay per view.

"Why didn't Bigelow do much in his 1987-88 run?" Isaac asked.

"Must have pissed off Andre or something" I joked. Kate returned from the restroom and the food arrived. Nothing like talking some old school wrestling to reunite a group of friends at odds over political differences.

Gabriel's bus arrived after we returned to the house. In the meantime, we toured the grounds, including the back yard and supply room adjacent to the house. Once we headed back inside, I pulled Isaac aside.

"When is your dad's funeral?" I asked.

"There isn't one right now," he answered. "Dad donated his body to U of L's medical school initially, because he didn't want a fancy funeral. This morning, I found out they didn't want his body after all. They said he had been deceased too long and his body too decomposed, so he was of no use to them."

"What a blow to the ego that would be," I slyly answered. "I can see him in the afterlife now saying, 'What, my body isn't perfect enough for med school students?'"

"I know, it's lame. We may still do an informal service here at the house in January once the holidays are over and things calm down. With Callum due soon, I haven't had a chance to process the grief yet."

"You ready to go to a high school graduation when you are sixty-three years old?"

"There are worse fates," he answered.

I nearly left, but stopped in the living room once more, where Kate had resumed relaxing in the chair.

"Pat was living back in New York," she said. "Once Gabriel was born, I insisted he move back here. 'Do you want to spend time with your grandson or not? If so, then come back.'"

"You know, Kate," I said. "Something struck me."

"What's that?" she asked.

"You heard about Amanda's recent hospital stay with pneumonia, right? So wretched. Had to stay all night in the ER over at Southwest before being transferred to St. Mary's and Elizabeth. The doctor was afraid of her going septic."

"Oh, yes, that's awful. Is she okay now?"

"Yeah, she's mostly recovered. It put a few things in perspective. Of everyone in this house, I'm the only one who has never been in the hospital as a patient. Obviously, you've had Gabriel, and soon Callum. Isaac has had his epileptic fits. Chad had the aneurysm scare back in 2007. Gabriel has had his health scares at a young age. If we include Amanda, she's had Andrew. Gall bladder removed. Appendix removed. Now this bout of pneumonia. Other than an x-ray, I've never had anything done at a hospital, never stayed at one overnight as a patient. Nothing."

"Isn't that a good thing?" she asked.

"I suppose so, but what does it *mean*? Sometimes Amanda says, 'Someday you will have something bad happen, and you will understand what it's like.' But I don't *want* to know what it's like. Since I was a teenager, I've been around my dad in a wheelchair, my mom and her health problems, or Amanda's various surgeries. I've *had* to stay healthy. No choice. Other than the screwy Lasik."

"Knock on wood," she said.

I found a nearby table and did a minor knock for good luck. Afterwards, I bid the group adieu and headed home.

Twelve days later baby Callum was born, weighing 8 lbs. and twenty-one inches long. Isaac related a slight scare, as Callum's blood sugar stayed too low, so a doctor admitted him to the neonatal intensive care unit for a brief stay. He went home in time for Thanksgiving weekend. Kate posted on Facebook the next day, "Callum and I are doing okay, but I'm really sore!"

I heard sparingly from Isaac during the holidays. He was too busy with various family responsibilities, same as me. A Christmas greeting here, a "How's the family doing?" there. In late January I finally found time to give him another call.

"How's your mom?" I asked.

"Not good," he said. "She caught COVID almost immediately upon entering the nursing home and barely recovered. We are faced with a decision between lifesaving versus comfort care."

"What's the difference?"

"Well, lifesaving is basically to keep her alive in ways deemed necessary. Comfort care is mainly to keep her comfortable until the end."

"Until the end?"

"It's a step away from hospice, from what I gather."

"That's rough. I suck at this sort of discussion, but what if comfort care is all she can expect at this stage? What use is keeping someone alive, if they have no quality of life?"

"Yeah, I'm bracing for the worst."

"How's Callum doing?" I asked, changing the subject slightly.

"He has been doing pretty decently, but we are concerned that he's not putting on any weight. If he doesn't, we may have to take him to the hospital and see if anything is wrong."

"Surely, he'll be okay. Keep me posted, though."

"Will do."

By early February Bonnie was back in the hospital, due to a nasty combination of a urinary tract infection and a colon infection. Also, Callum hadn't gained enough weight, so he, too, wound up in the hospital, so Isaac found himself going back and forth between hospital rooms at St. Mary's and Elizabeth Hospital. From what I gathered, Callum's situation puzzled doctors, but it was nothing they considered life threatening. Bonnie's condition, however, could be, if sepsis set in.

A few days later, Isaac and I chatted again. I found him remarkably calm about this entire ordeal, but deep down I understood. I've experienced this exact feeling before with my dad after his stroke, where the situation is so stressful as to become mind numbing. The feeling goes beyond pain, to the point where you feel oddly calm and resigned to the situation.

"Any updates on your mom?"

"She's off the feeding tube, at least. Seems better, but we don't know if she's absorbing enough nutrients."

"Hey, you need a break."

"I do. I still haven't cleaned out my dad's house. Might sell it."

"If the house isn't too obsolete, maybe contact a flipper? Eric and I may have to whenever my mom dies. Not sure there would be any point spending a bunch of money on what's left of the house."

"His house is outdated but hardly condemned. As far as Callum goes, they are running some tests, but who knows? Hopefully reflux, and not anything heart related."

After this conversation I sensed some slight relief in Isaac. Bonnie probably didn't have another ten years left, but losing both parents in the span of three months would be enough to wreck anyone. I never entirely understood the situation with his parents, even as a kid. They never lived together. Isaac's dad lived at the house near U of L, while Bonnie lived not far from me in Lynnview. Yet they weren't divorced. I've never asked, and Isaac has never discussed it.

Two days later, Isaac called me again.

"Mom's gone."

Dammit. Even though I hadn't been particularly close to Bonnie, this one hit me hard, as well. I had to collect myself for a few seconds.

"What ... what happened?" I asked. "I thought she was getting better?"

"She didn't get enough nutrients. Sepsis set in due to the colon infection, with an illusion of improvement for a day or so."

"I don't even know what to say. If there's anything you need, let me know."

"Kate can give me a ride home. But I will keep you posted on visitation and funeral details."

I barely remember the rest of the call. I remember texting Amanda afterwards, informing her of Bonnie's death. Amanda never met Bonnie, but she agreed we should stop by for the visitation. Over the weekend, Kate posted the details on her Facebook page. The visitation would be at Owen Funeral Home on February twelfth, with the funeral the next day at noon.

Given Andrew's ADHD meds would be worn off by 6 p.m., I didn't know if we should take him to the funeral home for the visitation. My mom agreed to watch him for the time we were gone, but as we ate at Mark's Feed Store before heading to the funeral home, Amanda expressed her doubts.

"That's too much backtracking and driving to take him to your mom's, then head to Owen, then back to your mom's to pick him up. Keep in mind I haven't been home since 7:45 a.m. Andrew can deal with the half hour we'll be there."

"All right. I'll call my mom and tell her he's coming with us after all."

I had spent entirely too much time at the Owen Funeral Home in recent years. *Any* time spent at a funeral home is too much time, unless you are the mortician. As we pulled into the parking lot, we noticed Isaac wandering to the car of another friend of his, a man wearing a kilt. I worried that Andrew would ask us to leave repeatedly, or potentially act a fool, but thankfully, he was on his best behavior. He mostly wandered around the chapel, keeping to himself while Amanda and I chatted with Kate. There were scattered people roaming in and out of the room, paying respects to Bonnie in the coffin, or talking to each other while we stayed near the exit.

"If you are wondering where Isaac is, he and a friend went out to the car for a quick shot of whiskey," Kate said.

"Yeah, we saw him outside," I answered.

"Gabriel and Callum are staying with my family while we're here tonight, as well as tomorrow afternoon during the funeral." Soon after, Isaac entered the chapel.

"Hey, man, how are you holding up?" I asked.

"I'll let you all talk," Kate said, leaving the room. "I have to look in on the food we brought."

"I haven't had a chance to process any of this yet. Eventually the grief will hit me, though, and I'm worried about when it does."

"It happens to everyone," I replied. "You were at my dad's funeral. It happened to me then. I broke down. Get the grief out of your system, but don't dwell too much."

The man's previous few months rivaled my own 1996 for death and life altering events. From November to February, he lost both of his parents and now had an infant at home. That year I lost my paternal grandparents, and my dad had a paralyzing stroke. We can debate who had the crappier year, but at least the baby gives Isaac one positive mark on the ledger.

The kilt wearing friend popped back in and conversed with Isaac, followed by another man who mostly talked about how antisocial he and Isaac both were. I didn't know any of these people. The thought occurred to me that regardless of how long I knew Isaac, did I actually *know* him? These people paid their respects and left, while I struggled to think of a decent Bonnie story to tell. One finally came to mind.

"Want to hear my favorite memory of your mom?" I asked.

"Sure, what is it?"

"This will sound silly, but your mom illustrated for me what having the infamous 'wrong kind of heat' is in wrestling. Remember when Chad and I came over for the Over the Edge 1998 Pay Per View? Austin versus Dude Love main event?"

"Yeah, I think you won five dollars betting on Kane to beat Vader."

"That's the show. Anyway, during the whole Sable and Marc Mero segment where she needed to find someone to champion her in a match against Mero, your mom left the room. This was during the whole domestic abuse storyline between Marc Mero and Sable. Bonnie said, 'I can't stomach watching *that* man!' and walked. That moment crystallized for me the idea of a wrestler having the wrong kind of heat. Mero didn't make her want to see him get beaten up, she left the room not wanting to see him at all!"

"I remember now," Isaac said, chuckling.

"Has Chad been here yet?" I asked.

"I think he and Harley were delayed by all the traffic in this misty weather. But he said they would be here."

"I have to work tomorrow, but are you coming back for the funeral?" Amanda pondered.

"Yes," I replied. "Noon, right?"

"Noon. We'll see you there."

"I'll be there for the ceremony, but remember I have to pick up Andrew tomorrow for this carpool, so I can't travel all the way for the interment at Evergreen on Preston."

"That's fine."

We stopped by the dining area, where Kate prepared the food for whoever wanted to stop by. I reiterated my participation at the funeral to her, then we left. Later, Chad sent me a text saying, "Sorry we missed you, but the traffic was rough in this weather. We were two ships passing in the night."

I dragged a dress shirt and pants out of mothballs for the funeral. Even wore a tie, which I am typically loath to do. Wiped off a pair of dress shoes, dusty from lack of use. The weather was still cold, but at least the misty rain and fog from the previous day had stopped. My jacket would do, instead of a full-blown dress coat.

I felt odd being at the funeral. While the visitation consisted of various friends of Isaac's and Bonnie's, the funeral was mainly for her close family members. I had never met any of these people and felt somewhat out of place. I found the end chair, took off my coat, and sat there trying not to be noticed. Isaac's uncle asked him about me.

"This is Brian. I've known him since U of L daycare when we were about two."

"I'm not sure it's been *that* long," I said, slightly laughing. "I have no recollection of being at the U of L daycare so far back. My first memories of the place were going to kindergarten there."

"I've known Chad since age two. Either way, we've known each other for decades."

"Glad to have you here," an aunt said, as I walked back over to my seat on the far left.

"Why don't you come sit with us?" Kate asked.

I shrugged and moved my coat over to the empty chair near Isaac and Kate, then had a seat. Bonnie's minister presided over the ceremony. He started with a few memories of Bonnie and then a biblical verse, I forget which. He intrigued me by discussing a song Bonnie wanted played at her funeral.

"She wanted you all to hear this," the minister said. "I feel as though it reflects her good-natured humor."

Sheb Wooley's "Purple People Eater" played over the sound system. The entire audience let out a laugh at this marvelous trolling Bonnie pulled off from the afterlife. After the song ended, the minister gave us a couple of minutes before he continued the ceremony. He discussed how Bonnie was a kind and thoughtful person, quoted some other scripture, then we paid our respects to Bonnie before departing. Isaac and Kate made the trip to Preston Highway for the interment.

On my way out of Owen, I passed by the caged parrot by the entrance. Isaac's aunt and a younger female cousin with a nose ring stopped me on my way to the car.

"You are welcome to come to our get together after the funeral," the aunt said. "The house is five minutes from here."

"Oh, such a get-together should be for close family," I said. "I didn't know Bonnie well." Various others asked, but I wasn't comfortable attending.

"Thank you for coming," the younger woman said. "Let me give you a hug." We embraced slightly, as I eyed my car, ready to leave. After the hug, I drove home.

That afternoon I put Bonnie's death in perspective, as I sat alone in the bedroom. I realized it's a matter of time before my own mother ends up on display at Owen Funeral Home, her arrangements having been made around the time my dad died in 2018. Such a morbid thought, planning one's own funeral.

I wondered what will become of Eric after she dies. He doesn't have a life outside of tending to Mom. No job skills, no social skills. Sometimes I wonder if tending to Mom was why he was put on this earth. Eric is a gentle soul and undoubtedly has some deep-seeded trauma from living with ailing parents much of his life. I have bemoaned this situation in the past. Eric never does. Amanda views Eric as an unkempt caveman, a future homeless bum. Believe me, I understand, to some extent, but she's never walked a mile in his shoes, nor does she fully understand the lifetime of pain he's endured without complaint. Honestly, he's a better man than I'll ever be.

"Two ships passing in the night." Chad's words described so many connections in my life over the years, in particular my old friend Jeremy Stigler, whose recent death was on my mind that night. I've spent too much time at Owen Funeral Home in recent years. Amanda's grandmother. My dad. Bonnie. And yes, Jeremy, who died in August 2023. I took time on my birthday to stop by his visitation at Owen. One of the great mysteries of my life is why Jeremy and I drifted apart after our last summer at U of L daycare. There was no argument, no blow-up. I called him one day in late 1992, we talked for five minutes, and he said, "Okay, I gotta go," and that was it. I never called him again. He never called me. We both went to high school at Butler but were in different graduating classes and never interacted much. I talked to him a few times on campus at U of L, usually about wrestling or movies, but we never made plans to hang out.

I ran into Jeremy in July 2022 at Tire Discounters, of all places, having not seen him in over twenty years. We reminisced about our base-ball playing days and exchanged email addresses. His son started kinder-garten at Stonestreet a month later and I routinely saw Jeremy in the car rider line or at open house. Always friendly and cordial. We never made plans. In retrospect, encountering him that last year of his life was like saying one long, quiet goodbye.

I've never known what to do with myself in the summer, not since I was twelve. My friends from back then are still my friends today, except there are fewer of them now. Every summer since 1992 has felt like something was missing. One last game of kickball. One more jump off the diving board at Crawford Gym. One more day spent with a friend who drifted away over the years, two ships passing in the night.

AFTERWORD

As I reviewed the contents of this book, as well as *Salvaged From the Flood*, several thoughts raced through my head. The first notion troubled me. For the first time in ages, I have run out of big picture ideas, wacky schemes, or passion projects. I'm mentally and emotionally spent. The old pot of gold at the end of the rainbow? It isn't in sight. I have a creeping sense of permanence right now. Hey, I've never sold out. I can say that much. Some people can sell out, others can't. Me personally? Hell, I don't even know how. I've never been able to sell much of anything.

Amanda and I are doing decent enough, though God knows what she would think of the contents of this book. I already told her, "You don't want to read this book, believe me." She has little knowledge of my conversations with Janet and I'd rather keep it that way. We get along some days, argue others. We're ... married. True love? Who knows? More of a work in progress, like any sustained relationship. I realize that now. I do feel as though I know Amanda through and through. Ironically, I don't think she has ever entirely known or understood me.

Amanda's bout of pneumonia back in November has been a constant frustration. Anthem deemed basic IV treatments and a second night in the hospital as "not medically necessary," the EMS ambulance company attempting to charge $1,800.00 for a ten-minute ride from Southwest Hospital to St. Mary's. I've long said, "I never want to get sick and end up in the hospital. It's not worth the money. Just let me die. Cremate me, buy a Folgers can, then scatter the ashes like in *The Big Lebowski*. Isaac plans to do this with his dad's ashes. He and Kate will head back to his dad's native New York state to scatter his ashes later this year.

After nearly eighteen years at Rutherford Elementary, Amanda is finally set to transfer out to Hartstern Elementary for the 2025-26 school year. She will have to work on a cart, travel from class to class, and have no room of her own. "Be careful what you wish for," I warned.

As for Andrew, he's doing well at Farnsley Middle. Straight A's all around. He never brings home any work, so I haven't the foggiest idea what he does there. We're doing well enough to take him to school and pick him up, with our constantly changing carpool situation involving some other people in the area.

The absurd $3,600.00 in pandemic unemployment has been repaid to the state, but I still haven't heard about my PUA case. I seemingly won a referee appeal after being denied PUA funds for the second half of 2020, but the decision was "corrected" later and sent back to the Adjudication Branch for further discussion. That was a year ago. They have sat on the case and done nothing, while all my phone calls lead to nowhere.

I haven't heard anything else from Janet since that fateful Sunday in late September. I assume she is out of my life for good. Would I want to talk to her again? I don't know. There is so much bad blood at the moment, I have no idea how to approach her, or if I want to, since much of the bad blood is on her end. I could easily apologize for the *My Old Ass* gag. That wouldn't be a problem. These other accusations of attempting to use her, and contacting various people mentioned in her book, however? I haven't done these things, so I don't feel the need to apologize. If I owe her one apology, she owes me ten. I miss talking to her, but we might be a toxic combination, two people destined to alienate each other, only to eventually try again, in a vicious cycle.

Rochelle and I are still friendly enough, though she rarely has time to text or talk much these days. I understand. She has a husband and two kids, as well as a full-time nursing job, so clearly she has a full plate. We'll never be as close as we were up through the first trip in 2003. At least I haven't said anything to drive her away permanently, a minor miracle, given my penchant for saying the wrong thing. Maybe we've never quite figured out what we mean to each other. However, even when we drift apart, I know deep down Rochelle would be there if I am feeling down, and vice versa. I would enjoy having a quality phone conversation that doesn't involve someone dying or discussing deep personal woes.

The worst thing for me to do is become seriously emotionally invested in someone. When I care about someone, I *really* care. Not like Kate walking miles in the rain to check on Isaac at 3:00 a.m., but I definitely obsess at times and have a tendency to scare people away. I would imagine these obsessive moments stem from spending so many years alone in my apartment and wanting deeper communication with people I feel are special. Ironically, the relative lack of obsessive behavior is one reason Amanda and I have lasted this long. I've never intensely cared about Amanda to wild extremes. Sometimes I feel as if I don't care enough. Perhaps she views this as me caring the right amount?

I finally participated on Vic's fan forum podcast, discussing *Abbott and Costello Meet Frankenstein*, though I felt ill at ease. I'm usually nervous in such situations, and in this case, I was surrounded by a group of film expert Boomers whose childhood memories of watching the film on local NYC TV in the '60s outweighed my own ("Um, I rented the movie from Blockbuster in 1990"). This experience underscored the same generational divide I referenced in my W & W piece, which Janet found strangely offensive. Vic never posted the show online, due to echo problems in the audio.

Looking back at these various projects, I can't help but notice a frustrating trend. When I have attempted a project I could complete single handed, I have been able to produce an end result I deem acceptable. For years I ran my own website nearly all by myself, with a hands-off webmaster I paid $20.00 a month. *Sonic Screamer*? I recorded all of those demos by myself, with minimal help from Eric here and there. Obviously, writing this book and *Salvaged* were individual tasks. Multiple editors mucked up the proceedings later.

But when I needed to rely on others? That's where plans go awry. Attempting to film *Welcome to Paradise* flopped, my friends being too preoccupied with their own troubles to spend time on my foibles. More recently, the entire podcast idea with Janet, which never came to fruition. I could attempt a solo podcast, though I have no idea who would listen or watch. When the time comes for creative endeavors, I would rather walk a lonely mile.

As I said, at the moment I am out of ideas, even dubious ones. The Justice of the Peace election is in the fall of 2026. I'll look into the race and see if I can gain ballot access. November 2026 is still a ways from now, however. Until then, all I can do is bide my time and deal with these carpool people. Due to their changing schedules, they, too, are wildly unreliable, but I can't take Andrew to Farnsley Middle and back every day and stay sane.

Other than that, I'll get up in the morning, ride my five miles a day, and stay healthy. As of this writing I am down to 148 lbs., which is the lowest I've been in forever. You could say I've been working on myself. My mom thinks I'm too thin now. Amanda hasn't been thrilled either. Does my newly svelte look make her feel self-conscious? She can't ride a stationary bike easily with a prosthetic leg.

Isaac has had difficulty coping with losing his mom and dad in such a short amount of time. Recently he posted a gut-wrenching statement of grief on Facebook: "The hardest part of losing both parents recently has been the guilt. When I start to miss one, I feel guilty I'm only missing that one and not the other. Then I start missing them both, and the cycle repeats. Mom and dad, I miss you so much. I love you both."

All I can do is be there if he needs me. I told him to focus on funny moments from the past as a coping mechanism, which I have done in the past over my dad. To that end, ever since Bonnie's funeral I can't help but think of a conversation Isaac and I had during the downtime after the minister played "Purple People Eater."

"I have given this considerable thought recently, especially after Jeremy died," I said. "I know exactly what music I want played at my funeral." Isaac smiled slightly, knowing where the conversation was headed.

"Demos!" we said simultaneously, both laughing.

"Mom wasn't as big a fan of your album as me," Isaac said.

"Wait, you played it for her?" I asked, incredulously.

"Sure, I used to play the CD around the house while doing chores. The first time I played it she immediately put her head in her hands and said, 'He thinks *this* is music?'"

"Ah, the exact reaction I wanted."

"What song would you want played?" he asked.

"'Metamorphosis.' All five parts of my nine-and-a-half-minute noise rock opus. I figure anyone still left in the room after it ends was with me until the bitter end."

APPENDIX

MY LIFETIME LOVE OF WHEELER AND WOOLSEY

This piece was submitted to Classic Images in October 2024, published in June 2025.

The comedy team of Bert Wheeler and Robert Woolsey have largely been relegated to the dustbin of film history, with occasional revivals of their films, and a cult fanbase to go along with general apathy. As film critic Ken Hanke noted, "Wheeler and Woolsey have either been totally forgotten or willfully ignored." Ask most older film buffs about W & W, and it isn't uncommon to receive a baffled response of "Who?" Or, if they know W & W, a groan, instead.

There does exist a certain age range who reconnected with W & W's films and their brand of Depression era comedy. There exists a sweet spot of people born in the late '70s or early '80s that grew up with W & W movies being more or less fixtures on cable TV. I am one of them, and this is the story of my experiences being a W & W fan.

I started middle school in August 1990, a period of time coinciding with my burgeoning interest in classic films. Like a lot of kids who became interested in classic Hollywood, I started watching movies like *Dracula* (1931), which I first read about at summer daycare. Other films such as *Scarface* (1932), and *The Hunchback of*

Notre Dame (1939), were my introduction to American Movie Classics, back when the station actually showed classic movies. For the purposes of this piece, the film that introduced me to classic comedian comedy was the Marx Bros. film *Animal Crackers* (1930). I adored that film, and still do, though at the time the concepts of things like anarchistic comedy were beyond me. From there I devoured all the Marx Bros. movies and was eager to find out about other comedians of the era.

AMC used to share TV time with the Travel Channel, 3:00 p.m. being the demarcation point when AMC started for the day. I usually got home from school around 2:45, by this point being a typical latchkey kid, my parents at work. I turned on AMC one day in late 1990 and the film up next was *Half Shot at Sunrise* (1930), the first W & W movie of which I became aware. Oddly, I didn't bother watching or recording it but looked the film up in our copy of Leonard Maltin's book. Maltin gave it **1/2, calling it a "Pretty funny Wheeler & Woolsey vehicle." Ah, so there was another comedy team from the same era as the Marx Bros. I needed to know more.

By early 1991, AMC had gone to the full twenty-four hour a day format, and by this point I was hooked. I convinced my parents to get me a subscription to AMC Magazine, the first issue being March 1991. I sifted through the listings and circled anything potentially interesting, including two W & W movies I noticed: *High Flyers* (1937), on March 1, and *Cockeyed Cavaliers* (1934), on March 5. As I would come to realize, AMC often showed W & W at either the crack of dawn or late at night, I would assume as filler programming. Now I can look back and realize AMC had no access to Turner's Warner Bros. or MGM properties, so they made do by grabbing old RKO movies because not even Turner's people cared about old RKO stuff.

I convinced my dad to tape *High Flyers* while I was at school, on his day off from the car dealership. His verdict wasn't especially encouraging: "Why did you want me to record those two weasels?" As I later learned, the film was W & W's last, though ironically enough, my first exposure to the team. I had no idea what to make of it. The film wasn't great or anything, but it had some moments I enjoyed, such as W & W accidentally getting high in the plane, Bert's wacky Chaplin impersonation, and Bob's song and dance with Lupe Velez. Either way, I already had *Cockeyed Cavaliers* on the docket.

Needless to say, *Cavs* is a much better movie, representing the duo at their peak. This being AMC, the film aired at 10:30 p.m. on a school night, so I saw half of it before having to go to bed. My dad watched the film with me, and this time he heavily invested in the wacky 17th Century goings on. The next day I reviewed the tape and highly enjoyed the wisecracks, the running gag of Bert's kleptomania, and the enjoyable songs "The Big Bad Wolf Was Dead," and "Dilly Dally." My dad's verdict this time? "Well, that was better than the first one, I guess."

And yet ... I wasn't convinced. I needed to see more. I didn't know what to make of W & W, nor did I know which was which (I searched for them in an almanac, and since Woolsey's birth date marked him older, I figured he was the one with the glasses). The next films of theirs on AMC were during spring break. The big budget *Dixiana* (1930) didn't entirely thrill me, possibly due to AMC showing the version without the two-color Technicolor ending. The restored version debuted on AMC in late 1991, and I watched it all the way through, although the movie started at 10:00 at night, while my dad argued with Aunt Carolyn on the phone. Once the color scene hit, even he looked over at the screen as if to say, "Whoa!"

The clincher arrived a few days later. AMC showed Peach-O-Reno (1931), as well as Woolsey's solo outing, *Everything's Rosie* (1931), back-to-back. Once again, early in the AM, so I set the VCR to record both in LP mode. Hindsight being 20/20, I should have found a way to record *Peach* in SP mode, and *Rosie* in LP mode. *Peach* immediately became one of my all-time favorite comedies, the epitome of the Pre-Code insanity W & W specialized in. I personally consider Bert Wheeler's drag performance in that film as Ms. Hanover the greatest performance of that sort since he *became* the character. The zany dance routine the duo performed, the anarchic courtroom climax, Bert and Dorothy Lee's entertaining "From Niagara Falls to Reno" number. Everything clicked. Now I understood why these guys were popular in the 1930s. Classic cinema doctrine dictated thou must love Marx Bros., Laurel and Hardy, or Abbott and Costello. Not me. Not after *Peach-O-Reno*. W & W were my boys.

During that summer, a woman who worked at the University of Louisville daycare talked to me about W & W, since her parents grew up watching them. *Peach* was also one of their favorites, so I let her borrow my tape. She watched both films, and the next day remarked about the Woolsey solo outing. "He needed Wheeler to reign him in. Too unhinged on his own." I found Wheeler and Dorothy's outing, *Too Many Cooks* (1931), the exact opposite. Bert came off dull without Woolsey. Sweetheart, they needed each other. Alas, the same summer I screwed up my tape of Peach. I wanted to pause the tape briefly, but instead tapped record by accident, and ended up with fifteen seconds of *The Gauntlet* (1977) in the middle of the film! Right as the law office is changing into the casino, here comes a biker gang to terrorize Clint Eastwood and Sondra Locke. If only I knew to remove the tab from the side of a VHS tape back then ...

Throughout 1991 and 1992 I dutifully checked AMC Magazine each month for more W & W movies. During that time, I noticed AMC Magazine publishing articles on forgotten comedians such as W &W, the Ritz Bros., etc. In the Dec. 1991 magazine, I became aware of critic William Drew and his writings on the duo ("The Screwball Satirists"). As Drew noted, "The military, the prison system, ineffectual peace conferences, South American coup d'etats ... all were targets for satire in their films." On occasion, other viewers wrote in and asked about films such as *Diplomaniacs* (1933), wanting to know more about the team. *Diplomaniacs,* one of the few W & W films available from Turner Home Video, I found at Suncoast in Green Tree Mall, in Clarksville, IN.

My middle school years were not great ones for me, personally. My grandfather died in August 1991, and I may well have had trouble coping with his death. I was also sick, due to constant sinus infections, and as such missed a considerable amount of school. Wheeler & Woolsey movies (and classic cinema in general) were a coping mechanism for me, a way to escape. Over those years of comic exploration, I became more and more aware of their work and used Ephraim Katz's *Film Encyclopedia* to put together a list of what I still needed to see. I tried in vain to convert some classmates and friends to the W & W cause, with limited success. Note to self: Don't start someone out on

Cracked Nuts (1931) as their first W & W movie. It is way too weird. Try something easier like *Hips, Hips, Hooray* (1934), instead.

I have stories of some sort about finding most of their movies. I got *Kentucky Kernels* (1934) on a factory VHS tape for my birthday on August 20, 1991. The VHS tape arrived right as my family returned from Holiday World, where we had spent the day. I also found *Hook, Line and Sinker* (1930) at the newly opened Suncoast in Jefferson Mall here in Louisville. The manager transferred from the Clarksville location, and remembered I had bought *Diplomaniacs*, so when another W & W movie came out on Turner Home Video, he ordered three copies. I bought one. The other two stayed on the shelf there for years.

In July 1992, my dad recorded *Hold 'Em Jail* (1932) on AMC while at daycare, and he had a doctor's appointment. He was misdiagnosed with a urinary tract infection, when he actually had diverticulitis, a scary illness that nearly killed him. But on that day at least, we had a blast watching the movie. I scoured the TV Guide each week to see if there were some other showings, and I found both *Mummy's Boys* (1936) and *Silly Billies* (1936) via TNT airings. Sadly, *Silly Billies* aired around 3 a.m., and an NBA game ran over, cutting the ending of the movie off my VHS tape!

By early 1993 AMC seemingly ran out of W & W movies to air, or at least ones I hadn't seen. *The Nitwits* (1935) was the last of their films I saw on AMC. For the next couple of years, I obsessed over their movies I had not seen, including their first two films *Rio Rita* (1929) and *The Cuckoos* (1930). I also hadn't seen *Girl Crazy* (1932), and the duo's lone oddball Columbia release, *So This Is Africa* (1933).

I started high school later that year, and other priorities took center stage (comics, pro wrestling, alternative rock). But I kept the light burning in the window for W & W and converted a few friends of mine into full-fledged fans. Almost by chance, I made a wonderful discovery in April 1995, when I went to the now defunct Hawley-Cooke Bookstore on Bardstown Road. Back then they had a plethora of magazines, including *Classic Images*. This particular issue had a Bert Wheeler 100th birthday celebration article, so I made sure to buy it.

What a revelation! I enjoyed the article on Bert, but I also noticed an ad in the magazine for the Ed Watz book *Wheeler & Woolsey: The*

Vaudeville Comic Duo and Their Films. Wait, hold on. There was a book about W & W? I had to have it. Further, in the back of the magazine I saw a two-page ad for Foothill Video (Are they now defunct? I would assume so). I scoured the listings and gasped. *Rio Rita*! *The Cuckoos*! *Girl Crazy*! *So This Is Africa*! I can upgrade my botched copy of *Silly Billies*! Eureka, I've struck gold! And only about eight bucks per movie!

Problem: My parents wouldn't give me the money for all of these things. Since I was interested in a book, they agreed to buy it, but I had to raise money for the movies themselves (which frankly were more important to me). I wound up selling my various Alice In Chains CDs to Ear-X-Tacy (*Facelift*, *Dirt*, *Jar of Flies*), along with Hole's *Live Through This* to raise the money. I later reacquired the Hole album. My brother has his own copies of the Alice In Chains albums.

The book and movies arrived during Derby Week in 1995. The week started on Sunday with the big free concert in Cherokee Park headlined by Bush, and a few days later the Watz book arrived in the mail. I practically inhaled the book, reading it from cover to cover in days. It quickly became one of my favorite books, even though I found Watz himself too harshly critical of some of their films. By Thursday the movies themselves arrived, the same day a Canadian man in town for the Derby rear ended my dad right at the Fern Valley Road exit on I-65. Not a serious accident, no one was hurt. But we didn't let that ruin the day, and on Friday we spent Oaks Day watching nothing but W & W movies.

We started with *Silly Billies* as a routine opener, since I had already seen it, then moved up to *Girl Crazy*, then the insane and bonkers *So This is Africa* (read more about the film's crazy censorship history on elbrendel.blogspot.com). *The Cuckoos* frustrated me, since it was a C & C Movietime print missing most of the color scenes, aside from Dottie's showstopper "Dancing the Devil Away." The print was missing the "Goodbye" color scene, as well as the ending of the movie back at the estate. *The Cuckoos* has never been one of my favorites due to this.

But the real piece de resistance was *Rio Rita*. We saved the best for last. I watched it with my dad in the back bedroom late at night. I already knew from the Watz book that the film was shorter than originally released, with over thirty minutes of footage cut for reissue (thanks Selznick!). But I also knew it was a massive blockbuster in its time, a fascinating time capsule of 1920s era Broadway musical comedy. In Watz's book, he noted the audience in a revival theater became hooked on the W & W scenes but sat bored during the draggy operetta. My dad and I enjoyed all of it. W & W were on fire, with one brilliant routine after another carried over from the stage version. This film completed the missing piece of the puzzle. Now I understood fully why they were successful on Broadway as a team.

Overall, that day is one of my fondest memories. I started out watching *High Flyers*, their last movie, and ended with *Rio Rita*, their first movie. Who would have ever planned it? I bought a better copy of *Peach-O-Reno* from Foothill as well, one without a biker gang.

During the summer, I noticed the fairly new Turner Classic Movies airing on the preview channel in my area. TKR Cable started to expand the lineup with the advent of fiber optic wiring, but we hadn't gotten full access to TCM when they aired a W & W marathon in late July. So, yes, I spent an entire day watching W & W movies on a scrambled signal, the highlight of which included "seeing" a restored version of *The Cuckoos,* complete with the Technicolor sequences, which Watz fretted about in his book cost too much to print. Some teenagers might watch scrambled cable for dubious reasons. I watched it for TCM.

TCM became available about a month or two later, but not in time for the festival. Eventually digital cable replaced what we had, and I spent years upgrading my VHS tapes to better quality copies. All except *So This Is Africa*, the lone W & W movie I have never seen on TV. I believe it aired in 1994 when TCM was not available in my area, but never again. I've never stopped being a fan, never stopped trying to convert others into fans.

Why did some people my age become invested in W & W? Perhaps a fluke situation, with the rise in cable TV and home video making their movies more available than previously. But I think it goes beyond that. To me, personally, I thought W & W had a character relationship, which made more sense to me as a jaded Gen X type. They may have skewered antagonistic Colonels, wardens, and rich landowners. But they were usually cool with each other, a noted difference from other duos of the era. I found them much easier to digest than some other teams, whose relationships seemed toxic to me, at times devolving into little more than one partner berating the other, or physical assault played for laughs. Woolsey might bust Wheeler's chops sometimes, but it's sly and amusing instead of mean spirited, *On Again—Off Again* being the lone exception.

I don't see any way a modern film would ever do this mean-spirited stuff and expect to draw money, whereas updated W & W type movies such as *Wedding Crashers* (2005), featuring Owen Wilson and Vince Vaughn as divorce attorneys, can still be successful. Ironic for those who say W & W's style is wildly dated. If anything, I think their style is highly modern and can still work. The "Two guys and a girl" formula with Dorothy Lee being a precursor to the formula used all over film genres, from the *Road* movies (Bing Crosby, Bob Hope, Dorothy Lamour) to *Star Wars* (Luke, Han, Leia). I think some in the W & W fandom get carried away with hyperbole ("They're the greatest comedians ever!"). I'm fine saying they are my personal favorites, knowing taste is subjective. Their place in film history is what it is at this point.

ABOUT THE AUTHOR

Brian Paige is an author who lives in Louisville, Kentucky, with his wife, Amanda, and son, Andrew. He is a 2001 graduate of the University of Louisville with a Bachelor of Arts in Communications, 2011 U of L graduate with a Master of Arts in Communication, and 2016 graduate of the University of the Cumberlands with a Master of Arts in Teaching in secondary social studies. He also has a self-produced album under the name Sonic Screamer, *Demos*, as well as a previous book, *Salvaged From the Flood*.

www.ingramcontent.com/pod-product-compliance
Lightning Source LLC
Chambersburg PA
CBHW021616120626
46545CB00001B/254